Praise

'a succinct and readi_ and key issues associated with chemical and biological weapons from World War I to the present . . . an excellent overview of an often underappreciated segment of 20th- and 21st-century security studies . . . It deserves the thoughtful attention of both students and professionals.'
– *Military Review*

'This concise work, with its extensive references and bibliography, will be of interest to all students and professionals in the fields of history, political science, public policy, toxicology, and chemical technology. Recommended.' – *Choice*

'provides a compelling case for governments across the globe not to overlook the potential threat of biological and chemical weapons . . . the book is more than just a history of these weapons, but also an important addition to the literature on the types of threat we are likely to face in the future . . . an important reminder of the substantial destructive and psychological power of chemical and biological weapons, as well as an accessible history about how states have thought about their use and utility in the past.' – *Political Studies Review*

'a comprehensive overview of the development, future, and implications of biological and chemical weapons. Spiers's book traces the origins of chemical and biological warfare from their ancient beginnings to the first major use of gas in 1915 in World War I, to more recent uses and suspicions of use.' – *Arms Control*

AGENTS OF WAR

A HISTORY OF CHEMICAL
AND BIOLOGICAL WEAPONS

REVISED AND EXPANDED SECOND EDITION

EDWARD M. SPIERS

REAKTION BOOKS

Published by
Reaktion Books Ltd
Unit 32, Waterside
44–48 Wharf Road
London N1 7UX, UK

www.reaktionbooks.co.uk

First published 2010
Revised and expanded second edition first published in paperback 2021
Transferred to digital printing 2024
Copyright © Edward M. Spiers 2010

Printed and bound in the USA by University of Chicago Press

A catalogue record for this book is available from the British Library

ISBN 978 1 78914 298 3

Contents

Preface

This book is a contribution to the continuing debate over chemical and biological weapons. It is written and presented in a way that makes it broadly accessible, a study that presents both forms of weaponry within their recent historical contexts and then elaborates upon the challenges that they have posed during periods of peace and war. It recognizes that these are highly versatile weapons that can be dispersed by many delivery systems, ranging from missiles, bombs and shells to aerosol dispensers, impregnated foodstuffs, insects and even umbrellas. If chemical weapons have been employed in inter-state and intra-state warfare, the military potential of biological weapons has been demonstrated by all means short of war, and both weapon systems have been employed by terrorists to inflict casualties, cause economic loss, and create widespread panic and disruption.

By reflecting upon the sinister image of chemical and biological weapons, the book reviews the debates about their usage and the allegations of covert development and employment that have period-ically erupted into propaganda battles. It examines (and seeks to interpret) the attempts to deter recourse to chemical and biological warfare during the Second World War and the Cold War, to stifle the proliferation of these weapons in recent years, and to promote international disarmament. It seeks to explain how these political and diplomatic initiatives have fared in light of the uncertainties caused by the rapidly evolving scientific and technological develop-ments of recent years, and by the diffusion of scientific expertise and industrial capabilities throughout much of the developing world.

As a revised edition, this volume adds chapters on the use of chemical weapons in the Syrian Civil War, and the Novichok poison-ings, as well as reflections upon literature that has appeared since the preparation of the first edition.

Abbreviations

AEF	American Expeditionary Force
ARP	Air Raid Precautions
BTWC	Biological and Toxin Weapons Convention
BW	Biological Warfare
CB	Chemical Biological
CBM	Confidence Building Measure
CBRN	Chemical, Biological, Radiological and Nuclear
CBW	Chemical and Biological Warfare
CDC	Centers for Disease Control and Prevention
CS	orthochlorobenzylidene malononitrile
CW	Chemical Warfare
DHS	Department of Homeland Security
DIA	Defense Intelligence Agency
DM	diphenylchloroarsine (adamsite)
DNA	deoxyribonucleic acid
DOD	Department of Defense
EOD	Explosive Ordnance Disposal
FMDV	Foot and Mouth Disease Virus
FSB	Federalnaya Shuzhba Bezopasnosti
GAO	General Accounting (later Accountability) Office
GPPi	Global Public Policy institute
GRU	Glavnoe Razvedyvatelnoe Upravlenie
HUMINT	Human Intelligence (collection method)
IAEA	International Atomic Energy Agency
ICBM	Intercontinental Ballistic Missile
ICI	Imperial Chemical Industries
IED	Improvised Explosive Device
IG	Interessengemeinschaft der Deutschen Teerfarbenfabriken
ISG	Iraq Survey Group

ISIS	Islamic State in Iraq and Syria
JIC	Joint Intelligence Committee
JIM	Joint Investigative Mission
JMIS	Joint Mission in Syria
KGB	Komitet Gosudarstvennoi Bezopasnosti
KTO	Kuwaiti Theatre of Operations
MOPP	Mission Oriented Protective Posture
MSE	Al Muthanna State Establishment
NBC	Nuclear, Biological and Chemical
NIE	National Intelligence Estimate
NTM	National Technical Means (intelligence collection)
OPCW	Organization for the Prohibition of Chemical Weapons
OTA	Office of Technology Assessment
R&D	Research and Development
RRL	Roodeplaat Research Laboratories
SCR	Security Council Resolution
SIPRI	Stockholm Institute for Peace Research
TNA	The National Archives
UN	United Nations
UNMOVIC	United Nations Monitoring Verification and Inspection Commission
UNSCOM	United Nations Special Commission
USDA	United States Department of Agriculture
WET	Water Engineering Trading
WHO	World Health Organization
WMD	Weapons of Mass Destruction

Introduction

Chemical and biological weapons arouse a peculiar degree of ire and passion, so much so that unlike many conventional weapons they have been the subject of various attempts to ban their development, production and usage. Addressing both houses of Congress on 9 February 1989, President George H. W. Bush declared that the spread and 'even use of sophisticated weaponry threatens global security as never before. Chemical weapons must be banned from the face of the earth, never to be used again.'[1] Despite the passage of the Chemical Weapons Convention (CWC) in 1993, and its entry into force on 29 April 1997, chemical warfare in various forms remains an option. On 1 June 2002, President George W. Bush addressed the graduates of West Point, declaring that 'Containment is not possible when unbalanced dictators with weapons of mass destruction (WMD) can deliver those weapons on missiles or secretly provide them to terrorist allies.'[2] The prospect of Iraq reviving its chemical and biological weapons capability even served as the nominal justification for the invasion, known as Operation Iraqi Freedom, in March 2003. To reflect upon these events requires some understanding of the weapons themselves and their effects, how they have evolved historically through the twentieth century, what problems they have posed for intelligence communities, and the limited effectiveness of defensive, deterrent and disarmament options as ways of responding to them.

Chemical Weapons

Chemical weapons are those weapons capable of disseminating chemical warfare (CW) agents, defined by a United Nations report as 'chemical substances, whether gaseous, liquid, or solid, which might be employed because of their direct toxic effects on man, animals and plants'. This definition includes riot-control agents and herbicides, as both have been used for their toxic effects in war, most notably in the Vietnam War, acting as 'force multipliers' by compounding the effects of conventional ordnance. Chemical warfare agents, therefore, are quite distinct from biological warfare (BW) agents (such as bacteria, viruses and rickettsia), which are defined as 'living organisms, whatever their nature, or infective material derived from them, which are intended to cause disease or death in man, animals or plants, and which depend for their effects on their ability to multiply in the person, animal or plant attacked'.[3]

Within the spectrum from chemical to biological warfare agents, there are, as the Chemical and Biological Defence Establishment (Porton Down) claims, many potential 'mid-spectrum' agents. These include highly toxic industrial, pharmaceutical and agricultural chemicals; agents of biological origin (such as peptides, the precursors of proteins made up of amino acids that could be manipulated genetically to affect mental processes or the regulatory factors of mood, consciousness, temperature control, sleep or emotions); toxins (chemical substances produced by living organisms that are inanimate and cannot multiply); and genetically modified bacteria, viruses or combinations of substances (designed to mask detection, enhance virulence, be resistant to antibiotics and environmental stability [see variable effects, pp. 24–5]). The mid-spectrum agents underscore the range and diversity of agents that might be employed by state or by non-state actors, and certain industrial chemicals are so toxic that the accidental release of 30 tons of methyl isocyanate – a chemical some hundred times less deadly than modern nerve agent – at the Union Carbide plant, Bhopal, India on 3 December 1984 killed 6,000 people. Moreover, this spectrum of agents illustrates the range of toxicity inasmuch as BW agents are kilo-for-kilo more potent than CW agents since they multiply after dispersion (in favourable environmental conditions), and so smaller and less costly amounts can inflict casualties over a much more extensive area.[4]

Of the several thousand highly toxic substances, only about 70 were employed or stored as CW agents in the twentieth century. Employed on an extensive scale in the First World War, chlorine and phosgene, both lung irritants, were initially the principal agents employed to inflict casualties. Gases at ambient temperature and normal pressure, their usage evoked the terminology 'war gases' and 'gas warfare'.[5] Subsequent research and development refined the requirements for militarily effective chemical agents, including ease of production from available raw materials and of supply in the quantities required for military purposes. Another prerequisite was stability in storage between production and use unless the substances were to be used almost as soon as they were produced. Ideally, cw agents should be capable of being handled and transported safely, with little or no corrosive effects on containers or munitions. They should be capable of being dispersed from a practical military device, and in sufficient concentration, to produce the desired effects on the target. Those handling these agents had to understand their mechanism of action, taking the appropriate measures to protect themselves physically and medically from any adverse effects, while the intended enemy would experience maximum physiological and/or psychological effects if the agents were difficult to detect and protect against.[6]

Biological Weapons

bw agents resemble their chemical counterparts inasmuch as they are capable of being dispersed in the air and travel with the prevailing wind. Able to penetrate any area where the air can circulate, they may contaminate terrain, clothing, food, water and equipment. Primarily effective against living organisms, whether humans, animals or plants, their effects, like those of cw agents, can be offset by protective clothing and collective protection devices. Although potentially more potent on a weight-for-weight basis than chemical agents, biological agents often have an incubation period, and act more slowly on their victims than rapid-acting nerve agents. They are also more susceptible to sunlight, temperature and other environmental factors; a biological agent, once disseminated, may retain its viability (that is, its ability to live and multiply) while losing its virulence (ability to produce disease and injury). On the other hand, as they infect living organisms, some contagious pathogens can spread from person to person, causing epidemics, or be carried by travellers, migratory birds and animals to distant localities. Biological agents, finally, lend themselves to covert use because the small amounts of material required can be easily concealed, transported, and used in sabotage, assassination or terrorist operations.

Like cw agents, only certain organisms or substances are likely to prove effective as bw agents. Whether targeting man, animals or plant crops, the agents require ease of production, adequate supply and stability in storage and in transportation. They must be easily disseminated by various means, remain stable after dissemination, infect the target preferably by more than one portal of entry, and produce death or disability consistently as well as the desired psychological effects. Ideally, the BW agents should prove difficult to detect and to protect against in time, especially if the attacker employed 'unusual disease agents, mixtures of various agents, very high infective dosages and unusual portals of entry or methods of infection'. Such tactics would complicate the tasks of identifying the organisms as well as of diagnosing the diseases that they produce.[7]

Characteristics of Chemical Weapons

Toxic chemicals vary enormously in their properties, in their physiological effects, and in their persistence once disseminated. Whereas some may cause their victims sensory irritation, others may incapacitate and some incapacitate or kill. They vary, too, in the persistence of their effects: some are relatively transient on impact; others may contaminate areas for several hours, days or many weeks. As the degree of persistence varies with meteorological, environmental and other factors, CW agents are classified by their physiological effects. The incapacitating agents (formerly known as vomiting agents, tear gases and irritants) temporarily impair the ability of the body to function effectively. Only lethal in extremely high concentrations, their action is generally rapid and their effects non-persistent and comparatively brief in duration. They are often subdivided into physical (or physiochemical) agents that cause irritation and abnormal bodily behaviour, and psychochemical agents, such as BZ, once standardized as an American CW agent, that cause mental disorientation. Orthochlorobenzylidene malononitrile, more commonly known as CS after its discoverers, B. B. Corson and R. W. Stoughton, is a particularly effective irritant. Commonly used in riot control, it is less toxic than chloroacetophenone (CN), but its effects occur almost instantly. Depending on dosage, these effects range from a prickling sensation in the eyes and nose to a gripping pain in the chest, copious flow of tears, coughing, streaming nose, retching and vomiting.[8]

Of more importance militarily is the wide array of lethal agents. Used extensively in the First World War, the lung agents (chlorine, phosgene and the related diphosgene) irritate the eyes and throat, and, in high concentrations, inflame the lung tissues, leading to pulmonary oedema, accumulation of fluid in the lungs, and eventually death from lack of oxygen. The blood gases (hydrogen cyanide or cyanogen chloride) proved more volatile and faster acting than phosgene; if inhaled in lethal dosages, they blocked the circulation of oxygen within the body and caused death very rapidly. Blister agents or vesicants such as mustard gas (*bis* (2-chloroethyl) sulphide) also appeared initially in the First World War. Known as 'king of the war gases', mustard gas acts insidiously as a general cell poison, with its delayed effects damaging any kind of body tissue but primarily the eyes and skin, producing burns, blisters and even temporary blindness, which may last for a week or more. As mustard gas is not very volatile, its effects may persist in the field for lengthy periods of time (depending upon the climatic conditions). In sufficiently high concentrations, it kills by inhalation or absorption through the skin, producing death from respiratory complications or infection.

More toxic than mustard gas or phosgene are the nerve gases (G- and v-agents) that impair the transmission of nerve impulses, causing uncontrollable muscular activity that can kill through respiratory failure. Practically odourless and colourless, the nerve agents act more quickly than mustard gas or phosgene, penetrating the body by inhalation or percutaneously (by absorption through the skin). By inhibiting the enzyme acetylcholinesterase, they cause a loss of control over the affected part of the nervous system and permit acetylcholine, a powerful poison, to accumulate within the body. Very low dosages cause a running of the nose, tightness of the chest, dimness of vision, and contraction of the eye pupils. At higher dosages, the symptoms progress through difficulty in breathing, nausea and vomiting, cramps and involuntary defecation, tremors, headache, convulsions and finally death. Respiratory lethal dosages may kill within fifteen minutes while percutaneous lethal dosages could kill quickly but are likely to prove fatal within one to two hours. The v-agents are more toxic than the G-agents: they act as rapidly as the G-agents if inhaled, but act much faster through the skin and are more effective in smaller dosages. Possessing volatility similar to that of heavy motor oil, the v-agents could be employed as a highly effective form of persistent ground contamination. vx, discovered in Britain during the 1950s, can incapacitate or kill in minute quantities (about 5 mg-min/m^3 and 15 mg/man respectively).[9]

Toxins constitute another potential category of chemical warfare agents. As the non-living products of micro-organisms, plants or living animals, they can also be synthesized chemically. Inanimate and unable to multiply, they are 'more easily controlled and faster-acting than microbiological agents' and so have a greater potential military utility.[10] Numerous toxic substances exist in nature: of those produced by bacteria, the botulinal toxins are considerably more poisonous than nerve gases and staphylococcal enterotoxin B, though not normally lethal, can incapacitate temporarily by causing a sudden and severe bout of food poisoning. Other toxins are generated by marine organisms (such as saxitoxin, a lethal toxin produced by certain algae), by fungi (aflatoxin and the trichothecene mycotoxins), by castor beans (ricin), by poisonous plants and by venomous snakes, insects and spiders.

Anti-plant agents have also been used in chemical warfare. These are agricultural chemicals that act in various ways upon plant life and vegetables. Some act as defoliants, causing the leaves of plants to fall prematurely; others act as dessicants, drying out the tissues of a plant to leave its leaves brittle, shrivelled, and more easily detached by the wind. Some cause abnormal growth of buds or roots so that the plant dies from the disruption and plugging of its vascular tissues. Many chemicals act as herbicides, damaging or killing a plant when applied to the air, soil and water, or to the plant itself. In the Vietnam War, herbicides known as Agent Orange and Agent Purple, which included mixtures of phenoxy acids, like 2,4-D and 2,4,5-T, were employed to defoliate forest and bush growth; Agent Blue, containing a hundred per cent sodium salt of cacodylic acid, was used to destroy rice crops. Some chemicals (such as Bromacil or Monuron) may also act as soil sterilants, preventing or retarding the growth or regrowth of plants by chemical treatment of the soil.[11]

By comparison with conventional ordnance, chemical weapons are capable of inflicting casualties over large areas, enveloping dispersed formations or small targets whose precise location is unknown. Unlike conventional weapons, including fuel-air explosives, which have significant area coverage, chemical weapons will not damage vital economic or military objectives such as bridges, ports, factories, railways and airfields. They may act as 'search weapons', penetrating shelters, buildings, trenches and other types of fortification. Unlike explosives, clouds of nerve gas or biological agent can surprise an enemy by an off-target attack (that is, by letting the agent drift downwind). Conversely, if delivered on target, chemical agent may build up rapidly, and in a concentrated form, over a target in fifteen to thirty seconds. Casualties will occur, especially if an enemy is caught unawares, either lacking protective kit or if they don or adjust masks improperly as they seek cover from the fragmentation effects of exploding-type munitions.[12] Persistent agents may also be employed as weapons of area denial, contaminating large areas of ground and foreclosing avenues of movement and resupply. Chemical weapons may also be employed alongside conventional ordnance as 'force multipliers', complementing and compounding the effects of conventional weapons. In counter-insurgency campaigns, they could be used against enemies in remote and relatively inaccessible areas or supported by local populations. Above all, chemical weapons inspire more fear than conventional munitions; they could terrorize civilians and demoralize ill-trained or poorly protected combat units.

Characteristics of Biological Weapons

Potentially, BW agents also have specific attractions as military weapons. On account of their extreme potency only small quantities are necessary to take effect and, as living organisms, they can injure or kill over far greater distances than CW agents. As Judge William Webster, when director of the Central Intelligence Agency, commented, 'biological warfare agents, including toxins, are more potent than the most deadly chemical warfare agents, and provide the broadest area coverage per pound of payload of any weapons system'.[13] The delayed effects of BW agents may mean that they leave only a minimal 'signature', especially if a naturally occurring disease is selected. Militarily useful quantities of BW agents may also be produced in dual-use facilities (that is, plants that could be employed for legitimate civilian purposes), and manufactured more cheaply than chemical or nuclear weapons. They could be employed in diverse ways: either covertly in advance of hostilities, or in tactical strikes on isolated targets, or in more localized and specifically targeted actions (such as the assassination of Georgi Markov with ricin in September 1978). Like chemical incapacitants, they could be employed to inflict extensive casualties, with the aim of overloading medical services and disrupting the movements and co-ordination of mobilized forces prior to the outbreak of hostilities.

Yet BW agents have not been used extensively in war, and their potential military impact has only been demonstrated 'by all means short of their actual use in war'.[14] More susceptible than CW agents to sunlight, temperature and other environmental factors, BW agents are often described as unpredictable and indiscriminate weapons but the use of modern meteorological techniques, coupled with the appropriate choice of agents and munitions, could make these weapons highly effective. For example, anthrax spores are not infectious (and so their disease could not be passed from man to man); they also remain alive in soil or water for many years and so could be employed with a degree of discrimination. Highly potent (estimates of the mean lethal dose of anthrax range from 8,000 to 20,000 spores but even the larger number weighs about one hundred-millionth of a gram), its pulmonary form could prove fatal in 95 per cent of cases over seven days. Although vaccines are now available, they ought to be administered before exposure and antibiotics should be administered before the signs of the disease become apparent. In 1993 the US Office of Technology Assessment (OTA) calculated that if an aeroplane were able to disperse 100 kg of anthrax spores in a line to the windward of a city of the size and population density of Washington, DC, the effects would be catastrophic: on a clear sunny day with a light breeze, 46 km² would be affected and between 130,000 and 460,000 people could die; on an overcast day or at night, with a moderate wind, 140 km² would be affected and 420,000 to 1,400,000 could die; and on a clear, calm night, 300 km² would be affected and between one and three million could die.[15]

Dispersing Chemical and Biological Warfare Agents

Compounding the attractions of chemical weapons are their flexibility in the method of dispersal: they can be adapted for delivery by mines, mortars, artillery, rockets, missiles, bombs and aerial spray tanks. In theory, any delivery system may be employed that can deliver a payload of bulk solid or liquid agent over a designated target area, and disseminate it in a form that utilizes the toxic properties of the agent effectively. In releasing the CW agent, the munition must convert the payload into an even distribution of droplets or solid particles in the appropriate size for the target hazard. The size should range from one to five microns in diameter for inhalation and lung penetration, and droplets of at least 70 microns in diameter or larger for penetration through the skin. The belligerents of the First World War experimented with three methods of dispersing a chemical agent – vaporization, pressure and explosion. Initially, they employed burning-type munitions in the form of grenades whereby irritant agent, mixed into a pyrotechnic composition, was ejected into the atmosphere by a fusing mechanism, whereupon it cooled rapidly and recondensed into aerosol droplets or solid particles. Such weapons are still employed by some police forces to disperse cs smokes for purposes of riot control. As some cw agents were liable to decompose in heat, they either had to be disseminated by a special pyrotechnic composition that burned at low temperatures, or be placed in a separate compartment above the composition. In the latter process, used in mechanical smoke generators, the vapour was forced out into the atmosphere through a slot or nozzle for rapid cooling and condensation. Although these munitions produced particles of uniform size, they dispersed the agent relatively slowly and their clouds were visible, at least initially.[16]

Discovered by the British towards the end of the First World War, the thermo-generator, or the 'M' device as it was then known, had the attractions of being relatively cheap to produce and light to install. Brigadier-General Charles H. Foulkes, the director of the British Gas Services, envisaged that 'hundreds of thousands' of toxic smoke candles could be employed in a surprise attack to 'open the road for our infantry in the minimum of time, without any warning and practically without loss'.[17] Though unused in France, toxic candles were employed as the first aerial gas weapons when dropped as bombs (with vanes to retard their flight and so time the burning of the agent) in the allied intervention against Bolshevik Russia in August and September 1919. They were also employed by the Japanese in operations against the Chinese in the late 1930s. In both cases they reportedly caused panic among unprotected enemies but the toxic clouds proved highly susceptible to variations in meteorological and topographical conditions.[18]

Much larger toxic clouds had been launched during the First World War from batteries of cylinders, with some 6,000 cylinders deployed along a 6-kilometre front at Ypres on 22 April 1915 constituting the first major cloud-gas attack of the conflict. Whereas the Germans ejected their liquid gas by using compressed air, the British, employing much larger cylinders, relied upon the pressure of the toxic gas itself to empty their cylinders. Under favourable climatic conditions, these batteries of cylinders could disperse large gas clouds over a distance roughly equal to the front from which they were discharged. Yet cylinder-based operations had profound disadvantages: the full cylinders were cumbersome to carry, laborious to install (usually at night as their installation in front-line trenches could not be concealed), had to remain in place until favourable conditions occurred (so placing nearby soldiers at risk from accidents, leaks or cylinders bursting under direct hits), and then emitted a distinctive hissing sound when the gas was released, so inviting an artillery barrage in response. The effects of cylinders were also blunted by the development of anti-gas defences, including warning systems, the training of soldiers in anti-gas drills, and the use of gas masks and other protective measures. Cylinders, nonetheless, remained a relatively cheap delivery system, and were used to harass an enemy by forcing him to wear a respirator for protracted periods of time. In spite of experiments to reduce the logistical burden and move batteries by ropeways and trench tramways, cylinders were generally more suited to fighting from fixed positions than fighting in a war of movement.

For more precise and accurate gas attacks, the belligerents came to rely upon artillery, mortars and gas projectors. Although gas artillery accounted for only 4.54 per cent of the artillery ammunition expended in the conflict, it caused some 85 per cent of the gas deaths and injuries (about 1,230,000 casualties overall).[19] Gunners experimented with tear gas shells, lethal gas shells, mixtures of gases, and refinements in the fusing and the design of shell casings. When the Germans launched bombardments with mustard gas from July 1917, they inflicted their heaviest casualties and began to deny the enemy ground by contaminating large tracts of terrain. The 4-inch Stokes mortar proved even more effective as a rapid means of establishing a high vapour concentration over a target, albeit over a limited range. Specially designed for gas warfare, it was a practical weapon that could be carried fairly easily and was not heavily dependent upon favourable meteorological conditions. Another specially designed chemical weapon was the Livens projector, named after its inventor, Captain William Howard Livens, and first employed by the British at the preliminary bombardment for the battle of Arras on 4 April 1917. By employing batteries of Livens projectors, the British could launch massive concentrations of agent over a large target area with maximum surprise in a way that neither artillery nor mortar units could emulate. Unlike cylinders, these were not weather-dependent weapons and could be discharged from behind the front lines by means of an electrical detonating wire. In the First World War, though, the projectors, each weighing 60 pounds and containing another 30 pounds of agent, were laborious to install, had a limited range of 1,700 yards, and could fire only at pre-determined targets.

Like other chemical weapons the Livens projector would be refined after the war, with its range increased to 2,500 yards and a stand, base block and drum provided for each device to enable it to be used, if required, in more mobile warfare. Gunners received time-and-percussion quick fuses that greatly enhanced the ability of artillery shells to disseminate chemical fillings. By means of these fuses, they could fire chemical shells for overhead bursts like shrapnel or for bursts on the surface of the ground (and not in the bottom of craters). They also fired more accurately, exploiting improvements in post-war ballistics. However, the Germans devised a whole range of munitions to supplement their use of artillery shells and exploit the potential of mustard gas as a means of ground contamination. They built bulk contamination vehicles, fitted with pressure nozzle attachments that could spray a belt of ground 700 metres long by 22 metres wide, with a contamination of 100 grams of mustard gas per square metre. They also devised a range of mines that could be laid at the last minute or by motorized transport, relying upon a spike on the bottom end of the mine to penetrate the ground and keep the mine upright. Finally they developed multi-barrel rocket launchers (MRLS) that were potentially more effective than guns or howitzers in delivering surprise chemical strikes because of their optimum rate of fire and agent-ammunition ratio. Although they employed these rockets to deliver conventional ordnance during the war, both the Americans and the Soviets enhanced the range and rate of fire of multiple rocket launchers after the war. As the Soviet BM-21 had a capacity to fire 40 rounds in twenty seconds over a range of 20.5 kilometres, the 18 MRLS of a Soviet motor-rifle division could fire 720 rounds (of which about 15 per cent of each would be chemical fill) in some twenty seconds. By delivering chemical agents so quickly, and in such quantities, the MRLS could lay down an effective concentration of fast-acting and quickly evaporating agents, like sarin or hydrogen cyanide.[20]

Yet the innovation that transformed the potential of chemical (and biological) warfare lay in the realm of aerial warfare. Giulio Douhet, the famous Italian advocate of air power, was only one of many writers who forecast that aerial gas attacks would become an integral aspect of strategic bombing in the future.[21] These attacks could involve either use of spray apparatus, involving pressure or non-pressure as a mode of release or bombs. Low-level spraying at subsonic speeds had an enhanced capacity for area coverage, and could achieve surprise through an off-target attack. Before, during and after the Second World War the major powers experimented with various forms of spray apparatus, and the Soviets perfected a 'line source' mode of attack, whereby they could disperse biological agents from tanks or Ilyushin bombers along a straight line for hundreds of miles. By such operations the Soviets envisaged the possibility of large-scale anti-livestock or anti-crop attacks to wipe out agricultural activity over wide areas in a matter of months.[22] The fast-acting properties of nerve agents had even more potential in an anti-personnel mode within the context of a high-intensity battlefield. 4,000 kg of sarin, if sprayed by eight low-flying aircraft across wind over six km of open or lightly wooded terrain, on an overcast day with a gentle breeze (about ten km/hour), could inflict heavy casualties on soldiers five km downwind. If the troops attacked only donned their respirators when they felt the first symptoms of nerve-agent poisoning, and if other medical counter-measures proved efficient, they could anticipate 20–30 per cent severe or fatal casualties and 70–80 per cent light casualties. With inefficient countermeasures, they might experience 80 per cent severe and 20 per cent light casualties.[23]

Bombing remained an attractive alternative because chemical bombs could use conventional bomb racks, be dropped from high level, and, as they did not rotate in the air like artillery shells, had negligible difference between liquid-filled and solid-filled ordnance. Chemical bombing involved much less risk than low-level spraying and possessed the potential of mounting attacks upon an enemy throughout the entire depth of his deployment, including specific targets such as railheads, supply points, air bases, headquarters and ports. The typical chemical bomb of the Second World War had a large streamlined container with a central high-explosive burster, liquid chemical filling, fin assembly and fuse. It could be used to disseminate various agents, including mustard or thickened mustard gas, for the purposes of ground contamination. To reduce the problem of over-dosage around the point of burst, cluster bombs, and later bomblets, spread the area of coverage. Indeed, bomblets, whether dispersed by aerial bombs or by missile warheads in off-target attacks, across the wind and upwind of the target area, could create an intense upwind source of agent. The Americans later developed the MK-116 Weteye bomb and the BLU-80/B Bigeye bomb, which released aerosol sprays on detonation.

Missiles and rockets were another means of delivering chemical and biological payloads in long-range strikes without imperilling either aircraft or pilots. The Soviet armed forces possessed an extensive array of such delivery systems. Each division had four Frog 7 free-flight rockets, capable of delivering a chemical warhead over a range of 65 kilometres. The Scud B missile was able to deliver a chemical warhead of 500 kg over a range of 280 kilometres. Both the Scud B and the Scaleboard missile, with a range of 800 km and a larger payload, delivered their agents in bulk form or as small bomblets, which could be released in flight 'creating a lethal rain over several square kilometres'.[24] If the large warheads of these missiles compensated for their inaccuracy, their replacements – the ss-21 for the Frog rocket and the ss-23 for the Scud – combined longer ranges with larger payloads and much greater capability, so extending the potential threat throughout the enemy's operational theatre. Even more devastating potentially was the extensive Soviet testing of cruise and intercontinental ballistic missiles (ICBMs) as a means of delivering biological agents. As defectors revealed, the Soviets envisaged the launch of BW attacks with cruise missiles, exploiting their onboard electronic guidance and mapping systems to fly sub-sonically at very low levels, evading most radar systems. Consequently, whether launched from the air, sea or land, cruise missiles had the potential to launch surprise biological attacks by spraying aerosol clouds over their target areas. An alternative method of attacking large strategic areas was by means of launching ICBMs loaded with biological agent. After several decades of flight-testing, the Soviets allegedly possessed the capacity to deliver anthrax, plague and smallpox by their ICBMs: as Dr Ken Alibek, the former first deputy chief of the Soviet Biopreparat agency, observed, 'A hundred kilograms of anthrax spores would, in optimal atmospheric conditions, kill up to three million people in any of the densely populated metropolitan areas of the United States.'[25]

Variable Effects of Chemical and Biological Weapons

Underpinning the reference to optimal atmospheric conditions is one of the major imponderables affecting the impact and effectiveness of chemical and biological weapons, namely their susceptibility to atmospheric and topographical conditions. In this respect they differ markedly from any other form of weaponry, earning a reputation for unpredictability and unreliability on the field of battle. The amount of agent used, even the feasibility of an attack at all, may depend upon the weather and terrain: variables in wind strength and direction, temperature and rain, coupled with the nature of the ground, could all have a bearing on the effects of an agent. Once a toxic agent is released in the air, it will form a toxic cloud whose effectiveness depends on its concentration and the length of time it takes to pass its target. A sarin attack of 500 kg/km would only pose a significant hazard 100 kilometres downwind in highly stable atmospheric conditions, that is, when the cloud is propelled by gentle winds (seven km/hour) over a period of about fourteen hours. Such conditions are likely to occur at the end of a sunny day, when a temperature inversion occurs and a layer of cooler air becomes trapped beneath a mass of hot light air (and the cooler air, because of its greater density, fails to rise, so leaving the atmosphere in a stable equilibrium). Similar conditions may persist at night or for several days during overcast weather in winter and often in valleys or plains surrounded by high peaks. Whereas high temperatures will accelerate evaporation, snow will inhibit it and increase the persistence of ground contamination. Similarly, light rain will disperse and spread a chemical agent; heavy rain will dilute and displace the agent, facilitating ground penetration but accelerating the destruction of water-sensitive compounds such as lewisite.[26]

Topographical factors, including the contour of the ground, vegetation and man-made structures, will compound the effects of meteorological factors. While gas clouds can move steadily over flat countryside under stable atmospheric conditions, they divide to avoid high ground, flow down valleys and accumulate in hollows, low ground and depressions. The persistence of the agent will be influenced by the texture and porosity of the soil, and by the presence or absence of vegetation. Chemical contaminants, though slow to penetrate the canopy of woods or forests, will persist for much longer in woods than if dispersed over barren terrain. They will also persist for longer in urban areas, despite their higher surface temperatures, than over open ground because building materials are frequently porous and tend to retain liquid chemical agents. Moreover, the factors that tend to reduce the persistence of contamination in open country (sunshine and wind over the ground) are of less importance in a city, where local inversions may occur in narrow streets during the night. Variables in climate and terrain may alter the persistence of contamination of the same agent over periods ranging from several days to weeks, or even months, depending upon local circumstances. Hence a UN report concluded 'that *a priori* classification of chemical agents as persistent or non-persistent, solely on the basis of different degrees of volatility, is somewhat arbitrary'.[27] Though true, this hardly detracts from the fact that persistent agents, such as mustard gas or VX nerve agent, dispersed in the form of liquid droplets, are less susceptible to the vagaries of the weather than non-persistent agents.

As living organisms, biological agents are more vulnerable than chemical agents to sunlight, temperature, humidity and other environmental factors, especially the effects of ultraviolet light. Biological agents have several characteristics, notably infectivity (the ability to infect a human host and cause disease), virulence (severity of the resulting disease), transmissibility (the ability of the disease to spread from person to person) and persistence (the duration of a microbe's survival once released into the environment).[28] Once disseminated, a BW agent can retain its ability to live and multiply but lose its virulence, and so the effectiveness of aerosol-borne BW agents depends upon their ability to survive in the air. Accordingly, the use of modern meteorological forecasting, coupled with the choice of appropriate agents and delivery systems, would be a prerequisite in the planning of a biological attack. Admittedly, abrupt changes in climatic conditions could prejudice the prospects of a successful attack but the BW agents need not decay in the process. Soviet scientists found that special additives could prevent their BW agents from decaying when they were transported over long distances and keep them alive in adverse weather conditions.[29] With sufficient scientific resources, access to micrometeorological techniques and adequate planning, climatic obstacles can be surmounted but they can never be discounted entirely, even if less significant in small-scale covert or terrorist operations.

The capacity of Soviet scientists to manipulate microorganisms to make them more stable and more lethal underscores another dynamic in biological weaponry, namely the application of biotechnology and genetic engineering to improve the efficiency of potential BW agents. Mooted by Joshua Lederberg as early as 1970, this use of genetic engineering aroused intense debate in the last two decades of the twentieth century. If such usage seemed unlikely to produce novel BW agents with greater potency than naturally occurring agents, genetic engineering might facilitate, as the OTA argued, the modification of 'standard agents to make them more stable during dissemination or more difficult to detect or defend against'.[30] They could do so by altering their antigene structures to overcome immunity barriers, changing the markers normally used in diagnostics, enhancing their resistance to antibiotics, making them more resistant to ultraviolet radiation and desiccation (and so more usable in aerosol form), restricting them to particular target organs or tissues, or unrestricting them and making them easier to produce and store. The JASON study by several American scientists in 1997 agreed that bacteria and viruses could be engineered to imbue them 'with such "desirable" attributes as safer handling, increased virulence, improved ability to target the host, greater difficulty of detection and easier distribution'.[31] More recently the scientists who have created live, artificial viruses or discovered how to preserve the potency of botulinum toxin have warned that their findings could be misused for the purposes of bioterrorism.[32] Were terrorists able to acquire and use genetically engineered microbes or viruses, they might bypass bio-defences designed to detect and counter traditional agents.

In short, chemical and biological weapons have constituted an evolving military capability whose effects were difficult to predict and whose impact ranged from the negligible or inconsequential through a variable level of casualties, both physical and psychological, within specific target areas. BW agents, in particular, if dispersed in favourable conditions by an effective means of delivery, could cause casualties over an extensive area: as a Pentagon report, issued in November 1997, concluded,

> Biological weapons have the greatest potential for lethality of any weapon . . . there are few barriers to developing such weapons with a modest level of effort. The current level of sophistication for many biological agents is low, but there is enormous potential – based on advances in modern molecular biology, fermentation, and drug delivery technology – for making sophisticated weapons.[33]

1

The Legacy of Gas Warfare in the First World War

The First World War represented a watershed in the history of chemical (and to a lesser extent, biological) warfare. Although the use of chemical and biological weapons, including attempts to contaminate water supplies, had lengthy historical precedents, with examples or allegations from ancient warfare through the Middle Ages to the South African War (1899–1902), chemical warfare occurred in the Great War on a scale, and with a sustained application of scientific expertise and effort, never previously witnessed. This total war, then known as the war to end all wars, has been dubbed as the first 'interstate industrial war', with entire state economies and populations committed to the conflict.[1] Chemical weaponry represented only a part, and a relatively small part, of the weaponry engaged. It involved the expenditure of some 125,000 tons of poison gas compared with two million tons of high explosive and 50,000 million rounds of small arms ammunition,[2] but reflected a large-scale investment of scientific and industrial resources in an innovative form of warfare. The conduct of offensive biological operations took place on an even smaller scale and never required the construction of the large organizations that sustained the chemical conflict. The latter form of war evolved and adapted throughout three and a half years, arousing intense passions at the time, and in its aftermath, and provoking lasting debates about its utility and potential. 'The history of chemical warfare', wrote Major Victor Lefebure, a wartime cw authority and later an executive in Imperial Chemical Industries (ICI) Ltd, 'becomes one of continual attempts, on both sides, to achieve surprise, and to counter it by some accurate forecast in protective methods. It is a struggle for the initiative.'[3]

Historical Antecedents

However shocking the first major use of gas in 1915, chemical and biological warfare has an historical pedigree stretching back over several millennia. In ancient warfare European, Indian and Chinese commentators described the recurrent use of poisonous smokes, with Thucydides recounting how the Peloponnesians had tried to reduce the town of Plataea with sulphur fumes in the fifth century BC. The Byzantines employed Greek Fire, an incendiary weapon (possibly based on petroleum with resins added as a thickener) in naval and military battles, and it reportedly contributed to the salvation of Constantinople from two Arab sieges. Insect bombs were used in the defence of walled cities, with bees released in tunnels to disperse sappers or secreted in booby traps, while bombs containing 'stinging' insects were hurled at scaling parties (possibly including scorpions in the defence of Hatra against Roman assault). The Greeks and Romans also utilized a wide range of poisonous substances in military operations, notably the Athenians in dumping cartloads of poisonous hellebore into the river that supplied the besieged city of Kirrha, near Delphi in Greece (c. 600 BC). The contaminated water induced violent diarrhoea, incapacitating so many defenders that the Athenians were able to overrun the city and slaughter its inhabitants.[4]

The deliberate spreading of infectious disease assumed different forms in land battles and naval warfare as combatants sought to debilitate their adversaries. The catapulting of beehives recurred between 1000 and 1300 AD, exploiting the vulnerability of horses even when soldiers wore protection in heavy clothing and armour. In 1346 the besieged Genoese seaport of Caffa (now Feodosia) on the Crimean coast incurred a biological onslaught when plague-stricken Mongols began hurling infected cadavers over their walls (probably using the trebuchet, a much more powerful machine with a longer range than a catapult). As the disease took hold survivors fled by boat, constituting one of several sources of infection that spread the disease through the Mediterranean basin. Less well documented are the allegations and effects of similar tactics at other sieges, notably those of Karlstein (1422) and Reval (1710): at the former an epidemic did not erupt and city held out, at the latter plague did occur but its contribution to the fall of the city is not so clear.[5]

Where suitable poisons could be found, they were employed to enhance the effects of weapons such as arrows, spears and darts, and in this role remained a longstanding feature of combat in parts of the developing world. Limited in range and sometimes uncertain in effect, these tactics seemed eclipsed by the development of cannons and gunpowder and hardly appropriate within the rules of European warfare as codified by Hugo Grotius, *De jure belli ac pacis* (1625) and Emmerich de Vattel, *The Law of Nations* (1758). These works included strictures, condemning the use of poisoned weapons and the poisoning of water supplies, but they only applied to 'just' wars between 'civilized' nations. In wars against 'savage' or 'heathen' peoples European rules licensed extreme measures as reprisals to punish or even exterminate adversaries. Within this context came the best-documented account of biological warfare in North America, namely the distribution of blankets and a handkerchief infected with smallpox from Fort Pitt in June 1763 during Pontiac's rebellion. The subsequent eruption of smallpox among the Delaware, Shawnee and Mingo Indians may have had other contributory factors but the epidemic accorded with the vituperative comments of Major-General Jeffery Amherst in his New York headquarters, exhorting the use of every method that would 'extirpate this execrable race'. The recurrent outbreaks of smallpox during the American Revolutionary War also led to allegations of deliberate infection.[6]

Natural outbreaks of disease continued to afflict mass armies from the French Revolutionary and Napoleonic wars onwards, often accounting for the majority of casualties and fatalities incurred. The multiple infections known as 'Walcheren fever', with malaria as the major component, destroyed a British expeditionary force in 1809, while bubonic plague swept through Napoleon's forces in his Egyptian expedition (1799), yellow fever devastated French forces in Haiti (1802–3), and various diseases, including typhus, accounted for over half of the 400,000 fatalities among the *Grande Armée* in Russia (1812). Whenever concentrated forces moved across terrain where disease was endemic, intermixed with other peoples, congregated at polluted supplies of water (like the British army outside Bloemfontein in 1900), and lacked high standards of hygiene and medical care, casualties from disease multiplied rapidly. Disease accounted for ten times as many men as the British lost in action during the Crimean War (1853–6), for nearly two-thirds of the fatalities on both sides in the American Civil War (1861–5) and for about two-thirds of fatalities in the South African War. In these circumstances, the deliberate spreading of poison was likely to arouse further ire. Raised as an issue at the peace conferences of 1868 and 1874, and at the Hague conference of 1899, all the principal belligerents, except Britain and the United States, agreed to 'abstain from the use of projectiles the sole object of which is the diffusion of asphyxiating or deleterious gas'. Britain later adhered to a similar declaration at the Peace Conference of 1907.[7]

The First Major Gas Attack

In light of these pronouncements Germany incurred most of the opprobrium for initiating large-scale chemical warfare, but both Britain and Germany had conducted pre-war experiments with irritant agents while France had developed the first practical chemical weapon – a hand grenade containing a relatively mild tear gas (ethyl bromoacetate) for use by the French police from 1912. By August 1914, the French army had procured 30,000 26-mm cartridges filled with the liquid agent and fired them from special rifles (*fusils lance-cartouches éclairantes*) on the Western Front in 1914 and in the Argonne sector in March 1915. In September 1914 Lieutenant-General Douglas M.B.H. Cochrane, 12th Earl of Dundonald, informed Lord Kitchener of the plans left by his grandfather, Admiral Sir Thomas Cochrane, during the Napoleonic Wars for the use of sulphur dioxide clouds to drive an enemy from fortified positions. Although Kitchener discounted these, Winston Churchill, then First Lord of the Admiralty, kept the scheme alive and eventually the proposal, in a modified form, was implemented not as lethal gas clouds but as naval smoke screens.[8]

Yet the major innovation of the gas war was the first large-scale use of chlorine gas, discharged from cylinders at Ypres on 22 April 1915. German interest in chemical munitions had quickened after the onset of trench warfare, following their reverse at the Marne in September 1914. Early experiments with irritant agents proved ineffectual, notably the shelling of the French at Neuve-Chapelle with 3,000 rounds of *Ni-Shrapnell* (27 October 1914), the bombardment of the Russians at Bolimow with 18,000 *T-Stoff* shells (31 January 1915), and the firing of tear gas at Nieuport against the French (March 1915). However, Professor Fritz Haber convinced the German military authorities that cloud-gas attacks with chlorine launched from cylinders emplaced in the front line would prove more effective. Although the allied intelligence had detected preparations for the impending attack (they could hardly miss the installation of several thousand cylinders in the enemy's trenches), they totally underestimated its potential effects and their forces lacked any form of protection. When the Germans released the chlorine from 5,730 cylinders along a 6-kilometre front, they precipitated the flight of the French forces (the 45th Algerian and the 87th Territorial Divisions), opening up a gap of some 8 to 9 kilometres and enabling their infantry to capture some 50 guns, 2,000 prisoners and a substantial tract of the Ypres Salient. But the Germans lacked reserves and dug in at night rather than press on to Ypres, only 2,500 yards away, thereby allowing the allies to regroup, to bring forward ten battalions to cover the gap and counter-attack.[9]

Like the allies, the German high command failed to anticipate the surprise effects of the first major gas attack. By approving the attack as an experiment that would divert attention from the transportation of German forces to Galicia,[10] they wasted its potential. By 24 April, when the Germans launched another chlorine attack, the Canadians, aided by improvised protection, resisted with only minimal loss of ground, and neither this attack nor the four subsequent gas attacks in May broke the deadlock of the trenches. The Germans, as Brigadier Harold Hartley asserted after the war,

> made almost every possible mistake in their earliest gas attacks. They chose a gas against which protection could be obtained with comparative ease, they used it in small quantities on narrow fronts in discharges of long duration and low concentration, thus losing the effect in depth, and finally they failed to exploit the partial advantage they gained. Within three weeks we were protected.[11]

The Germans also handed the allies a propaganda coup. Both in the wake of these attacks, and after the war, the allies protested over the German initiation of 'frightfulness' (as gas warfare was dubbed) and about the breach of international law (the spirit, if not the letter, as projectiles were not involved). Although the number of gas casualties in the first attack could not be assessed accurately as the French failed to keep any records, and the Algerians retired too quickly to have lost many men, spurious accounts of the gas casualties were published. The claim that 5,000 men died out of 15,000 gas casualties, still reproduced in some histories of chemical warfare, is almost certainly an exaggeration as British field ambulances and casualty-clearing stations only treated about 7,000 gas casualties, of whom 350 died.[12] Numbers of casualties, though, were less important than the demonstration of large-scale gas warfare: as a German officer, Rudolph Binding, wrote in his diary on 24 April 1914, 'I am not pleased with the idea of poisoning men. Of course, the entire world will rage about it at first and then imitate us.'[13]

Organization of the Gas War

Imitation involved the organization of scientific, military and industrial expertise to support the evolving gas war; the design, development and refinement of chemical protective kit, with the preparation of accompanying warning systems and anti-gas training; and the research, development and production of various methods to retaliate-in-kind. Based in the Kaiser Wilhelm Institute for Physical Chemistry, Haber, promoted to the army rank of captain, had perceived the need to organize and concentrate German resources in the gas war. He drove forward the research and development of war gases, advised on the requirements for weapon-development, assisted in the formation of special forces (later Pioneer Regiments 35 and 36) to undertake gas operations in the field, and collaborated with industry in the design of protective devices against chemical agents, both Germany's gases and later those of the enemy. His institute expanded steadily, became fully committed to the military in February 1916, and evolved into nine departments at various locations in Berlin and its suburbs. By the end of the war it employed 150 academically trained staff, 1,300 non-commissioned officers, soldiers, other workers and additional support personnel. Despite the commitment of skilled scientists, relatively simple lines of command and some delegation of responsibility to section heads in 1916, the organization reflected Haber's autocratic, if inspiring, leadership, and the increasingly military tone, secrecy and compartmentalization of its activities. Although German research sometimes pursued unproductive lines of inquiry, relied excessively on diphosgene and responded slowly to the Livens projector, it seized the initiative repeatedly in the gas war, introducing chlorine, phosgene and later mustard gas.[14]

Neither Britain nor France possessed a commanding authority to lead, inspire and organize their chemical warfare responses. The extreme centralization of French science enabled scientists and laboratories to forge close links between the offensive and defensive research, with another department responsible for application and pilot-plant operation, and a third for purchases and dispatch. By contrast, the British organization evolved with entirely separate groups working upon the defensive and offensive aspects of gas warfare, according defensive research priority and leaving offensive research isolated, producing 'duplication, vexation, and delay'.[15] Despite even more problems in the production of chlorine, and the supply of cylinders, the British pressed ahead with plans to retaliate-in-kind, exploiting the generally favourable westerly winds in the cloud-gas war. Initially they formed four 'Special Companies' to undertake the gas operations in France. Under the command of Major (later Major-General) Charles H. Foulkes, Royal Engineers, who would become a doughty champion of cloud-gas warfare, the companies included soldiers posted from other units and men with scientific experience or qualifications, who were enlisted as corporals with higher rates of pay. Within five months of the first German use of gas, the British were able to retaliate at the battle of Loos (25 September 1915).[16]

In the following year the War Office acquired an initial 2,886 acres at Porton Down as an experimental ground with hutted laboratories. The site would be expanded steadily over the course of the war, eventually occupying 6,196 acres, with another 310 acres at the nearby Arundel farm for animal breeding. It enabled Britain to conduct field trials of chemical weapons (cylinders, shells and Livens projectors), the examination of 147 toxic substances, assisted by work in the first physiological laboratory erected on the site, a meteorological section, and individual and collective protection when the Anti-Gas Department was moved to Porton from the Royal Army Medical College in 1917. By the Armistice, Britain had 916 officers and other ranks, 500 civilians and 33 women of Queen Mary's Auxiliary Corps working at Porton. Although there were frustrations in the British gas effort, reflecting the original separation of the offensive and defensive research, the wide range of departments involved, both at home and on the Western Front, and shortcomings in the productivity of the chemical and munition industries, this was a remarkable period of experimentation and often imitation in response to the German gas initiatives.[17]

In an industrial war, though, Germany possessed an indisputable advantage in the scale and productivity of its manufacturing plant. Of an estimated 150,000 tons of gases manufactured during the war, Germany produced 68,100 tons or about 45 per cent, with the Bayer plant alone producing 32,317 tons of gases – more than Britain (25,735 tons) and only marginally less than France (36,955 tons).[18]

Close contacts between Carl Duisberg, the chief executive of Bayer, with Haber and the military high command, facilitated the responsiveness of industry to the many demands of chemical warfare. Even so, the legendary organization of the German industry only evolved slowly and it was not until well into 1916 that Bayer and other dye-stuff plants, now working at less than full capacity, combined to form IG (Interessengemeinschaft der Deutschen Teerfarbenfabriken). Plants within this massive combine specialized in the production of precursor chemicals, war gases, munition filling and gas-mask components. Newly built plants, including Adlershof near Berlin and Breloh on the Lüneberger Heide in northern Germany, were placed under military control. The French never matched the German economies of scale and developed a mixture of government-owned and small-scale independent enterprises, while the British industry had to expand rapidly from its initial reliance upon Castner-Kellner of Runcorn as the sole source of liquid chlorine, eventually engaging 70 factories in the CW effort. However, Britain and France struggled to respond to the German introduction of mustard gas (12/13 July 1917) and sustained use thereafter, exploiting ample supplies of thiodiglycol, a key precursor in the German manufacturing method. French production only began in May 1918 and the British in September 1918, after 710 of the 1,100 workers at the Avonmouth plant had incurred mustard gas-related illnesses, producing a mere 500 tons by the Armistice. The United States, entering the war in 1917, followed neither the French nor British approach; it chose to build a federal gas factory alongside the principal shell-filling plant at Edgewood, Maryland. Rapidly built and efficiently managed, this factory employed over 7,000 personnel at its peak, and began producing phosgene, chloropicrin and mustard gas in August 1918.[19]

Anti-gas Defences

As an early victim of poison gas, Britain regarded anti-gas protection as its main priority. Within 36 hours of the first gas attack, the army issued impregnated pads to its troops in France. These were followed by hoods with a mica window (the 'Hypo' Helmet), then the Phenate Helmet, which saved many lives when the Germans launched their first phosgene attack on 19 December 1915, and later the Phenate-Hexamine or 'PH' Helmet that gave enhanced protection against phosgene. Despite the manufacture of 14 million 'PH' Helmets, further refinements in 1916 included the 'PHG' Helmet, with goggles to protect the eyes against lachrymators; the Large Box Respirator, a somewhat cumbersome attempt to emulate the high standard of protection achieved by the German cartridge design; and finally, the Small Box Respirator, a highly efficient mask relying upon charcoal and other chemicals as adsorbents in the box and much lighter to wear than the German mask with its canister screwed into the facepiece. Sixteen million Small Box Respirators were issued to British and American troops before the Armistice.[20]

Although these respirators protected the eyes and respiratory tract against the effects of mustard gas, the ability of mustard to burn and blister, even through clothing, confounded wartime research. When the Germans became victims of French mustard-gas attacks, they issued boxes of bleaching powder or permanganate so that soldiers could treat any contaminated skin with reactive chemicals. This proved impractical as supplies of bleach never matched requirements and the boxes only added to the burdens of the soldiery. Similarly, attempts to protect soldiers by issuing them with a cream or protective paste before an assault failed to provide sustained protection in the field. Mobile bathing units, as employed by the Americans, were another attempt to decontaminate soldiers and keep them in the field but the units were few in number, extremely heavy and confined to roads. The only real solution was to equip soldiers with mustard-gas-proof clothing but the oiled suits prepared during the war proved too cumbersome and were only worn by a few artillery formations.

With the coming of mustard gas, decontamination became a much more daunting task as ammunition dumps, gun emplacements and factories all became liable to contamination. Bleaching powder, which broke down dichlorodiethyl sulphide into sulphur chlorides and ethylene dichloride, became the primary decontaminant. After barrages with mustard-gas (or Yellow Cross) shells, guns and camouflage had to be cleaned (often with chloride of lime) and both the ground round the gun emplacements and the impact points of the shells dusted with bleaching powder. The white patches from the decontaminants then had to be covered with earth to conceal them from aerial observation. Similar precautions had to be taken in any sheltered place where the gas could penetrate.

Physical protection, though, was never the sole concern in anti-gas defence. As soldiers could wear their masks for only limited periods of time, they required adequate warning of an impending gas attack. If it were a cloud-gas attack, like the first German phosgene attack when the cloud travelled over 8,500 yards, gongs and klaxons in the front-line trenches would not alert men in the rear. The British duly installed Strombos horns, with their distinctively loud noise caused by compressed air, in both the front-line trenches and at intervals towards their rear. Likewise, when the Germans found that shell-fire rendered their system of bells and sirens inaudible, they introduced a warning system based upon electric bells and light signals in the dug-outs. Following these warnings, soldiers were supposed to perform anti-gas drills but the response was always variable. Commanding officers and gas specialists regularly attributed a significant proportion of their gas casualties to men being caught by surprise, lapses in gas discipline, and the loss, neglect or misuse of their anti-gas equipment. Although general service officers, staff and men received anti-gas instruction from specialist chemical advisers in gas schools, the instruction often seemed theoretical, and another burden, until a gas attack was experienced at first hand. As this experience varied considerably, anti-gas discipline remained erratic. For example, Anglo-American soldiers repeatedly used the satchels that accompanied their box respirators to carry extraneous items that damaged the respirator inadvertently or impeded its rapid removal, but German soldiers were just as prone to mistakes. As a gas officer of the Sixth German Army recorded in November 1916,

> The casualties were mainly due to the men being surprised in dug-outs, to the neglect of gas discipline, masks not being at hand, to faulty masks, and to the use of old pattern drums which could not afford protection against the type of gas employed by the enemy.[21]

Offensive Gas Tactics

The tactical use of gas evolved as the war gases and new munitions became available, taking account of the integration of chemical and conventional operations, the enduring problems of communications across 'No Man's Land', and the supply shortages, particularly of shells, that recurred throughout much of the war. Any hopes that poison gas as a new weapon of war could break the stalemate of the trenches quickly vanished in 1915. The failure of the initial German attack at Ypres, followed by the failure of a British chlorine attack at

Loos, eroded confidence in gas as a breakthrough weapon. In the preparations for the Loos attack Sir Douglas Haig, once a sceptic about gas, had become an enthusiastic convert, and insisted that the attack could not be mounted without the aid of gas. He was aware, nonetheless, that cloud-gas attacks were highly weather-dependent. Although the winds helped on the right flank at Loos and provided assistance in the centre, they proved a liability on the left, blowing back on the British troops. Over the next three weeks of inconclusive fighting, some 2,000 British soldiers succumbed as casualties of their own gas, ten fatally and 55 severely wounded.[22]

By persevering with cloud-gas attacks thereafter, the British exploited the prevailing westerly winds in France and compensated for their continuing problems in shell production, but their aims became those of harassment and attrition. During the battle of the Somme and its immediate aftermath, Britain launched 110 cylinder operations between 24 June 1916 and 19 March 1917. Given the depth of the attacks and the aim to incapacitate, demoralize or exhaust the enemy's reserves, inflicting casualties whenever men were caught by surprise, field commanders could only gather fitful information about the effects of the gas from raiding parties, deserters or prisoners of war. While some commanders, like Sir Henry Wilson, commended these attacks, others doubted their value and the commander of the First Army reckoned that the advantages were uncertain, variable and a matter of conjecture. Any losses and demoralization inflicted on the enemy, he argued, were outweighed by the labour of installing cylinders in the front line and the danger they posed to British troops.[23]

More accurate attacks that infantry could follow up required the use of lethal gas shells (introduced by the Germans and French in 1916) or projectors (first used experimentally at the Somme and then on a large scale by the British at the preliminary bombardment before the battle of Arras, 4 April 1917). Initially, the Germans wasted the effects of lethal gas shells by bombarding wide areas and so failing to achieve high concentrations of gas. By the autumn of 1916 the French sought to exploit the rate of fire by slow, steady shelling of the German batteries over several hours, and replaced the use of hydrogen cyanide, a highly toxic blood agent (as used at Verdun in February 1916), which seldom achieved the requisite concentrations. The Germans experimented with phosgene, diphosgene (another lung irritant) and diphenylchloroarsine (DA), sometimes mixing the agents, sometimes using them separately, notably DA shells marked with a blue cross and diphosgene shells marked with a green cross. When they introduced mustard gas (known by its shell marking as Yellow Cross) in attacks upon the area around Ypres (July 1917), they found that this was a potent means of inflicting casualties.

Colonel Georg Bruchmüller refined the gas artillery tactics in pounding Russian positions during the autumn and winter of 1917 before introducing them on the Western Front in the spring offensive of 1918. By mounting short, intense bombardments, they achieved surprise concentrations of gas in their counter-battery fire; by bombarding enemy positions with non-persistent gas shell (Green Cross), they paved the way for follow-up infantry assaults. In the famous attack across the Dvina at Riga on 1 September 1917, the German counter-battery fire began at 4 a.m., the bombardment of the Russian infantry at 6 a.m. and the crossing of the river at 9.10 a.m., encountering a very weak counter-barrage from the Russian guns.

In the subsequent spring offensive on the Western Front, Bruchmüller allocated about 100 guns per kilometre and launched short, intense pre-dawn bombardments in the five major attacks (21 March, 9 April, 27 May, 9 June and 15 July 1918). German gunners fired the arsenic Blue Cross shells in the hope of penetrating enemy respirators, causing the victims to sneeze and remove their respirators, so breathing in the lethal Green Cross gas. They also bombarded allied artillery with Blue and Green Cross shells, targeting each allied battery in rectangles with co-ordinated fire from three or four German batteries, before pounding targets some 600 yards from the German infantry with Blue Cross and Green Cross shells, and then launching the attacks with creeping barrages of Blue Cross shells some 600 yards ahead of the advancing infantry. They also inflicted heavy casualties on the flanks of these attacks, with massive barrages of Yellow Cross shells, pounding Armentières so heavily between 7 and 9 April that gutters reportedly ran with mustard gas. Although the Blue Cross shells never fulfilled expectations, allied soldiers had to wear respirators for protracted periods, adding to their strain and fatigue and impeding their movement and communications.

When the allies launched their own offensive in August 1918, the Germans began using their gas shells, particularly Yellow Cross shells, defensively. Although they still employed large quantities of Blue Cross, and sometimes Green and Blue Cross, shells in defensive barrages and in preparation for counter-battery attacks, they relied primarily upon Yellow Cross shells to disorganize the allied operations. They employed these shells in pounding front-line positions, counter-battery work, horse-drawn resupply and creating barriers of mustard gas to impede the forward movement of allied forces. Only by maintaining very high standards of gas discipline at night (when most of the attacks occurred) could allied forces contain their gas-casualty rates. As the allied offensive progressed, German gas shelling, hampered by dwindling stocks of gas shells, became less organized as it sacrificed large-scale bombardments for smaller and more disparate ones. Hartley reckoned that the enemy had failed to exploit 'an extremely fine defensive weapon' as 'they neglected its use on roads and did not hamper our communications nearly as much as they might have done'.[24]

The British found themselves doubly handicapped in the offensive gas war. The lack of mustard gas meant that they could not retaliate-in-kind until late September 1918, and their shell-manufacturing difficulties compelled an undue reliance upon cylinders and shorter-range weapons such as Stokes 4-inch mortars and projectors. They mounted some gas artillery attacks but initially neglected variations in the rate of fire; only subsequent refinements in tactics enabled them to produce surprise concentrations of gas at night to interfere with enemy movements and in counter-battery bombardments. When they moved onto the offensive, though, the British did not employ projectors in creeping barrages and the speed of movement rendered gas operations increasingly difficult. In this respect the British approach differed from that of the American Expeditionary Force (AEF), late entrants into the war, who had suffered disproportionately from gas, incurring 26.8 per cent of its casualties, including dead and wounded, from gas. The 1st Gas Regiment realized the potential of Stokes mortars and projectors as a means of supporting the offensive war, and envisaged discharging gas, in conjunction with smoke and thermite, to force enemy troops to don their respirators and so reduce their morale, vision and operational effectiveness. The Americans believed, too, that by moving their Stokes mortars with advancing troops they could build up local concentrations of gas in attacks upon machine-gun nests, strong-points, trench intersections and other sensitive points in the German defences. After an initial gas operation at San Mihiel (12 September 1918), Company F was called upon to support the French XVII Corps in the Meuse-Argonne sector. Having installed 230 Livens projectors in two nights, they launched the largest American gas bombardment of the war on 16 October 1918, so prompting requests for further gas support. With his six companies badly in need of rest, Brigadier-General Amos A. Fries, the American Director of Gas Services, asked his British counterpart to transfer any of the underused British Special Companies to the American front. Although nine were despatched, they were not employed before the Armistice took effect.[25]

Imagery of Gas War

If one legacy of the gas war was the massive scientific, industrial and military effort involved over a period of four years, another legacy, which in some respects was more enduring, was the imagery of the gas war. From the first major use of gas at Ypres in April 1915, the allies had depicted this new form of war as peculiarly odious, a breach of international law, and yet another atrocity perpetrated by the Germans. Senior British military commanders, like Sir John French, castigated the Germans for playing 'a very dirty "low down" game' in shooting out 'that damnable gas' before seeking both respirators and a capacity to retaliate-in-kind.[26] *The Times*, possibly unaware of the likely British response, denounced 'an atrocious method of warfare' that would 'fill all races with a new horror of the German name'; Wellington House, the propaganda bureau of the Foreign Office, drew attention to these 'inhumane' methods of war in the hope of influencing opinion in the neutral United States; and 'Eye-Witness', the British government's official war correspondent, described how a German officer had laughed at the sufferings of British gas wounded. All these charges and allegations, coupled with other allied atrocity stories, like the crucifixion of a Canadian soldier and the publicity accorded to the sinking of the RMS *Lusitania*, ensured that gas remained a central issue in allied propaganda. Despite the readiness of the allies to retaliate-in-kind, and to introduce new weapons of war, including the flame-thrower, Germany would be arraigned for introducing poison gas as one of 32 crimes by the Commission of Responsibilities at the post-war peace conference.[27]

Of more importance as an influence upon the lasting image of gas warfare were the writings, poetry and paintings associated with gas. Few of these works placed the injuries inflicted by gas in any form of context; in other words, they failed to mention that gas shells, though responsible for some 85 per cent of gas casualties, constituted a mere 4.54 per cent of the artillery ammunition expended. Whether employed by gunners or by engineer-combat forces, gas comprised only a small fraction of the ordnance used and inflicted a mere 5.7 per cent of nonfatal battle injuries and 1.32 per cent of battle deaths.[28] Instead the wartime writers, poets and painters dwelt upon the peculiar agonies inflicted by gas. Sir Arthur Conan Doyle, writing on the *British Campaign in France and Flanders 1915* (1917), described the 'agonies of asphyxiation' inflicted by a 'mechanical and inhuman' ordeal; Wilfred Owen, in 'Dulce et Decorum Est' (1917), one of the great war poems, depicts the feelings of fear, exhaustion and choking to death from gas (but greatly compresses the likely period of a gassed soldier's demise); and John Singer Sargent, in his memorable painting *Gassed* (1918), portrays blinded and helpless men on their way to a casualty-clearing station – an image that fails to reveal that most victims of mustard gas recovered from temporary blindness within two weeks.[29]

Post-war writing reached a far wider audience. Erich Maria Remarque described both the fear of gas and the suffering of its victims in *All Quiet on the Western Front*, which was translated into English in 1929 and sold two and a half million copies within eighteen months of publication. In *Goodbye to All That* (1929), Robert Graves denounced gas as 'a nightmare', evincing little confidence in respirators and claiming that 'accessories' (as the cylinders were called) were unwelcome in the trenches as their gas could blow back on British soldiers and attract artillery fire from the enemy. Although Graves vividly described the 'yellow-faced and choking' gas victims with buttons tarnished green, and trenches stinking 'with a gas-blood-lyddite-latrine smell', he was not a dispassionate commentator on poison gas. Afflicted by a breathing difficulty, he could not wear the respirator issued on the eve of the Somme and a nose operation spared him from service on the first day of the battle. He retained an obsessive fear of gas, even trembling in later life from the strong scent of flowers. In *Memoirs of an Infantry Officer* (1930), Siegfried Sassoon expressed similar distaste for the changes wrought by modern warfare: by the winter of 1916–17, he wrote, war had become 'undisguisedly mechanical and inhuman'.[30]

Buttressing these sentiments were popular and perceived fears of poison gas that lived on into the interwar years. Military impressions of gas varied considerably: some veterans, imbued with fatalism, came to regard gas as a tiresome and chancy facet of war; others remained stricken with fears of gas. Whereas Edmund Blunden, in *Undertones of War* (1928), reckoned that he had suffered no ill effects from gas shelling in 1917, others in receipt of post-war pensions for the 'effects of gas' ascribed all manner of long-term illnesses to wartime gassing. In a study of 103 such pensioners, all of whom had respiratory conditions that might have been affected by smoking, industrial pollution or bad housing, and of whom only eleven died before the age of 70, they attributed their enduring illnesses and continuing ill health to the debilitating effects of wartime gassing. Their feelings doubtless conveyed to friends and family, and more broadly reflected in popular folk memory, sustained 'popular convictions' about the 'potency and systemic effects' of gas poisoning.[31]

Was Gas Warfare a Failure?

Another legacy of the war, though less apparent to contemporaries, was the perception that chemical warfare had proved a failure. 'Gas', wrote Brigadier-General James Edmonds, the official war historian, 'achieved but local success; it made war uncomfortable, to no purpose.' This view, though endorsed by another historian who served in the trenches, was probably too dismissive,[32] but it was taken up by Ludwig Haber, the son of Fritz Haber and author of the seminal study *The Poisonous Cloud* (1986). Having reviewed the chemical war in its scientific, industrial and operational dimensions, Haber sought to explain how Germany repeatedly seized the initiative in the conflict but failed to secure any decisive successes. This outcome he ascribed to the fitful commitment of the German high command, the 'mutual incomprehension of officers and scientists', the unreliability of the weapon system, weaknesses in the manufacturing and organization process, and the superiority of gas defences by 1918. On its own, argued Haber, gas was a failure; only in combination with artillery did it cause casualties and deny access to terrain that high explosive would have 'churned over'. He compared gas unfavourably with the tank, aircraft or light machine guns that 'changed the face of war in 1918', and cast doubt on predictions of an allied gas breakthrough in 1919.[33]

Few contemporaries would have endorsed this assertion: after the first aerial gas attacks upon the Bolsheviks (August and September 1919), Fries anticipated that gas would be used by every branch of the armed services in a future war.[34] The Great War had witnessed a steady increase in the use of gas, almost doubling from 32,500 tons in 1917 to 61,000 tons in 1918. By July 1918, gas shells comprised 50 per cent of the ammunition in some German ordnance dumps and, by the Armistice, they comprised 35 per cent of the French, 25 per cent of the British and fifteen per cent of the American ammunition expended. Had the war continued into 1919, the Americans, British and French had plans to expand their production of mustard gas and use of gas shell considerably. The British hoped to support a mobile war by use of a sled-mounted projector (a battery of sixteen tubes towed by a supply tank) and by dispersing a powerful sternutator, adamsite, code-named DM, from its Handley Page bombers, against which the German respirator offered no protection. The chemical conflict may or may not have become a 'ubiquitous condition of warfare on the Western Front',[35] but, by mid-September 1918, Canadian forces were encountering mustard-gas attacks every night, regardless of the atmospheric conditions as the German tried to disrupt their offensive preparations. Throughout that month Canadian gunners endured 'continuous chemical bombardments', suffering 2,389 casualties, of whom 344 were due to gas, and throughout the 'Last Hundred Days' of open warfare, the Canadian forces suffered 'both physically and mentally', losing at least 2,500 casualties to gas.[36]

In his excellent study of the Canadian gas experience, Tim Cook underlines the utility of gas both offensively and defensively. From the seizure of Vimy Ridge (9–13 April 1917), where Canadian gunners pounded the German artillery with gas to consolidate their triumph, they honed their gas drills thereafter. By integrating gas shelling into their fire-plans, the Canadian artillery employed it to bombard German batteries, deny jumping-off points for German infantry, disrupt lines of communication, damage morale and degrade the Germans' ability to fight. In the successful actions at Hill 70 (15 August 1917), and later at Passchendaele (30 October–10 November 1917), gas provided crucial assistance in Canadian counter-battery work and in harassing enemy jumping-off points. Similarly, in preparing for the breakthrough at the Canal du Nord (27 September–1 October 1918), the Canadians bombarded German gun positions in Bourlon Wood with some 17,000 gas shells over fifteen days before launching another 7,600 lachrymatory and lethal gas shells into the woods on the morning of the successful attack. In this assault, and in others spearheaded by the Canadians in the 'Final Push', they restricted their number of gas casualties by virtue of the intense gas doctrine drilled into the men by the Canadian Gas Services. Even so, Cook concedes that gas caused acute psychological fears and depressed morale, not only among victims but also among those who tended those casualties – stretcher-bearers, medical staff and padres. Gas encumbered logistics, particularly in the removal of casualties to the rear, disrupted communications and crippled fighting efficiency whenever men had to fight wearing their respirators.[37]

To claim, nonetheless, that gas failed because it failed single-handedly to break through the trenches is to measure it by an unreasonable yardstick. Gas was only introduced because conventional ordnance had failed to break the deadlock in 1915, and neither the tank nor the aeroplane 'changed the face of war' subsequently. The Germans used only nine tanks in their spring offensive of 1918, while the British failed to exploit their initial successes with tanks (at Cambrai on 20 November 1917 and at Amiens on 8 August 1918) because they lost so many machines (of the 414 sent into battle on 8 August, only 145 followed up one day later and a mere six by 12 August). As John Terraine wrote, 'The German empire was not going to be overthrown by six tanks, any more than by Trenchard's ten bomber squadrons at Nancy.'[38]

Chemical warfare was only one of several new forms of warfare introduced during the First World War. Having failed to break the deadlock of trench warfare in 1915, it was used increasingly as an ancillary weapon to harass the enemy, inflict casualties and support operations. It was not used on every front – although the British considered the use of gas at Gallipoli on several occasions, they rejected it because of difficulties in supply, training and employment, and the loss of prestige in using gas other than as a weapon of retaliation. Only as precautionary measures were several hundred thousand respirators and some 600 cylinders sent to the Gallipoli theatre: gas was not used there.[39] Wherever gas was employed, though, it influenced the military experience, not least upon the principal victims – the poorly prepared Russians, who incurred horrendous gas casualties (possibly 475,340, of whom some 56,000 died), and the Italians, whose disastrous defeat at Caporetto was precipitated by a projector attack upon their forces in a gorge at Zaga (24 October 1917). That attack caught the Italians by surprise and the gas failed to dissipate because of the nearby mountain range, so inflicting heavy casualties and facilitating the Austrian advance.[40] Quite apart from these effects, the war had demonstrated how chemical weapons could be integrated in methods of war. Chemists on both sides had investigated over 3,000 chemical substances, selecting 30 for use in combat of which about a dozen achieved the desired results. By refining these options, and by developing mustard gas that would be used in war 70 years later, they had demonstrated the military utility of certain agents. By exploiting this R&D and massively expanding their industrial production, the main belligerents employed gas increasingly as an ancillary weapon, both offensively and defensively. Whether it had become a 'standard weapon' is debatable[41] but few contemporaries doubted that it would be used in a future war.

Sabotage with Biological Weapons

Unlike the large-scale battlefield operations involving chemical weapons, those involving biological agents were smaller in scale, covert in form, and directed against draft, cavalry and military livestock. Launched by the Germans (and possibly the French), these were veterinary sabotage missions. The German programme was particularly ambitious; it was sustained over the period 1915–18 and spread across three continents, mainly against neutral suppliers of the allies but later against the belligerents as well. The best-documented accounts involve the role of German agents, trying to inoculate horses with glanders and anthrax in the United States prior to that country's entry into the war, but similar operations were mounted in Argentina, Romania, Norway and possibly Spain. By confining the programme to livestock, the German general staff sought to circumvent legal proscriptions that prohibited the use of pathogens against humans; indeed, the German military authorities rejected several proposals to employ anti-human pathogens (partly for legal reasons, partly for practical concerns lest these weapons acted too slowly and unpredictably, and posed a risk to German troops).[42]

From the summer of 1915 to the autumn of 1916, the first major sabotage operation was undertaken on the eastern seaboard of the United States. Anton Dilger, a physician, brought the bacilli into the country, set up a covert laboratory in the Chevy Chase district of Washington, DC, and produced cultures of *Bacillus anthracis* and *Pseudomonas mallei*, the causative agents of anthrax and glanders. These cultures were suspended in liquid and packaged into tubes for distribution by Captain Hinsch to German agents, who hired teams of men at various shipping points to inoculate remounts destined for the allied war effort. The Germans also undertook a similar operation in Romania, profiting from the surface transport connection to grow cultures in Germany and transport them overland to agents in Romania. If the surviving evidence about operations in Norway, and possibly Spain, is less conclusive, cultures in the form of ampoules embedded in sugar cubes were shipped to Argentina over the period from mid-June 1916 to 1918. Unlike the American cultures, these cubes were to be used directly for purposes of sabotage. One such shipment, thought to be on board a commercial steamship, and reportedly concealed in the false lid of a trunk belonging to the mistress of the German naval attaché, evaded the Royal Navy in a fog and reached Buenos Aires in early 1918. As Mark Wheelis observes, 'The effectiveness of the biological sabotage programme in Argentina is, like its American and European progenitors, impossible to assess.'[43]

Neither these programmes nor the sporadic sabotage missions behind enemy lines on the Western Front were ever on a sufficient scale to cause widespread disruption, and the capture of agents often terminated the operations. Nevertheless, these activities constituted the first organized national programme of offensive biological warfare. Sustained over several years, exploiting a network of German agents in three continents, it was the first large-scale clandestine biological warfare operation, and one that was directed primarily against neutral countries, targeting animals and not humans. All this underscored the diverse potential of biological warfare agents to be employed covertly and indirectly as weapons of war.

2

Deterrence and Disarmament: Responses to Chemical and Biological Warfare, 1919–93

The 'war to end all wars' held out the prospect of fundamental change in the conduct of international relations. Politically, the armistice agreement committed the United States, its European partners and Germany to seek a peace based on the Fourteen Points and speeches of President Woodrow Wilson, which included a reduction of national armaments 'to the lowest point consistent with domestic safety' (point 4) and the creation of a 'general association of nations' (point 14). Underpinning many of the post-war hopes were the assumptions that enhanced co-operation through the future League of Nations would reduce international tensions, obviate the recurrence of arms races, and remove the incentives for waging aggressive wars. Such aspirations complemented beliefs that the world must never witness another conflict that replicated the nature, scale and costs of the Great War. That war had inculcated a loathing of the new 'horror' weapons – not only recourse to chemical and biological weapons but also the indiscriminate killing of civilians by submarine attacks on allied and neutral shipping, and the bombing of civilians far behind the battle lines from aircraft and dirigible airships. Both the rapidly expanding capacities of bomber aircraft and submarines, and the weakening of legal and moral distinctions between attacking combatants and non-combatants, underlined popular fears that warfare, if unchecked, could precipitate a descent into barbarism. Prominent among these fears were concerns that civilian populations would face new perils from even more lethal combinations of weapons, including chemical and biological warheads.[1] Such fears would inspire some politicians, writers, artists, poets, journalists and philosophers to campaign alongside pacifist organizations not merely for the limitation and prohibition of certain weapons but also for general and comprehensive disarmament.

Such fears were not shared universally; the British general staff was not alone in suspecting that 'no nation can take the risk of abandoning it [gas warfare] without the absolute certainty – which will be impossible to attain – that it will never be used by an adversary'.[2] In both official commentary, and the early interwar writings of Basil Liddell Hart and J.F.C. Fuller, gas was depicted as a weapon standardized by its usage from 1915 to 1919, one that was relatively humane (inasmuch as it achieved effects without causing as many fatalities and permanent disabilities as high explosives), versatile (since it could be dispersed by tanks, ships and aircraft), and a weapon of the future usable in offensive and defensive operations. Although military writers often differed about how chemical weapons might be employed, and some changed their opinions altogether,[3] they agreed generally that their armed forces should retain capabilities to protect themselves from these weapons and, if necessary, to retaliate-in-kind. By retaining these capabilities, nations sought to deter recourse to chemical and biological warfare.

Interwar Disarmament

Disarmament, though, took precedence as the British prime minister, David Lloyd George, sought to disarm Germany at the Paris Peace Conference. He sought reductions in the size of the German army and armaments as precursors to general disarmament, his ultimate objective, which he considered a means of crushing militarism throughout Europe, bolstering peace, and enabling Britain to concentrate upon its domestic difficulties. Supported by Woodrow Wilson, they managed to define the purpose of German disarmament not as a means of curbing German power but as a means of 'render[ing] possible the initiation of a general limitation of the armaments of all nations' (preamble to Part v of the Treaty of Versailles). Within this overall context, Article 171 of the treaty declared:

> The use of asphyxiating, poisonous or other gases and all analogous liquids, materials or devices being prohibited, their manufacture and importation are strictly forbidden in Germany.[4]

Making progress towards disarmament, whether of all weapons or of chemical and biological, proved immensely difficult. A British mission sent to inspect the German gas factories of the IG combination found extensive evidence of dual-capable processes. Just as many of the war gases (such as chlorine, phosgene and hydrogen cyanide) served perfectly legitimate purposes, so the bulk of the plant had existed pre-war, producing dyestuffs or pharmaceutical products. Consequently, as long as Germany was allowed to retain its dye industry, part of a policy to create a German democratic bulwark against Bolshevism, other countries would have to retain their chemical industries, so preserving a residual capacity to retaliate-in-kind. Unwilling to engage in unilateral disarmament, the victorious states retained their R&D facilities, albeit in Britain's case, preserving Porton Down on a much-reduced scale and in an unobtrusive manner. Nor were these states pressed unduly on the disarmament issue by the newly created League of Nations. Despite the League's commitment under Article 8 of its Covenant to 'formulate plans' for 'the reduction of national armaments to the lowest point consistent with national safety', and the passionate advocacy of disarmament by enthusiasts like Lord Robert Cecil (president of the League of Nations Union from 1923 to 1945), technical sub-committees of the League reported repeatedly that it would be impractical to prohibit the use of gas in war or to limit its manufacture in peace.[5]

Nevertheless, the United States, a non-member of the League (after the Senate failed to ratify the Treaty of Versailles), proved a champion of disarmament, most notably at the Washington Conference convened in November 1921. Despite the doubts of another technical committee about the practicality of gas disarmament, other committees deprecated the suffering caused by chemical weapons and their threat to non-combatants. When the US delegation, pandering to popular sentiments, promoted the abolition of gas warfare as one of several disarmament measures, the British empire delegation, though sceptical about gas constraints but eager for naval arms control, found itself in an impossible dilemma. Unable to resist a policy in line with the pre-war Hague declarations and Article 171 of the Treaty of Versailles, it supported the proposal but reserved the right to take precautions against any future violation by an 'unscrupulous enemy'. Article v of the Washington Treaty duly declared that

> The use in war of asphyxiating, poisonous or other gases, and all analogous liquids, materials or devices, having been justly condemned by the general opinion of the civilized world and a prohibition of such use having been declared in treaties to which a majority of the civilized powers are parties,

The Signatory Powers, to the end that this prohibition shall be universally accepted as a part of international law binding alike the conscience and practice of nations, declare their assent to such prohibition, agree to be bound thereby as between themselves and invite all other civilized nations to adhere thereto.[6]

Although this treaty never came into force since France refused to ratify the submarine clauses, gas disarmament remained on the agendas of the League and US foreign policy. When the issue was referred to a conference on the Control of the International Trade in Arms, Munitions and Implements of War, which convened at Geneva on 4 May 1925, the US delegation seized the initiative again. Its spokesman, Theodore E. Burton, urged the adoption of a convention that practically reproduced the wording of the Washington Treaty but extended it to include a ban on the trade in war gases. On the advice of another technical committee, deprecating any regulation of the trade in dual-use chemicals, the latter point was jettisoned, but, in passionate debates, several states supported the American resolution and the Polish representative advocated the inclusion of bacteriological as well as chemical warfare. Forty-four states, including the United States, France, Germany, Poland, Italy, Japan and the British empire, duly signed the Geneva Protocol on 17 June 1925, affirming that

Whereas the use of asphyxiating, poisonous or other gases, and of all analogous liquids, materials or devices, has been justly condemned by the general opinion of the civilized world; and . . . the prohibition of such use . . . shall be universally accepted as part of International Law, binding alike the conscience and the practice of nations . . . [and shall] extend this prohibition to the use of bacteriological methods of warfare, and agree to be bound as between themselves according to the terms of this declaration.

By only banning the use of chemical and biological weapons, the protocol was a distinctly limited agreement. It failed to address the R&D, production, possession or transfer of such weapons, avoided any reference to how the agreement could be verified or enforced, and allowed states who ratified it to enter one or both of the following reservations: first, that it was binding only in relation to other states who were a party to the protocol, and second, that it would cease to be binding whenever enemy states used gas warfare. In effect, the Geneva Protocol became known as a 'no first use' agreement.[7]

Although 43 states ratified the protocol in the interwar years, several, including Britain, entered reservations, and both the United States and Japan failed to ratify it at all. The failure of the United States Senate to ratify the protocol was both a major surprise and a blow to the credibility of the agreement (since Japan followed the American policy). Hitherto the results of opinion polls in the United States, supported by the declared views of General Jack Pershing at the Washington Conference, and the readiness of the Senate to ratify the Washington Treaty in 1922, had indicated the depth of popular antipathy towards poison gas. Yet in the Senate debate of 1926 proponents of chemical warfare, marshalled by Major-General Amos A. Fries of the Chemical Warfare Service, campaigned formidably against the protocol. Their briefing of sympathetic senators, and supply of copious testimony from the Veterans of Foreign Wars, the Association of Medical Surgeons and the American Chemical Society, prompted the chairman of the Senate Foreign Relations Committee to withdraw the treaty from the Senate's consideration.[8] It remained with the committee until 1947, when President Harry Truman withdrew the executive's request for Senate action on it. When resubmitted by President Richard Nixon on 19 August 1970, it was eventually ratified in 1975.

Nevertheless, the disarmament movement, driven on by Lord Cecil and others, ensured that the abolition of gas warfare remained on the international agenda, first in the Preparatory Disarmament Commission (1926–30) and then in the World Disarmament Conference (1932–6). In neither forum was much progress made, largely because disarmament became subsumed within broader, and more important, debates about security. The latter reflected the differing priorities of Britain, reluctant to become committed in Europe, and France, primarily concerned about her security vis-à-vis Germany. French anxieties reflected at least partially the many violations of the disarmament clauses of the Treaty of Versailles by Weimar Germany, not least in her collaboration with Russia under the Treaty of Rapallo (1922).[9] By the time of the ill-fated Disarmament Conference, overshadowed by the Manchurian crisis and Adolf Hitler's rise to power, Franco-German differences were becoming acute. While Germany demanded equality of treatment in matters of disarmament, France refused to countenance any agreement without the security guarantees that neither Britain nor the United States would supply. In these circumstances there was scant prospect of reaching any agreement upon gas disarmament, whether Cecil's proposal to abolish all weapons that would assist the offensive or President Herbert Hoover's sweeping disarmament plan. When Germany eventually withdrew from the conference in October 1933, and announced its decision to leave the League of Nations, the prospects for gas disarmament were left in ruins.

CBW Rearmament in the 1930s and '40s

Opposition to cw disarmament did not derive primarily from a desire to employ poison gas offensively. Although scientists, like J.B.S. Haldane, and some military commanders championed the use of gas as a normal weapon[10] – and it would be used against the Bolsheviks, and in several Third World conflicts during the 1920s and '30s (see chapter Three) – the scepticism reflected doubts about the practicality of relying upon international agreements that could be neither verified nor enforced. In attaching reservations to their ratifications of the protocol, most of the great powers affirmed their right to protect their own citizens and soldiers against gas attacks and to maintain a capacity to retaliate-in-kind if necessary. Similarly, preserving the option of gas preparedness underpinned much of the American opposition to the protocol. Yet preserving such options did not ensure that appropriate expenditure would follow, especially as no interwar us administration envisaged military commitments in Europe. For Britain, the return to 'normalcy' after the war had produced wholesale demobilization, and slashed defence expenditure, a trend accentuated by the Locarno agreements (1925) and the entry of Weimar Germany into the League of Nations. Any research on chemical weapons at Porton had to be done 'under the rose', and it was not until the gas bombing of the Italo-Ethiopian War (1935–6) that interest in gas preparedness revived. As the Prime Minister Stanley Baldwin observed: 'if a Great European nation, in spite of having given its signature to the Geneva protocol against the use of such gases, employs them in Africa, what guarantee have we that they may not be used in Europe?'[11]

Given the proximity of the great powers, and their capitals in Europe, air defence assumed an overwhelming priority. In Britain, where the response of local authorities was at best uneven, the government assumed increasing responsibilities, establishing anti-gas schools at Falfield and Easingwold in 1936 and 1937 to train the instructors, who then trained volunteers in the Air Raid Precautions (ARP) service. In 1937 it secured the passage of the Air Raid Precautions Act that compelled local authorities to prepare measures of local defence, and authorized the mass production of civilian gas masks. It distributed 38 million during the Munich crisis (September 1938), 50 million by the beginning of the war, and 1,400,000 anti-gas helmets for babies and two million 'small child's respirators' by January 1940. The aim was not merely protection for individual citizens, but also the bolstering of public morale (in the hope of mitigating panic if gas attacks ensued), and deterrence by publicizing the scope of these provisions. By contrast, French ARP provisions emphasized collective protection and the defence of the capital. They included the construction of public shelters in the Paris Métro, the approval of 60,000 cellars as shelters and the preparation of an evacuation plan for Paris. Civilian instruction and training paled by comparison with the British and German standards; indeed, Germany formed an Air Defence League with thirteen million members, aided by 5,000 schools and 28,000 instructors.[12]

Chemical rearmament in peacetime was a more formidable undertaking, partly because states were seeking to resolve international sources of tension and partly because it had to compete for scarce resources with other forms of military expenditure. It was also peculiarly complex, requiring critical choices and trials over several years to determine which chemical agents and weapons to develop and how they might be used alongside high-explosive and incendiary bombing. In some states, too, this required the construction and testing of the requisite manufacturing and storage capacity, involving additional plants, charging units, roads, rail and sewage facilities. In Britain, this proved a lengthy process for which Treasury approval was not forthcoming until 3 February 1939, so leaving Britain with a minimal stock of about 500 tons of gases when war broke out. France had production facilities for adamsite, mustard and lewisite at Le Bouchet but the large-scale production plant at Soussens remained incomplete by July 1940. In Germany, where Gerhard Schrader had discovered nerve gases – tabun in 1936 and sarin in 1938 – the tabun plant at Dyhernfurth, started in September 1939, would not begin production before April 1942 and the sarin plant, not authorized until 1942–3, was unable to begin production before March 1945.[13]

Of all the European powers, the Soviet Union had the potential to be more prepared for chemical warfare than any other. Motivated by Russia's horrendous casualties in the First World War, and by the allied gas attacks in 1919, the Soviet Union had every incentive to develop its CW capability. After the Treaty of Rapallo, it had access to German expertise and technology (until banned by Hitler in 1933), and with the foundation of the Military Chemical Agency of the Red Army under General Jacov M. Fishman in August 1925 it had an organization responsible in peacetime for the activities of chemical troops and platoons, anti-gas defences, CW R&D institutes, and the production and supply of CW materials. From the early 1920s civilian and military institutes, particularly the Moscow-based Chemical Scientific Research Institute, undertook R&D, while the testing facility at Tomka near Shikhany became the focus for studies of aerial spraying apparatus, mustard gases with enhanced persistence, decontaminants, toxic smoke generators, gas shells, protective clothing and various CW agents, especially those suited to cold weather conditions (including a mixture of mustard and lewisite).

The German engineer and entrepreneur Dr Hugo Stoltzenberg tried to build the first Soviet mustard-gas plant at Samara (later Chapaevsk) but, after its failure in 1928, Professor E. I. Spitalskij and the Chapaevsk manager launched a crash programme, building five factories by 1932. Thereafter the Soviets developed an extensive CW programme, encompassing the weaponization of fifteen chemical agents, an impressive array of anti-gas equipment, numerous ground and aerial delivery systems, and the integration of chemical weapons, albeit on a secondary level, into the operating doctrine devised by Marshal Nikolaevich Tukhachevskii and embodied in the 1936 *Provisional Field Service Regulations*. In 1937, though, the Stalinist purges undermined much of this work by executing twenty per cent of the Soviet military leadership and purging three-quarters of the high command, among them Marshal Tukhachevskii and General Fishman. Tukhachevskii's innovative doctrine was dismissed as 'bourgeois' and 'subversive', but the CW infrastructure remained.[14]

Covert preparations and intelligence misperceptions compounded the difficulties of rearmament. Such factors detracted from the ability of the great powers to choose priorities and allocate appropriate resources to mitigate the perceived threats from potential belligerents. Just as British intelligence completely missed the German discovery of nerve agents, confidently quoting a Polish assessment in 1937 that 'no highly effective new gases have been discovered', so it failed to grasp Hitler's disdain for a form of warfare that had injured him in 1918, and the feeling within the German CW fraternity that its rearmament programme, launched in the mid-1930s, was fifteen development years behind those of the allies.[15]

Intelligence gaps and fears of enemy intentions and capabilities were even more prominent in the preparation for biological warfare. Memories of German biological sabotage efforts in the Great War stimulated an active French R&D and testing programme in the early 1920s under the leadership of André Trillat, director of the Naval Chemical Research Laboratory. Mutual fears and suspicions festered between Germany and the Soviet Union, as the Treaty of Rapallo never fostered any BW collaboration between them. These anxieties underpinned the drive of the Red Army to launch a widespread BW research, development and testing programme under the direction of General Fishman. The intelligence fears even became public in 1934 when Henry Wickham-Steed, a former editor of *The Times*, published an article in which he claimed that German documents had come into his possession that showed that they had conducted BW testing in the Paris Métro. This both revived the French BW programme, which appears to have become dormant after the signing of the Geneva Protocol, and prompted the organization of the British BW programme under Sir Maurice (later Lord) Hankey in 1936. The British programme was defensive until the outbreak of war, whereupon it became increasingly offensive in orientation, both in laboratory research and field testing, pursued partly with Canada and later the United States. Eventually the UK acquired a modest retaliatory capability of five million cattle cakes contaminated with anthrax spores, intended for use against livestock in the event of a biological attack on Britain.[16]

Ironically Germany was probably the least prepared of all the European great powers for biological warfare. Despite the sabotage efforts during the Great War, Germany's military scientific experts were not convinced that biological warfare was feasible until they gained access to French research and testing data following the fall of France in 1940. Even so, German biological warfare languished under Hitler's personal interdict against any BW offensive research, which precluded the option of retaliating in kind. The ban persisted despite alarmist (and largely inaccurate) intelligence reports about the BW activities of Britain, Canada, the Soviet Union and later the United

States, and despite encountering localized bw sabotage by Soviet and Polish resistance groups in 1943. Confined to a defensive remit, German bw research included aerial trials in the dispersal of Colorado potato beetles but never collaborated with the other axis powers. While Italian bw research and open-air testing remained relatively limited, the Japanese bw programme was probably the most extensive of all programmes in the Second World War (see chapter Three). British fears of German-Japanese collaboration proved unfounded as the Japanese and German officials exchanged little material, with the former never revealing the scope of the bw operations in China.[17]

Dr Heinrich Kliewe, the leading German bacteriologist who evaluated the French bw programme, which included research on anthrax, brucellosis, tularaemia and animal diseases, the loading of bombs and projectiles with bacteria, and the examination of bacterial aerosols as 'a usable means of attack', feared the Soviet bw programme above all others.[18] Begun in 1928 under Fishman's direction, the Soviet bw programme, led by Nikolay N. Ginsburg, focused on weaponizing *Bacillus anthracis* and *Clostridium botulinum* and on methods of disinfecting persons and equipment contaminated with pathogens. By the 1930s more specialist institutes were created in the Moscow region and Leningrad oblast – bodies that were moved east during the Second World War, when a major bw institute was formed in Kirov. In addition the Soviets established three open-air test sites before the war – Tomka in the 1920s, Gorodomlya Island north of Moscow, where pathogens were tested, causing foot and mouth disease, leprosy, plague and tularemia, and, finally, Vozrozhdeniye Island in the Aral Sea, which was operational from 1936 and became the favoured site. Used for large-scale, open-air testing of weaponized pathogens, it was closed during the war but reopened in the 1950s. Like its chemical counterpart, though, the bw programme suffered from the Stalinist purges, which removed both Fishman's leadership and many of the leading bacteriologists and microbiologists, who were charged with treasonable sabotage activities.[19]

Arguably the most sustained progress in bw research occurred in the allied camp. The Anglo-Canadian defensive research on anti-animal and anti-crop diseases began in the mid- to late 1930s, well before the American bw programme came into existence in 1942–3. All too aware of the uk's vulnerability to bw attack, Hankey secured the approval of the cabinet to undertake offensive bw research in case Britain had to retaliate-in-kind. Under Hankey's authorization, Dr (later Sir) Paul Fildes, who led Britain's BW programme at Porton, shared the results of the anthrax tests on Gruinard Island with Canada and the United States in May 1943.[20] Anglo-American liaisons were not always harmonious but they assisted the fledgling American BW programme, which began in the summer of 1942 in great secrecy under the guise of a civilian agency, the War Research Service, housed within the Federal Security Agency. Crippled by the lack of verifiable intelligence, but fearful lest the axis powers enjoyed a ten-year lead in BW activities, the US programme focused initially upon BW protective measures and R&D into the wartime feasibility of various anti-personnel, anti-animal and anti-plant agents. Once candidate agents were identified, the information was passed onto the Chemical Warfare Service (CWS) for field testing and pilot plant production. By mid-1944 the CWS had received the R&D on all promising projects, and by September 1944 the War Department had taken over the BW programme as a whole.

The United States had the resources to develop a far more extensive BW programme than the United Kingdom, investigating eighteen diseases as promising BW agents and two groups of potential herbicide agents: plant growth regulators and defoliants. It weaponized one compound, LN-8 (2,4-dichlorophenoxyacetic acid) for potential use against Japanese rice and other crops, although the war ended before this compound or any of the defoliants could be used. The US also developed facilities that could follow through on some of the laboratory work at Porton and had the potential to mass-produce the BW retaliatory agent sought by Winston Churchill (set at 500,000 4-lb 'N' (anthrax) bombs). At Fort Detrick, Maryland, the lethality, infectiousness and stability of agents disseminated in aerosol form were tested. Field testing was undertaken at Horn Island, in the Mississippi Sound, and later at the Granite Peak installation, a substation of the Dugway Proving Ground, Utah. The mass-production of BW agents was planned to take place at the Vigo Plant, Indiana, including the British request for 'N' bombs, but it was still only functioning as a pilot plant at the end of the war.[21]

Non-use of CBW during the Second World War

Lack of preparedness was a principal reason for non-use of chemical or biological weapons between the major belligerents in the Second World War. It affected states to different degrees during the course of hostilities but it was particularly apparent in September 1939, and at the entry of the United States into the war after the bombing of Pearl Harbor (7 December 1941). Diplomatic declarations to abide by the terms of the Geneva Protocol bought limited respite, especially in view of the continuing intelligence misperceptions, while the allies retained understandable fears about Hitler's intentions and Japanese militarism, the axis powers remained fearful of Soviet CBW capabilities. However, the startling successes of the German *blitzkrieg* in the early months of the war underscored the advantages of a fast-moving assault with conventional forces. Neither Britain nor France could initiate gas warfare at this time; their stocks of gas and gas munitions were distinctly low, and Britain's high-level aerial spraying capacity could not easily be employed in the vicinity of allied civilians. Britain wished neither to offend neutral American opinion by initiating gas warfare nor give the Luftwaffe justification for launching gas reprisals against Britain. Moreover, British political and military planners had every reason to fear lest a gas war started in one theatre might spread to the Mediterranean and Middle Eastern areas, where British anti-gas provisions were far less extensive than those at home.

Yet the prospect of Germans landing on British beaches after the fall of France provoked a review of whether gas should be used. While senior British officers debated the options of low-level spraying of German forces crowded on beaches, and of using liquid mustard gas to slow down any breakout, the chronic shortage of gas stocks prompted Winston Churchill, who became prime minister on 10 May 1940, to assume personal oversight of the CW programme. Bereft of any moral qualms about using gas, he harried officials, demanding weekly reports on gas production and pressing for a rapid build up of gas stocks (securing 15,262 tons by 26 December 1941 with 4,351 tons in storage and the remainder in a plentiful supply of gas-filled munitions for the army and Royal Air Force). By the end of the war Britain had amassed 35,000 tons of gas.[22]

Germany entered the war with a larger stock of gas than Britain – 2,900 tons and a production capacity of 515 tons per month – but it was inadequate for the ambitions of the *Nebeltruppe* (gas troops) and IG Farben, who wished to avoid the mistakes of the previous war and use gas decisively. In their view, decisive results required a massive use of gas initially, followed by continuous and uninterrupted attacks thereafter to overload the enemy's medical support, exhaust supplies of protective equipment and demoralize enemy forces. Accordingly IG Farben had to produce vast tonnages of chemical agent, a task that would involve twice as many scientists as Britain required and necessitate twenty factories to accumulate stocks of about 70,000 tons of poison gas and a vast array of gas-filled munitions by the end of the war. Apart from tabun and sarin, the Germans developed two new types of mustard gas (Lost) – sommer-lost for hot climates, winter-lost for cold – new gas weapons, and even tested their V1 and V2 rockets with chemical warheads. Yet Hitler, irrespective of his personal reservations about poison gas (and he never visited the CW proving ground at Raubkammer), had strategic, operational and logistic reasons for resisting the option of first use. Desperate to avoid a war on two fronts, and hence the willingness to conclude the Nazi–Soviet pact of 24 August 1939, he initially sought an accommodation with Britain, for which a gas war would have been an extra impediment. When he subsequently launched his drive for Lebensraum in the east (6 June 1941), speed was imperative as German assault forces pressed on towards Moscow and the industrial heartland. Any major use of gas would have encumbered German logistics as the supply lines lengthened from the Third Reich and risked provoking retaliation-in-kind from the much-feared Soviet CBW arsenal. The use of the latter became increasingly unlikely as the Red Army lost vast amounts of anti-gas clothing and equipment in the early defeats and later had to plan its counter-offensive on Soviet soil. Soviet first use, as Alibek claims, may have occurred on the eve of Stalingrad (1942), when an exceptionally large outbreak of tularemia affected German troops but a natural outbreak is also possible.[23] Generally the Soviets exercised restraint in CBW to avoid complicating operations in Russia and to refrain from giving the Allies another excuse to delay the Second Front so desired by Stalin.[24]

Deterrence was now the determining factor in the non-use of gas. In a broadcast on 10 May 1942, Churchill revealed that Britain had made gas preparations on 'a formidable scale', and would launch gas attacks against the towns and cities of Germany in the event of 'unprovoked' German use of gas against Russia. On 5 June 1942 President Franklin D. Roosevelt, though wedded to no first use of chemical weapons, issued a similar warning to Japan, threatening retaliation-in-kind if 'authoritative' reports confirmed the continuing use of gas by Japanese forces in China. In an era of woefully inadequate intelligence and fears of reprisals, such threats contained an element of bluff (as in May 1942 the United States possessed only 1,250 tons of mustard gas), but they were taken seriously, as General Hideki Tojo, Japan's war minister, confirmed in post-war interrogation. Japan appreciated the huge industrial potential of the United States.[25]

By exploiting its vast resources, and opening thirteen new cw plants, including the Pine Bluff Arsenal, Arkansas, and the Rocky Mountain Arsenal near Denver, Colorado, the United States accumulated the world's largest stock of poison gases (over 135,000 tons) and a multitude of gas-filled munitions by 1945. As the allies also acquired a growing aerial superiority, this provided cover for their most hazardous undertaking – the D-Day landings of June 1944 – and enabled them to reconsider the option of first use from a position of strength. Once again opinion was split: military reservations prevailed over Churchill's desire to use gas in retaliation for the V-rocket attacks on Britain, and, in the summer of 1945, us military planners reviewed the option of chemical attacks rather than further costly conventional assaults upon Japanese islands. The American debate was only feasible after Roosevelt's death (12 April 1945), and the ending of the war in Europe (7 May 1945), but the planners found that huge logistical and time-consuming difficulties would beset any movement of gases and munitions from continental United States to bases in the Far East. In any event the dropping of the atomic bombs upon Hiroshima and Nagasaki (6 and 9 August 1945) ended the war, so saving American lives more quickly than the moving of gas stocks across the Pacific.[26]

CBW Developments during the Cold War

Although nuclear weapons came to dominate international relations, triggering a massive arms race and serving as the principal means of deterrence during the Cold War, chemical and later biological weapons retained a prominence that they had not had after the First World War. The discovery of large German stocks of highly potent, odourless, colourless nerve agents provided a new focus for chemical R&D. The Soviets, having captured two plants capable of manufacturing tabun and sarin, dismantled the plants and removed them to the Soviet Union, where they were reassembled. When the United States, having deactivated much of its cw programme in the late 1940s, found itself embroiled in the Korean War, it restored the wartime status of key facilities, notably the Dugway Proving Ground, with an additional 279,000 acres of land. At the Rocky Mountain Arsenal, it resumed production of artillery shells filled with distilled mustard and constructed a secret installation (1951 to 1953) for the mass-production of sarin from 1953 to 1957. In 1954 British research on nerve agents produced the even more potent 'V'-agent compounds, and shared this information with its American ally. US scientists selected one of these compounds, VX, for manufacture, producing tens of thousands of tons of the agent in the 1960s. As the Soviets developed exactly the same agent as the Americans had, East German espionage may have obtained the formula for mass-production from the mid-1960s onwards.[27]

Although Britain abandoned its offensive CW capability in 1957, preferring to rely upon a nuclear deterrent and the promotion of CB disarmament,[28] the two remaining superpowers modernized their CBW arsenals. In the 1950s and '60s, the United States filled howitzer rounds, mortar rounds, shells, battlefield rockets, bombs and air-borne spray tanks with mustard or nerve agent. It also produced M-23 land mines, containing VX, to counter human-wave infantry attacks similar to those encountered in Korea, and cluster munitions containing a non-lethal hallucinogenic agent called BZ that was later abandoned as too unpredictable for military use. Above all, American research produced the binary munition in which the warheads or bombs contained non-lethal chemicals in two separate compartments that did not mix and react to form a nerve agent until after launching. These munitions offered the prospect of greatly enhanced safety in production, storage, transportation and handling.[29]

Equally extensive were the post-war Anglo-American BW research, development and testing programmes. Porton's Microbiological Research Department, housed in a vast new building, completed in 1951, determined the infectious levels for some fifteen species of micro-organisms, and in five secret sea trials using pathogens off the Bahamas and the Scottish coast between 1948 and 1955, gained greater insights into the airborne travel of aerosol particles. Although Britain abandoned its BW retaliatory option in 1957, preferring to rely on a nuclear deterrent, subsequent trials using inert particles or harmless microorganisms as simulants demonstrated that biological agents could be employed strategically against the UK and that they had considerable potential as weapons of sabotage. The US programme involved the development of anti-personnel and anti-crop agents as potential weapons. It tested pathogens and simulants in hundreds of open-air trials between 1949 and 1969. These included onshore tests from ships and releases in urban areas, airports and subway systems, with further testing at the Dugway Proving Ground until 1962, in Florida and California, and, after 1963, in the Caribbean, Central America, and over parts of the Atlantic and Pacific Oceans. The Pacific tests confirmed that biological weapons, though much cheaper than their nuclear counterparts, had a similar strategic potential, with a capacity to spread over a vast area. From 1954 to 1969 the US stockpiled anti-crop agents (36,000 kg of wheat rust and some 900 kg of rice blast pathogen), and manufactured and loaded BW munitions with anti-personnel bacteria, viruses and toxins at the Pine Bluff Arsenal.[30]

On 25 November 1969, at a time when the United States was incurring widespread censure for its use of herbicides and riot-control agents in the Vietnam War (see chapter Three), President Richard M. Nixon announced the termination of the American BW programme. In a policy statement that reaffirmed the renunciation of the first use of lethal chemical weapons, he extended that policy to include non-lethal incapacitating agents and renounced all methods of biological warfare (extended to include toxins in the following year). Nixon affirmed that the US would destroy its existing agent stockpiles and munitions, and convert its biological R&D to focus exclusively upon biological defence. In a declaration that effectively halted any further production of chemical weapons, Nixon also announced that he would resubmit the Geneva Protocol to the Senate for ratification. In bowing before domestic public protests and congressional criticism, the Nixon administration set aside the findings of its secret research and testing programme and claimed that biological warfare posed 'massive, unpredictable and potentially uncontrollable consequences'. Heeding the advice of Matthew Meselson, a Harvard professor with security clearances, it chose to rely upon the US nuclear deterrent and to promote BW disarmament in the hope of deterring smaller nations from acquiring a relatively cheap weapons technology with immense strategic potential.[31]

CBW Disarmament and Secret CBW Programmes

Hitherto chemical and biological disarmament had been debated in various fora under the auspices of the United Nations, but in July 1969 Britain proposed that the two weapon systems should be treated separately. The unilateral renunciation of the US BW programme enhanced the prospects for reaching a BW agreement, especially as the two superpowers were negotiating bilateral strategic agreements on nuclear weapons, the Strategic Arms Limitation Talks (SALT I). Within this spirit of superpower détente, agreement was duly reached on the Biological and Toxin Weapons Convention (BTWC) of 10 April 1972, which banned the development, production and stockpiling of biological and toxin weapons but permitted defensive BW research. Containing no means of verification or enforcement, the BTWC entered into force on 26 March 1975, and, by 2007, 155 states had signed and ratified it, becoming 'states parties', and another sixteen had signed it.

At least two states, the Soviet Union and Iraq (see chapter Five), were willing to join the treaty regime without any willingness to abide by its rules and precepts. Indeed the Soviets proceeded to develop the world's largest and most ambitious offensive BW programme. Its roots lay in the aftermath of the Second World War, with the construction of facilities at Sverdlovsk in 1946 and Kirov in 1953. Further R&D institutes were established under the ministries of Defence, Agriculture and Health, and under the Biopreparat group, an ostensibly civilian pharmaceutical agency which had vast production factories in some 40 sites. Altogether 60,000 scientists, technicians and support staff worked in over 100 institutions; they produced hundreds of tons of classical BW agents, conducted open-air tests of pathogens at Vozrozhdeniye Island in the Aral Sea, and the engineering of munitions to deliver anthrax, smallpox and plague. In 1972 the Soviets launched a new offensive, second-generation BW programme under the leadership of Yuri Ovchinnikov, a bioscientist academician, and the military direction of Colonel-General Yefim I. Smirnov. This was a long-term programme to apply new biotechnology techniques to BW-related R&D. It aimed to counter any illicit US BW programmes (possibly by private companies), contribute to the drive for military superiority in the 1980s and offset potential threats from China. The programme enhanced the infectiveness, virulence and hardiness of first-generation BW agents. By inserting genes taken from haemorrhagic fever into the variola virus (which causes smallpox), it made the latter more deadly than the viral strains found in nature, and by inserting genes into the Y. pestis cells (which causes pneumonic plague) it made the bacterium more resistant to common antibiotics. It also weaponized anti-crop agents (wheat rust, rice blast and rye blast), anti-animal agents such as African swine fever, rinderpest and foot and mouth disease (FMDV), and highly virulent agents such as the Marburg virus, for which there was neither a vaccine nor effective treatment. In effect, it weaponized a wide range of BW agents, both lethal and incapacitating, for use in strategic, operational or tactical missions.[32]

Conducted under the greatest secrecy, the Soviet BW programme aroused the suspicions of Western intelligence, notably over allegations that an outbreak of anthrax, causing numerous casualties in Sverdlovsk in April 1979, had come from an accident at the BW facility. An impassioned debate erupted between the Reagan administration and its critics, both internationally and within the United States. In 1985 an independent commission claimed that US intelligence in this area was 'strikingly deficient', and that 'the Department of Defense does not have an adequate grasp of the biological-warfare threat'.[33] It required two defections to reveal the extent of the Soviet programme, first by a Soviet biologist, Vladimir Pasechnik, to Britain in 1989, and then by Kanatjan Alibekov, the second-in-command at Biopreparat, who changed his name to Ken Alibek after defecting to the United States in 1992. Alibek confirmed that the Soviets had not only produced, tested and weaponized traditional anti-personnel, anti-animal and anti-plant BW agents but they had also created genetically altered, antibiotic-resistant strains of plague, anthrax, tularaemia and glanders. The research costs had not proved prohibitive: 'A few million dollars. This is what it cost us for making the smallpox-VEE chimera at Vector in 1990 and 1991.'[34] Such evidence enabled the United States and Britain to press the Russian regime of Boris Yeltsin into admitting that the former Soviet Union had violated the BTWC systematically. It also conceded that the outbreak of anthrax at Sverdlovsk had been caused by an accidental release from the BW facility (and not a natural outbreak as claimed by Soviet propagandists and believed by some Western commentators), and that Russia had maintained BW production facilities. President Yeltsin, seeking improved relations with the West, promised to close down all BW activity and, under a Trilateral Agreement of September 1992, Russia, Britain and the United States sought to resolve their differences over the programme.

Almost as impressive was the Soviet CW programme, which survived the nuclear obsessions of Nikita Khrushchev and emerged as the largest and most diverse capability in the world. The large, well-trained and equipped Soviet chemical troops, possibly numbering between 80,000 and 100,000 personnel, eclipsed the 5,000 chemical forces in the *Bundeswehr* and the 9,000 in the US Army. Assigned to front-line commands and the Air Force, they discharged major duties, often mounted in vehicles, in nuclear, biological and chemical (NBC) reconnaissance and large-scale decontamination. These troops and the widespread introduction of collective protection (air filtration and sealing devices) on main battle tanks, self-propelled artillery, armoured personnel carriers and anti-aircraft guns enhanced the Soviet capability to carry out tactical operations in a contaminated environment. Moreover, Soviet offensive CW seemed to enjoy a marked growth in investment from the mid-1960s onwards, involving at least fifteen R&D centres, the increase of storage capacity at nine major sites, and a substantial expansion of the testing facilities at the Shikhany Proving Ground.

This build-up gathered momentum at a time when NATO's doctrine of flexible response emphasized the possibility of a conventional phase at the outset of any war in Europe, employing weapons that were supposedly more predictable in their effects than chemical weapons. As the only retaliation-in-kind could come from the ageing CW capability of the United States, the main deterrent to a Soviet chemical strike lay in the risk that it might trigger nuclear escalation. There was little sign that this deterrent had had much effect upon Soviet doctrinal thinking. On the contrary, the Soviets envisaged using chemical weapons throughout the entire depth of the combat zone, including rear-area attacks upon enemy airfields, nuclear weapon sites, munitions depots, ports, command and control facilities and major road and rail junctions. They also seemed equipped to use chemical weapons to protect the flanks of fast-moving offensive operations, to degrade the combat effectiveness of NATO forces that would be compelled to wear their protective kit, and to exploit the many weaknesses in the hugely variable state of NATO's defensive readiness. The US Defense Intelligence Agency claimed, too, that the Soviets were ready to conduct such operations with chemical munitions stored in 32 forward areas in Eastern Europe.[35]

The exact size and composition of the Soviet CW stockpile remained a source of intense speculation, even after the announcement of Mikhail Gorbachev that the Soviet Union possessed chemical weapons in March 1987 (the first such admission), and that it would cease further production one month later. Initially, Soviet spokesmen declared that the Soviet capability amounted to 'no more than 50,000 tons' of agent (later reduced, without any visible means of destruction, to 40,000 tons). This was not only at the low end of Western estimates but it was also very much smaller than some Western estimates of 300,000 tons. When the Soviets subsequently displayed 'standard' chemical munitions at Shikhany in October 1987, sceptics immediately noticed that these only included elderly munitions and classical nerve agents, mustard gas, lewisite and cs. While the Bush administration sought clarification of Soviet data through a Memorandum of Understanding, signed by Secretary of State James Baker and Soviet Foreign Minister Eduard Shevardnadze at Jackson Hole, Wyoming (22–23 September 1989), Bush wanted to exploit the political symbolism of the agreement and to remove the 'scourge' of chemical weapons (see Introduction).[36]

Although the Bush administration had entered office committed to the modernization of the us chemical capability through the development of binary weapons, it knew that these weapons aroused fierce controversy in the House of Representatives. Congressional opponents had seized upon technical difficulties in the development of the Bigeye bomb, and had only authorized funding for the 155 mm artillery shell, with effect from 16 December 1987. As some of these difficulties persisted, congressional opposition to these 'morally repugnant' weapons grew, enabling the House to block funding for the entire programme in 1989. Making a virtue of necessity, and facing Soviet demands to terminate the binary programme, the Bush administration abandoned the programme as part of a bilateral pact with the Soviets, signed at the Washington summit (1 June 1990). By this accord, the two superpowers affirmed a mutual cessation of cw production and a readiness to exchange data, accept monitoring of declared stockpiles, and accelerate their mutual destruction programmes as soon as a multilateral ban entered into force.[37]

The pact had little long-term significance. It neither accelerated the destruction process (which was thwarted by mounting costs and a lack of political will in Yeltsin's Russia and by safety and environmental concerns in the United States) nor galvanized the disarmament process in Geneva. For over twenty years diplomats in the Conference on Disarmament (and its predecessors) had grappled with the complexities of cw disarmament without resolving key issues on retaliatory use and challenge inspection (a central component of the proposed verification regime). The credibility of the negotiations had also been put at issue by Iraq's use of chemical weapons without paying any political penalty during the Iran–Iraq War (1981–8). Accordingly, after the US-led coalition triumphed in the Gulf War (1991) without any recourse to chemical warfare (see chapter Four), spokesmen for the Bush administration promptly claimed that chemical weapons had lost their former utility. As Ronald Lehman, director of the US Arms Control and Disarmament Agency, asserted:

> A lot of nations looked at the Gulf War and have come to the conclusion they don't want to go down the chemical weapons path – the risks are too great – and they want to make sure nobody else does, either. It is this attitude that has given us a boost for the Chemical Weapons Convention.[38]

This may have been a premature judgement (see chapter Four) but the Bush administration had to make further concessions and compromises before it could accelerate the negotiations in Geneva. On 13 May 1991 it renounced the right to retain a small stockpile of chemical weapons for security purposes and the right to retaliate-in-kind. It then modified several proposals that the US had formerly required of the draft convention, including the dilution of the 'any-where/anytime' principle on challenge inspection. By breaking the impasse in Geneva, the administration could claim credit for facilitating the negotiations that led to the multilateral agreement. A Chemical Weapons Convention (CWC) was opened for signature in Paris on 13 January 1993 and came into force, when 65 states had ratified it, on 29 April 1997.

The Chemical Weapons Convention

The 174-page document, comprising 50,000 words in the English-language version, bans the development, production, use, transfer, retention or stockpiling of chemical weapons, and requires the destruction of all production facilities and chemical weapons within a period of ten years. It established an international body, the Organization for the Prohibition of Chemical Weapons (OPCW), located in The Hague, with a Technical Secretariat of 500 staff, including 200 inspectors responsible for the implementation of the verification provisions. These provisions encompass the on-site inspection of declared storage and closed production sites, the destruction of production facilities (or the monitoring of those converted for civilian purposes), the destruction of stockpiles of declared agent and weapons, and the routine onsite inspection of facilities that handle specific chemicals. These chemicals are arranged in three schedules: first, very toxic chemicals that have been, or have the potential to be, chemical weapons (but are retained in strictly controlled amounts for research, medical, pharmaceutical or protective purposes); second, chemicals produced in limited quantities for peaceful purposes but that could be used militarily or as key precursor chemicals; and third, dual-use chemicals produced in large amounts for industrial purposes. The routine on-site inspections for each of these schedules varied in frequency and intensity. Unprecedented in its intrusiveness, this verification regime, coupled with the scope of a treaty affirming an international norm against the possession and use of chemical weapons, attracted the adherence of 182 states-parties in its first decade of existence.

The CWC, nonetheless, is a limited agreement. As a voluntary treaty between states, it was aimed primarily at the activities of states and not sub-state groups such as terrorists. Secondly, it concentrated upon chemicals that had been used in war, or those perceived at the time as possible candidates for military usage, but many other toxic chemicals could be used as chemical weapons or as precursors for such weapons. Thirdly, the routine inspections were intended to confirm that the activities at declared plants were consistent with their permitted activities, and that the risk of detection would deter the diversion of militarily significant quantities of agent for weapon-production. These inspections, though, would not necessarily detect the diversion of small quantities of these chemicals for the purposes of terrorists or sub-state actors (including the use of chlorine tankers as suicide weapons in Iraq in 2008). Finally, the first two decades of the treaty regime passed without any request by a state party for a challenge inspection at any location, whether declared or not, of another state party. As making such a challenge would be politically contentious (and might backfire on account of faulty intelligence or the extended lead times allowed for the challenge inspections in the treaty), states have sought to resolve non-compliance concerns by bilateral discussions.[39]

Politics, in sum, had always figured prominently in the response of states to the prospect of chemical and biological warfare. Rarely were political leaders supplied with accurate intelligence about the CBW programmes of potential adversaries. Often they had to act in conditions of considerable uncertainty, seeking to exploit better relations with measures of disarmament, whether in the mid-1920s or in the wake of the Cold War. Whenever war loomed or occurred, deterrence became a natural response, not least because of the additional burdens, the psychological fears and the immense uncertainties associated with any recurrence of chemical warfare. Though biological warfare was potentially an even greater threat, whose feasibility and area coverage had been demonstrated by all measures short of war, chemical warfare had recurred in various theatres throughout the twentieth century. The legacy of those conflicts, and the rapid pace of scientific and technological change (see chapter Seven), would ensure that the use of chemical weapons remained an option beyond the signing of the Chemical Weapons Convention.

3

Chemical Warfare in
Third World Conflicts

In debates about the utility of chemical weapons, and their purported failure in the First World War, critics claimed that these weapons had not only failed to prove decisive but that they had also not been assimilated as 'normal' weapons of war. Examples of incomprehension between scientists and the military, the additional logistic burdens, risks and uncertain effects of some cw operations, particularly those dependent upon gas cylinders, and the effectiveness of anti-gas defences prior to the impact of mustard gas seemingly buttressed the sceptical case. Even the German advantage in mustard gas failed to stem the allied onslaught in the autumn of 1918; retaliation-in-kind eventually followed, gas never reproduced its impact as a weapon of surprise, and would not be used in the Second World War (see chapter Two). Contemporary critics dwelt less upon the shortcomings and burdens of chemical weapons than upon their horrific effects, and their potential to injure and kill, especially if delivered by aircraft in assaults upon defenceless civilians. While such criticism encouraged some states to promote disarmament, or at least to adjust their military priorities while disarmament diplomacy was underway, recourse to chemical warfare persisted, albeit without any blaze of publicity.

Following the First World War, when the great powers were engaged in wholesale demobilization, limited intervention on behalf of the White Russians posed immense operational and logistical problems. Those allied armies based in Archangel and Murmansk faced difficult fighting against larger Bolshevik forces in heavily forested terrain. Senior commanders pressed for aerial support to drop thermo-generators, or 'M' devices as bombs, capable of emitting toxic smoke clouds containing the vomiting agent adamsite or diphenylamine chlorarsine (DM). The sole concern of Winston Churchill, then Secretary for War and Air, was whether any limited application of the gas in northern Russia would reveal the secret of Britain's new gas weapon, but, under pressure from his military advisors, he approved its use.[1] His concerns were vindicated inasmuch as Britain lacked sufficient aircraft to conduct aerial gas operations effectively in northern Russia. In eight bombing attacks from 27 August to 2 September 1919, pairs of aircraft, and on one occasion three aircraft, dropped 361 bombs to release clouds of toxic smoke, but these clouds were limited in area coverage and concentration. As the aircraft were unable to land at night, the bombs had to be dropped during the day, and the clouds tended to rise and become dispersed by the sunlight. Nevertheless, the non-lethal gas caused casualties and panic (as corroborated by enemy prisoners), prompting Lord Rawlinson, general officer in charge of Allied Forces, North Russia, to claim that 'the moral effects on the enemy was [sic] very great and materially assisted the operations'.[2] Although the intervention petered out as the allies withdrew, colonial powers would review and in some cases exploit their advantage in chemical weaponry against local insurgents.

Interwar Colonial CBW Conflicts

The defeat of the German and Ottoman empires had led to an increase in Britain's imperial responsibilities at a time when she was demobilizing her forces and reducing her garrison in India. Faced with growing commitments in Ireland, Churchill and his military advisors looked to technology in the form of air power and poison gas as partial substitutes for manpower in imperial policing. As early as May 1919, the War and Air ministries reviewed the option of employing gas bombs against 'recalcitrant Arabs' in Egypt. At that time, the Air Ministry lacked the requisite ordnance, and feared that it would take several months to produce. Military opinion was split; while Major-General W.G.H. Salmond, the commander of the Middle East Royal Flying Corps, deplored the use of gas and contended that conventional bombs would suffice, the army council favoured the use of 'gas against uncivilized tribes'. Churchill was

> strongly in favour of using poisoned gas against uncivilised tribes. The moral effect should be so good that the loss of life should be reduced to a minimum. It is not necessary to use only the most deadly gases; gases can be used which cause great inconvenience and would spread a lively terror

and yet would leave no serious permanent effects on most of those affected.[3]

As the waging of the Third Afghan War (May–August 1919) had imposed a considerable strain upon the available manpower, Churchill sent Brigadier-General Foulkes to promote the case for chemical warfare in India. After a two-month tour of the north-west frontier, Foulkes issued a stream of reports, confirming the potential effectiveness of mustard gas in the prevailing high temperatures (where the gas would vaporize more rapidly than on the Western Front, causing severe inflammation, blistering and skin lesions). He claimed, too, that British soldiers could be trained and equipped for gas warfare, that the problems of logistics and supply could be overcome, and that gas could be used to seal the flanks of attacking columns, to protect lines of communication and outpost pickets, and to attack fortified positions and enemy encampments. The untrained and unprotected Afghans would have to evacuate the combat zone to avoid incurring casualties. Although Foulkes convinced several front-line commanders, persuading them to set aside beliefs in the purported chivalry of frontier fighting, he had less success with Lord Chelmsford, the viceroy, and Sir Charles Monro, the commander-in-chief. Like the political authorities in the India Office, they were primarily concerned about the political and moral implications of introducing gas warfare on the Indian sub-continent. As barely six months had elapsed since the disastrous killing of 400 unarmed Indians and the wounding of another 1,000 at Amritsar (13 April 1919), their concerns were reasonable even if the cabinet proved unwilling to renounce the use of gas without an international agreement. Ultimately gas equipment was sent to India but only for the purposes of retaliation and not as a weapon of surprise or as a means of quelling public disturbances.[4]

In 1920 Britain faced similar problems in Mesopotamia (later known as Iraq), which it had gained from the Ottoman empire. Desperate to reduce the costs of garrisoning Iraq, Churchill looked to the newly founded Royal Air Force to police the country, backed by a limited body of British and Indian troops. Once again Churchill favoured using gas bombs that would release a non-lethal asphyxiating agent, but neither these plans nor the ordnance were available when an Arab revolt erupted in the middle of 1920. Large numbers of ground troops and reinforcements from India had to quell the uprising. Although RAF squadrons were active before, during and after the revolt, undertaking reconnaissance, close support, the dropping of food and ammunition to beleaguered garrisons, and providing assistance in rapid pursuit, communications and in demonstration flights, they did not bomb the rebels with gas. As late as 29 August 1920, only weeks before the revolt ended, Churchill was still pressing RAF experts to work on the development of gas ordnance, including mustard-gas bombs. Over a year later, on 16 December 1921, he assured the RAF that he was 'ready to authorise the construction of such bombs at once; the question of their use to be decided when the occasion arises'.[5] Gas shells may have been used in Mesopotamia with 'excellent moral effect', but the claim that Britain bombed the Iraqis with gases, as made by one author, appears to confuse what Churchill wished with what was practical at the time.[6]

The Spanish authorities were much less inhibited. After the disaster at Anual in Spanish Morocco (22 July–9 August 1921), when Rif tribesmen massacred some 8,000 to 12,000 Spanish troops, Spain no longer wished to rely upon its poorly equipped army, operating in difficult terrain, to suppress the Rif revolt. Within a month of the disaster Spain established contacts with the Reichswehr, and soon signed a contract with Hugo Stoltzenberg to construct a mustard-gas plant near Madrid that would be named after the king, Alfonso XIII. Other plants were built to produce gas masks and weapons (both gas hand grenades and bombs), and further contracts were signed to procure equipment, materials and gas shells from France. In November 1921 Spain began its gas war. Initially gunners fired shells, emitting phosgene and chloropicrin. Two years later, Spanish pilots began dropping toxic bombs in low-level attacks, but had to do so selectively as they had only a limited supply. Mustard gas, dispersed by artillery, made its introduction reportedly at the battle of Tizzi Azza (15 July 1923), where the positive reports prompted military demands for large numbers of mustard-gas bombs. By 22 June 1924 the Spanish air force began its mustard-gas bombing, dropping 99 bombs (5,000 kilos of mustard gas) on the headquarters, house, home town and nearby villages of the Abdel Krim, the leader of the Rif revolt. Thereafter it launched a succession of massive bombing raids, involving high-explosive, incendiary and mustard-gas bombs, upon target areas – small towns, villages, often on market day, and cultivated areas during the harvesting season. Although villages were still targeted in the final two years of the revolt, 1926 and 1927, the bombing may have become more selective, increasingly focused upon fortifications and cannon emplacements.[7]

In his excellent account of the Spanish gas war, Sebastian Balfour explains that the Spanish authorities sought to conceal evidence of the chemical operations both at the time and retrospectively. Spain did not ratify the Geneva Protocol until 1929, two years after the colonial war had ended. Spanish military attitudes about the use of gas seemed to veer across a spectrum from those who sought revenge, and wished to exterminate an enemy deemed 'uncivilized' and barbaric in its treatment of prisoners, to those who believed that chemical attacks represented the most effective way of bringing the revolt to a rapid end, with a minimal loss of Spanish lives. Neither expectation was fulfilled. Gas certainly caused casualties, panic and fear among its victims, many of whom were women, children and elderly people, but the Rif learned to evacuate gassed areas and take to the hills. Moreover the gas campaign, according to British, French and German observers, was hardly a model of efficiency. Casualties occurred in the gas factories; the bombing was often inaccurate, especially if pilots proved unwilling to expose their aircraft to accurate rifle-fire in low-level operations; and co-ordination with conventional forces often proved defective, so Spanish troops, following gas attacks, suffered casualties from the vagaries of the wind or from precipitate offensives over contaminated terrain. The chemical war, nonetheless, acted as a force multiplier, compounding the effects of conventional weapons and starvation, thereby causing 'extreme suffering and want amongst Moroccan soldiers and civilians'. If the ultimate victory depended primarily upon Franco-Spanish collaboration, without the use of gas by the French, chemical weapons had weakened the resistance of Abdel Krim's supporters.[8]

Unlike the Spanish, the Italians embarked on their colonial campaigns of the interwar years with wartime experience of chemical warfare and of employing air power in colonial conflict, pioneering such activity in the conquest of Libya in 1911–12. Having been driven back over several years to the coastal towns of Tripolitania and several forts in Cyrenaica, the Italians launched the reconquest of both provinces in 1922. Despite the exploitation of tribal rivalries, the use of mobile columns and fiercely repressive policies, Italian expansion into the hinterland proceeded slowly. Over the vast spaces of the Libyan desert, air power provided reconnaissance for the planning and conduct of ground operations, transported ammunition and supplies, removed the wounded, and provided close air support, particularly in the pursuit of retreating guerrillas. It also bombed concentrations of the enemy, and in some actions bombed with phosgene gas under the orders of Governor Emilio De Bono. Occasionally Caproni aircraft, dropping gas bombs, may have proved effective, possibly scaring Zintan tribesmen into surrender in 1925,[9] but gas bombing remained a small ancillary component of the aerial operations. 'The absence of mass bombing action', argues John Gooch, 'was due not to lack of interest in such activities but rather to the fact that the air base at Hon lacked the fuel, explosives and landing-fields to support such operations.'[10]

Benito Mussolini, nonetheless, would ensure that Italian forces were much better equipped for the forthcoming invasion of Ethiopia, a war that would be described as a 'civilizing mission'. When Italy was criticized over the use of gas in the ensuing hostilities, such usage was at first denied and then described as a limited reprisal for the emasculation of captured Italian airmen. In fact Italy had prepared thoroughly in advance of the gas war, pre-positioning military supplies in its East African colonies over a period of several years. Over 1,000 bombs filled with mustard gas were sent to Mogadishu between 1930 and 1932; some 56,000 artillery shells filled with arsine gas were ordered for Eritrea in the summer of 1935 and another 20,000 for Italian Somaliland. Between 25 June and 25 December 1935, 45 tons of mustard gas, 265 tons of another poison gas and 7,483 gas bombs were shipped through the Suez Canal. After the first phase of the war from October 1935 to the fall of Addis Ababa, the Ethiopian capital, on 5 May 1936, the Italians replenished their stocks of gas and bombs, and used them extensively in seeking to pacify the remaining two thirds of the country. Over the next three years at least 459 gas bombs, (243 emitting mustard gas, 216 non-lethal arsine) were dropped on the Ethiopians.[11]

Gas comprised only part of an arsenal of modern weaponry that Mussolini wished to employ decisively in seeking a rapid victory in Ethiopia. In launching the invasion, he sought not merely to avenge the shame of Adowa (a disastrous Italian military defeat by the Ethiopians in 1896) but also to display the military prowess of fascist Italy. He had to get the bulk of his army back before the onset of the rainy season in the summer of 1936 (and so restore his forces on the Brenner Pass) and to resolve the conflict before sanctions passed by the League of Nations could take effect or be extended to include oil. Determined to use all available weapons, he resolved to exploit Italy's air superiority and its gas capabilities. Nevertheless, Italian forces had to experiment with various gases and modes of delivery on account of local meteorological conditions. In the north sudden and gusty winds, alternating with dead calm or sudden torrential showers, diffused vapour clouds, as did the hot equatorial sun rising in the daytime in the desert areas of the south. As these conditions militated against the effects of non-persistent agents, such as phosgene or chloropicrin, the Italians came to rely increasingly upon mustard gas, which burnt more rapidly in the hot sun than in European conditions, and upon aerial delivery. Initially the aerial attacks involved the dropping of metal drums, whose thin walls ruptured on contact with the ground to leave puddles of agent that experienced warriors soon learned to avoid. Thereafter the Regia Aeronautica dropped 100-, 200- and 500-kg bombs that contaminated areas up to 200 yards in radius, and finally sprayed agent from nine, fifteen or sometimes eighteen aircraft so that the gas spread more evenly over much wider areas.

In a two-front war, gas was employed on both fronts but primarily in the north as Italian forces crossed the high ground and passed through the mountainous defiles, using gas to protect their flanks. The Italians also used gas to terrorize civilians in the bombing of villages and to interdict enemy supply columns, killing cattle and pack animals, as well as frightening camp followers and disrupting communications. They dispersed gas over large enemy encampments to demoralize Ethiopian forces and encourage desertion; and, in major battles, followed up the artillery, machine gunners and high-explosive bombing by gassing the bare-footed and bare-shouldered warriors, thereby turning retreats into routs. Yet the actual effectiveness of the chemical attacks remains a matter of dispute as the Italians concealed evidence of the gas war, the Ethiopians kept few records, and most of the journalists on the Ethiopian side never ventured beyond Addis. As most of these correspondents had regurgitated optimistic reports from the Abyssinians in the earlier part of the war, they blamed the unexpected demise of Haile Selassie's armies, as did the emperor himself, upon the 'deadly rain'. If the gas was easier to blame than the emperor's strategic blunders, and his resolve to seek battle against a vastly superior army, chemical weapons proved a force multiplier in battle. They helped to drive the Ethiopians from their prepared positions and ensured that Selassie's armies, once beaten, could not easily reform and re-engage in further actions. Though the gas rarely proved fatal, its effects were horrific to experience and observe, and almost certainly undermined Ethiopian morale.[12]

Chemical and Biological Warfare in China

East Asia had been spared any recourse to chemical or biological warfare during the First World War. Japan's Imperial Army, though, had begun to study chemical weapons and their methods of production as early as May 1918, and Japanese incursions into Siberia during the civil war intervention left a recurring fear that the Red Army might employ chemical warfare against Japanese forces. Having sent military personnel to study gas warfare in France, Germany and the United States in the early 1920s, and having followed the United States in refusing to ratify the Geneva Protocol, Japan began small-scale gas experiments in the late 1920s. A chemical production facility was built near the town of Tandanoumi on the island of Okunoshima, and the production of chemical agent began in 1929. The plant was expanded in 1933, and again in 1935, by which time it was producing mustard gas, lewisite, several tear gases and hydrogen cyanide, all in the strictest secrecy. Trials of offensive and defensive equipment took place at various sites, including the tropical conditions on Formosa, and the army, always more interested in this option than the navy or air force, established a Chemical Warfare School at Narashino in August 1933. It produced some 3,350 CW experts over the next twelve years.[13]

Nevertheless, the Japanese failed to establish a balanced, co-ordinated and fully integrated CW capability. The Imperial Army never constituted a Chemical Warfare Service on the American model; its R&D programmes, which eschewed liaison with civilian scientists or industrial facilities, neither discovered any new gases nor invented new munitions; and its productive capacity neither produced rugged defensive kit nor sustained efficient, high-volume production. Yet when the so-called 'China Incident' erupted on 7 July 1937, Japanese gas units were sent into Manchuria and they served there and in other provinces throughout the war until 8 May 1945. The initial deployments were cautious, including the Number One Chemical Experimental Battalion, and their operations were relatively small scale, mounting only nine gas attacks in the first six months of the war, all using non-lethal gases. Among the units despatched were a field chemical laboratory sent to Shanghai in October 1937 to gather intelligence on the lamentable state of China's anti-gas defences; a field gas section of 119 officers and men armed with portable sprayers and toxic smoke candles; four chemical mortar battalions; and the Morita Detachment, a battalion of 1,031 officers and men sent to support the Central China Expeditionary Force.

Gas attacks expanded steadily in scope and diversity, with mustard gas employed against Guomindang and Communist forces from the summer of 1939 onwards. Dispersed primarily from short-range munitions – candles, gas grenades, mortar bombs and portable sprayers – the gas provided support at close range for ground operations. Although aerial gas attacks occurred, the close-support on the ground, often with weather-dependent weapons, reduced both the element of surprise and the scope of combined operations. As captured Japanese reports confirm, the Imperial Army employed gas to dislodge the enemy from fortified positions, facilitate river crossings, clear caves, engage numerically superior Chinese forces in encounter battles and, in the most extensive usage, deliver some 375 gas attacks during the four-month campaign to conquer Wuhan (12 June–25 October 1938). The Japanese also used gas defensively in defending exposed positions or in covering retreats, and occasionally, as at Yichang (October 1941), employed gas shells and bombs to surprise the enemy prior to a counter-attack.[14] The increasing recourse to, and more diversified use of, poison gas indicates that some field commanders appreciated the utility of gas as a means of exploiting Chinese vulnerabilities. If the gas caused relatively few fatalities,[15] and periodically failed to have any effect,[16] it could still harass, confuse and demoralize an ill-equipped and poorly trained adversary in localized engagements.

Potentially biological warfare was an even more effective option in a war waged over a vast terrain against a country sorely deficient in its public health and sanitation provisions. However Major (later Lieutenant-General) Shiro Ishii, who was the driving force behind the Japanese BW programme, was originally much more concerned about the potential of a weapon whose use had been banned at Geneva. Once the Kwantung Army seized Manchuria (1931–2), he had a more immediate task of devising a weapon that could be used against the Red Army. During the border clashes of 1934–5, and the fierce exchanges of the Nomonhan Incident (1939), both sides allegedly tried to spread diseases and to contaminate water supplies.[17] Ishii, supposedly working on water purification and epidemic prevention, gained approval from high-level officers in the Japanese Army to undertake BW research at centres in Manchuria. Initially he chose Harbin and later a village known as Beiyinhe, before acquiring more extensive facilities at Ping Fan (a collection of ten villages, 24 kilometres south of Harbin). Completed in 1939, this massive installation involved some 150 buildings (laboratories, dormitories, administrative blocks, barracks, barns, a large farm, greenhouses, a prison to hold the human test subjects, a power plant, three furnaces, recreational facilities for the staff and a railway connection to Harbin). It housed 3,000 scientists, technicians and soldiers, was self-sufficient in livestock, and was protected tightly on the ground and in the air, with regular aerial patrols over the plant. Ishii's department, later named Unit 731, was in charge of the undertaking, with an annual budget of ten million yen and substantial support from civilian scientists. The plant had a productive capacity of eight tons of bacteria per month and an ability to produce twenty million doses of vaccine per year.

The staff developed techniques for growing bacteria in aluminium tanks and harvesting them by scraping the tanks with metal rakes (a highly dangerous task). They conducted research on human reactions to plague, typhoid, smallpox, tularemia, anthrax, botulism, gas gangrene, dysentery, glanders, tuberculosis, frostbite and many other diseases. The death toll among the victims, known as *marutas* (or 'logs' by the Japanese), was almost certainly far above the 3,000 commonly given for Ping Fan. The Japanese conducted laboratory research in another eighteen facilities in China, the Dutch East Indies, Singapore and Rangoon, and sought to eliminate all trace of their activities towards the end of the war. As Sheldon Harris observes, the Ping Fan death toll overlooks the deaths in other branch camps within Manchuria, another 5,000 or 6,000 killed in factories at Mukden, Nanking and Changchun outside Ishii's control, and in the widespread murders of prisoners and Chinese workers that occurred in August 1945 as the Japanese tried to eliminate evidence of their experiments before the arrival of Chinese and Soviet troops.[18]

Cultivating and testing pathogens, though, proved much easier than developing viable means of dissemination. Ishii's staff examined two types of artillery shell, neither of which proved practical, and several types of bomb: steel-walled HA and Uji bombs, a ceramic and fin-guided Uji bomb, high-altitude Ro bombs supposed to release two quarts of bacteria-rich liquid, and a Mother and Daughter bomb, in which the daughter cluster was released on a radio signal from the mother bomb. Unit 731 also conducted (by their own admission) at least twelve field tests over civilian communities in China. In aerial operations, they dispersed contaminated wheat, millet and bits of paper, plague-infested fleas, and experimented with dropping bacterial bombs from low altitudes. Saboteurs spread BW materials among Chinese forces and civilians, lacing wells with typhoid, injecting people with germs instead of vaccines, releasing rats with plague-infested fleas, and injecting chocolate bars, dumplings and sweet cakes with anthrax and typhoid.

Unit 100, operating out of Changchun, worked closely with the Intelligence Division of the Kwantung Army in conducting many of these field tests and sabotage missions in the period 1940–42. Largely experimental, the tests proved of limited value as the Japanese never developed an efficient means of large-scale dissemination. In one ghastly act on 20 August 1945, after the official Japanese surrender, six members of Unit 100 infected 60 horses with glanders at their former headquarters, and then released them, along with hordes of rats infected with plague germs and other pathogens, into the Chinese countryside. The resulting epidemics left parts of Changchun and nearby towns uninhabitable until the mid-1950s. Yet the Japanese BW programme was notable primarily for the data gathered on tissue pathology from human experimentation. Once they were aware that this information might be available, US interrogators would offer immunity to Ishii and many of his colleagues in exchange for the data about the Japanese BW programme.[19]

Cold War Conflicts and Allegations

As the Cold War ensued, controversies attending chemical and biological warfare multiplied, often becoming a focal issue in the propaganda battle. The American debriefing of Ishii and his co-practitioners in the BW programme, which took several years, proved the first bone of contention. By promising immunity from war crimes indictments, and by refusing Soviet requests to interrogate Ishii and the other Japanese scientists, the Americans had to keep the evidence on human experimentation secret. The Soviets, though, had overrun the ruined Japanese facilities in Manchuria and captured twelve Japanese officers, including General Yamada Otozoo, commander-in-chief of the Kwantung Army, and other ranks, all of whom either knew about or were directly involved in the BW programme. When the Soviets conducted a show trial of these men at Khabarovsk (25–30 December 1949), they produced a comprehensive account of the activities of Unit 731 and Unit 100. The United States sought to dismiss this evidence as a mere distraction from the controversy over the fate of an estimated 376,000 Japanese soldiers and civilians captured by the Soviets.[20]

This dispute resurfaced during the Korean War (1950–53) when the Chinese and North Koreans alleged that the United States had waged biological warfare against them. First raised briefly in a radio cablegram to the president of the UN Security Council on 8 May 1951, the Communists then launched a massive propaganda campaign on 22 February 1952, carefully timed to coincide with a dispute over the release of prisoners during the Panmunjon negotiations. Led by official protests from the ministers for foreign affairs of North Korea (Pak Hen Yen) and China (Zhou Enlai), the campaign fomented worldwide protests from every Communist government and media outlet, supported by supposedly 'impartial' investigations by scientists, international lawyers and radical journalists, including the newspaper editor John W. Powell, and the Canadian clergyman James G. Endicott. Although only one of many atrocity charges against the United States and its UN allies, the BW allegations came to dominate the closing months of the war.

The Communists alleged that the United States had dispersed diseases from the air, and occasionally by artillery shells, and that aircraft had sprayed BW agents or dropped bacteria-laden bombs, containers or other packages throughout the target area. Numerous witnesses came forth, claiming that they had seen US aircraft dropping these bombs or containers that released a multitude of vectors, including flies, fleas, spiders, mosquitoes, butterflies, feathers, cotton wool, paper envelopes, clams, infected animals and even infected pancakes. From these carriers came a multitude of reported diseases: plague, anthrax, cholera, smallpox, encephalitis, typhoid and rickettsia, among others. Laboratory tests purportedly confirmed some of the evidence, with claims that the diseases or epidemics had erupted out of season or in anomalous circumstances or had been eradicated in the recent past, and that some of the insects appeared specially bred. Finally, the Chinese released confessions from captured American airmen, four of whom were interviewed by an International Scientific Commission.[21]

Disconcerted by these charges, the initial American response was of dignified silence, followed by indignant denials from US Secretary of State Dean Acheson on 4 March 1952. Neither these denials nor similar protests from the UN Command, the UN Secretary General, Trygve Lie, and the overwhelming majority of UN members proved sufficient. Only scientists and journalists who had the approval of the Chinese and North Korean authorities were allowed to investigate the evidence, and the UN was barred from undertaking any investigation. Meanwhile the reputation of the United States suffered from a continual onslaught in every UN forum. Although it never lost any votes, the United States could neither prove a negative nor determine the truth amidst the myriad of allegations. Faced with Soviet accusations that the US had neither ratified the Geneva Protocol nor renounced the use of biological warfare, and that it had both sheltered Japanese BW war criminals and used their expertise in their active BW programme, US spokesmen emphatically denied any use of biological weapons. They claimed that the alleged incidents involved naturally occurring diseases in wartime, and that the discovery of 'new' species reflected scant understanding of the natural insect faunae of North Korea and China, and the effects of a government-induced flurry of entomological collecting.[22] They also defended their BW programme as a prudent, defensive precaution within the Cold War, a more practical option than relying on the 'paper promise' of the Geneva Protocol. If the United States could never prove its case conclusively, even with recantations from captured airmen after the war, there are good reasons for doubting that the US initiated biological warfare in Korea. As John Ellis van Courtland Moon argues, such an operation would have broken with the existing policy of 'retaliation only' and required presidential approval. President Harry S. Truman would have had to give his consent despite the popular revulsion against this option in the United States and the qualms of European allies opposed to first use. He would also have risked escalation in a local war, in which all manner of restrictions had been placed upon US conventional bombing and naval operations, at a time when the US was more concerned about the longer-term needs of defending Europe.[23]

Controversy would again bedevil the United States when it employed riot-control agents and herbicides in the Vietnam War. Although the United States had supplied irritant agents to the Army of the Republic of Vietnam (ARVN) as early as 1962, the first use by

American forces occurred on 23 December 1964 when CS grenades were air-dropped in an abortive attempt to rescue American prisoners in An Xuyen Province. Described initially as a weapon of self defence, CS possessed an operational potential that was soon revealed. On 5 September 1965, Lieutenant-Colonel Leon Utter ordered the 2nd Battalion, 7th Marine Regiment to use CS in the first tunnel clearance exercise, securing the emergence of 400 people, including women and children held by the Viet Cong, from a complex of tunnels, bunkers and 'spider' holes without serious injury. Military Assistance Command promptly sought, and received permission (on 3 November 1965), to use riot-control agents more extensively in support of military operations. This authority was delegated to subordinate commanders.[24]

Once approved for purposes of area denial, CS and CN gases became highly flexible as weapons of choice, spawning refinements in munitions, delivery systems and the agents themselves. In tunnel-clearing operations the burning-type CS grenades would be used with smoke grenades and later a portable blower, the M106 Riot Control Agent Dispenser, dubbed Mighty Mite. As even these systems proved limited in clearing the multi-level tunnel systems, many of which had air locks, US forces detonated bags or cardboard containers filled with powdered CS1 to disperse an agent that could remain effective in a sealed tunnel for several months. Just as the powdered CS1 was more durable than the aerosol CS, so CS1 coated with silicone and known as CS2 proved more resistant to moisture and could remain active in the field for several weeks. To maximize its impact, CS1 or CS2 was often disseminated in bulk over known or suspected base camps, rest areas, or infiltration routes from CH-47 helicopters, with locally fabricated racks that could dispense 30 55-gallon drums, each containing 80 pounds of CS. The US Army also dispensed CS from the E8 riot control launcher, the XM-630 cartridge for the 4.2-inch mortar, the M79 grenade launcher and the XM-631 projectile for the 155 mm howitzer. For longer-range aerial operations, US forces employed the M-5 bulk agent disperser, the XM-15, XM-165 and E-158 canister launchers and the BLU-52 chemical bomb. CS became so valued as a tactical weapon that the US Army purchased 13,736,000 pounds over the period from Fiscal Year 1964 to Fiscal Year 1969.[25]

American commanders found that CS could be employed effectively in a whole array of offensive and defensive missions. Quite apart from using it to clear bunkers and caves, they employed it in suppressing enemy fire around helicopter landing zones, in the reduction of enemy resistance prior to taking prisoners, in releasing civilian hostages seized by the Viet Cong, and in support of house-to-house fighting, including Operation Hue City (3 to 15 February 1968). Defensively, they found CS even more useful in the perimeter defence of fixed installations, in protecting patrols against ambush, and in reconnoitring suspect areas within the tropical rain forest (where conventional firing was often blunted by the trees and failed to penetrate dug-in positions). American forces utilized CS to break contact with the enemy, as a favourite tactic of the North Vietnamese Army was to ambush small US forces and stay close to them to escape air or artillery counter-attack. Similarly, air rescue units found that CS could assist in the retrieval of wounded personnel or airmen shot down in enemy-controlled territory. Yet the life-saving purposes of CS, as promoted in press briefings,[26] represented only part of their tactical properties. Just as American tactics became increasingly systematic, so CS dispersal, often in vast quantities, became integrated into 'search and destroy' missions; it dislodged the enemy from entrenched positions and heavily forested terrain into the open, followed by artillery bombardments, B-52 bombing or sweeps of the targeted area by infantry forces. As these tactics incurred increasing controversy, Rear Admiral William E. Lemos admitted in congressional testimony that CS had become an ancillary weapon 'authorized for use in combat'.[27]

Spraying herbicides for the purposes of defoliation and crop destruction was another response to the peculiar demands of fighting in Vietnam. The Americans had developed and tested anti-plant agents for possible use against the Japanese during the Second World War, and the British had experimented with herbicides when fighting Communist insurgents in Malaya. Faced with similar problems that the Americans would encounter in Vietnam, British military authorities had sought the assistance of ICI in providing herbicides that would clear roadside vegetation (to reduce the scope for ambushes) and destroy the crops grown by the insurgents. Within six months ICI had tested and supplied appropriate chemicals, sodium trichloroacetate and a mixture of Trioxone and diesolene (to kill crops and keep the soil infertile), and spraying commenced using fire engines at selected roadside ambush sites and helicopters in crop destruction missions (1952–3). However, a shortage of helicopters and the indeterminate nature of the results (including the difficulty of distinguishing the crops of insurgents from those of peasants) limited the scope of the aerial operations. British forces also found that it was cheaper to cut trees by hand than spray with expensive chemicals ($664 per mile as against $1,700 per mile for chemical spray).[28]

The Americans were not so constrained. After testing various herbicide and spraying systems in 1962, President John F. Kennedy approved requests from the government of South Vietnam that US assets and expertise should be deployed in crop destruction missions. As approved on 2 October 1962, this was to be a restricted programme carried out by South Vietnamese personnel, but, as the American involvement in the war deepened, particularly after the Tonken Gulf incident (August 1964), the first American aircraft, carrying temporary South Vietnamese markings, flew crop destruction missions (3 October 1964). The restrictions on herbicides operations were gradually relaxed as the area of operations was expanded. By December 1965, American aircraft, principally the twin-engine C-123, later designated the UC-123, began spraying the trails and footpaths of the Ho Chi Minh Trail in southern Laos; by the following year they were spraying along the Demilitarized Zone that separated North Vietnam from South Vietnam in the hope of uncovering infiltration routes and supply depots. In 1967 Operation Ranch Hand reached its peak, defoliating 1,486,446 acres of vegetation and destroying 221,312 acres of crops, and over the period from 1962 to 1971 as a whole, it sprayed nearly six million acres of South Vietnam.[29]

Of the 18.85 million gallons of herbicides sprayed over Vietnam and adjacent areas, nearly 88 per cent was devoted to defoliation. Spraying Agent Orange and Agent Purple (which included mixtures of phenoxy acids, like 2,4-D and 2,4,5-T), and Agent White (which included a less volatile form of 2,4-D and picloram for longer-term forest destruction) served a multitude of purposes. It defoliated a swathe several hundred yards wide along roads, railways, other lines of communication and tax collection points to reduce the scope for ambushes. It enhanced the defence of base perimeters by opening fields of fire and by facilitating observation from outposts. It revealed enemy base camps or bunkers, forcing him to move to avoid aerial observation, and uncovered infiltration routes, compelling the enemy to move by night or by different routes if he wished to avoid photographic surveillance and aerial bombardment. By 1968, the heavy use of spraying had denied the enemy cover in War Zones C and D and in Boi Loi Woods; increased the security of allied forces whether in base camps or moving along water and land routes of communication; and compelled the enemy, as confirmed by captured Viet Cong, to avoid certain areas and waste time and resources in non-combatant tasks, such as re-locating camps or waiting for the hours of darkness. Accordingly a US military subcommittee, reporting to US Ambassador Ellsworth Bunker, recognized 'the military worth of defoliation beyond any doubt'.[30]

Crop destruction, primarily employing Agent Blue (which contained a 100 per cent solution of cacodylic acid) for the destruction of rice crops, did not merely deny food to the Viet Cong and North Vietnam Army units. It diverted some of their manpower from combat missions to food production and food transportation. It compelled some farmers and their families to abandon contaminated fields and flee from the Viet Cong to government-controlled areas, where food and clothing were available. This deprived the Viet Cong of both food and labour and compounded the burdens upon their transportation networks. Yet these benefits were largely notional. Even at its peak, in 1967, when the crop destruction programme constituted fifteen per cent of the herbicidal effort, it destroyed only about 1.75 per cent of the South Vietnamese rice crop. It had not seriously encumbered the Viet Cong, who grew only about ten per cent of their own food and confiscated supplies to make up for any deficiencies. Indeed, several wartime reports concluded that the crop destruction programme had proved largely counter-productive. As civilian farmers and their families bore the brunt of the spraying, crop destruction left a lasting sense of bitterness over the loss of food and the product of many months of labour and cultivation.[31]

Even so, the controversy over the herbicidal programmes ranged far beyond their perceived effectiveness. As early as 1964, the Federation of American Scientists had denounced the herbicidal missions as field-testing for chemical and biological warfare.[32] They were followed by groups of American and other scientists, who condemned the use of herbicides as immoral, indiscriminate in their effects since it attacked combatants and non-combatants alike, and was liable to erode the barriers to the use of more lethal chemical weapons. Some anguished, too, about the ecological consequences of the herbicide campaign, prompting the Department of Defense and the American Association for the Advancement of Science to commission several wartime studies. After fears surfaced that some of the chemicals might damage human health, the programmes were suspended temporarily from 15 April 1970, with the last crop destruction mission flown on 7 January 1971. Engulfed by the swirl of adverse publicity, the programme was neither likely to be resumed nor repeated after the profusion of post-war lawsuits from Vietnam veterans, attributing physical and behavioural changes, cancers and birth deformities among their offspring to the effects of Agent Orange.[33]

Coinciding with the American gas operations in Vietnam was the gas bombing of royalist villages in the Yemen by the Egyptian air force. Authorized by President Gamal Abdel Nasser, these gas operations were directed against his ideological enemies, the royalists, who opposed the republican regime in Yemen. After an experimental gas attack upon the village of al Kawma on 8 June 1963, Egyptian gas bombing became more systematic in 1966, with a major chemical attack upon the village of Kitaf on 5 January 1967 and more sustained gas attacks until the Six-Day War with Israel began in the following June. The gas attacks supported the more extensive and costly conventional attacks, launched on the ground and in the air. By June 1967, the royalists claimed that their people had suffered over twenty CW attacks and more than 400 fatalities from poison gas. Despite corroboration in the Western press, and protests from the Saudi government, the UN Secretary General U Thant had refused to intervene, and, after the war with Israel, Egyptian planes resumed their attacks upon royalist villages with mustard gas and phosgene-filled bombs. While the United States, having recognized the Yemen Arab Republic, was preoccupied in Vietnam, Egypt encountered little more than moral condemnation from newspapers and parliamentarians in the United Kingdom. No state wished to intervene in an inter-Arab war from which Egypt was willing to withdraw after the Khartoum summit of August 1967.[34]

Controversy over chemical and biological warfare erupted again in the last decade of the Cold War. Within a few years of the end of the Vietnam War, refugees fleeing into Thailand alleged that the Vietnamese had employed chemical weapons in Laos since 1975 and Kampuchea since 1978. H'Mong refugees from Laos described how air-bursted rockets and spraying had released poisonous clouds over their villages. Western journalists described these clouds as 'yellow rain' because they were often, though not exclusively, yellow in colour, and sounded like raindrops as they fell on the roofs of huts and surrounding fields. As further charges of chemical warfare emanated from the mujahideen after the Soviet invasion of Afghanistan,

several governments investigated these charges. The Reagan administration made the first charges when Secretary of State Alexander
Haig informed the Berlin press association on 13 September 1981 that
the United States had gathered physical evidence to substantiate the
allegations, specifically samples containing three highly toxic mycotoxins. However the manner of the announcement (as a last-minute
insertion into a speech about NATO to forestall press revelations about
the mycotoxin evidence), the nature of the evidence presented in a
subsequent briefing (leaf and stem samples from Kampuchea), and
assertions that the trichothecene mycotoxins were not indigenous to
the region aroused the scepticism of some journalists and scientists.[35]

Thereafter the US State Department published a series of reports
claiming that bombs, spray, rockets and artillery had delivered several
hundred chemical attacks upon Laos, Kampuchea and Afghanistan,
spreading an array of chemical agents, including a rapid-acting incapacitant, as well as the mycotoxins. Eyewitnesses, journalists, defectors,
doctors and 'national technical means' established the time and place
of the attacks. The reports were corroborated from other sources,
including film of reported chemical attacks by a Dutch journalist,
Bernd de Bruin, in the Jalalabad area (15 and 21 June 1981), and cross-
checked with knowledge of the Soviet CBW data base and information
from the corresponding data base of the United States. More physical evidence was gathered from two gas masks, five environmental
samples and biomedical samples (blood, urine and/or tissue) from
sixteen individuals, showing the presence of trichothecene mycotoxins in Laos, Kampuchea and Afghanistan. The State Department
insisted that the evidence and accompanying control samples had
been collected, transported and analysed properly in independent
laboratories.[36]

Although other Western governments conducted their own
surveys of alleged attack sites, they failed to find anything other than
circumstantial evidence that CW attacks had occurred, and UN investigation teams, denied access to the war zones, had to rely upon the
voluminous circumstantial evidence. After several thorough investigations, the Canadians eventually detected the presence of mycotoxins
not only in samples handed to them from the war zones but also in
the blood of Thais who were not the victims of chemical attacks.
Sceptical scientists, including Matthew Meselson, now focused upon
the pollen found in the 'yellow rain' samples analysed by Thai,
Canadian and Australian scientists. As the spots of 'yellow rain'

resembled the natural excreta of bees of the genus *Apis*, and as Meselson demonstrated that the bees swarmed and defecated in Thailand, he argued that the 'yellow rain' was a natural phenomenon. In other words, at the time when the bees were swarming and illness was occurring from people eating mouldy bread, eyewitnesses erroneously linked the two actions with rumours of poison falling from the sky.[37]

The State Department and its scientific advisors demurred. They maintained that this alternative hypothesis left many questions unanswered – about the evidence from gas masks and water which contained no pollen, the coincidence of the reports of 'yellow rain' emanating solely from war zones after over-flights or attacks with artillery or rockets, and the many reports of illness and death.[38] Yet they were unable to resolve the controversy in the absence of independent investigations or incontrovertible evidence (such as intact munitions or remnants of munitions containing compounds used exclusively as cw agents). Only timely and unimpeded access to the sites of the alleged attacks could have facilitated this sample collection but many of the reported attacks occurred in remote areas (other than in Kampuchea) or required long journeys (sometimes twenty days in Laos) before refugees could bring samples or seek medical treatment. Moreover, as the preferred mode of the reported attacks in Laos and Afghanistan involved aerial spraying, it left neither munitions nor canisters for post-attack recovery.

Ironically the Cold War ended, as it began, with a propaganda battle, fuelled by allegations of chemical or biological warfare. Unable to prove their cases conclusively, the main protagonists relied on the manner in which they presented their allegations, the quality of the evidence, and a limited degree of external support. The controversy sparked in both cases, like the bitter debates aroused over the use of riot-control agents and herbicides in Vietnam, underscored the political costs of using these ancillary weapons or of alleging their usage. However effective tactically, as chemical weapons undoubtedly were in one-sided Third World conflicts, where the victims often lacked any means of defence and still less of any ability to retaliate-in-kind, the political costs often seemed to outweigh these tactical benefits.

4

The Proliferation of Chemical
and Biological Weapons

Concern about the proliferation of chemical (and later biological) weapons erupted in the 1980s and '90s, reflecting anxiety about the number of states that possessed these weapons or had a capability to produce them. Spokesmen for the Reagan administration, referring to classified intelligence information, began a process that has been sustained by successive US and allied governments, all of them alluding to a phenomenon whose momentum has varied over time but still appears to be underway. In giving evidence on 5 February 2008 before the US Senate Select Committee on Intelligence, J. Michael McConnell, the Director of National Intelligence, affirmed that

> the ongoing efforts of nation-states and terrorists to develop and/or acquire dangerous weapons and delivery systems constitute major threats to the safety of our nation, our deployed troops, and our friends. We are most concerned about the threat and destabilizing effect of nuclear proliferation. We are also concerned about the threat from biological and chemical agents . . . The time when only a few states had access to the most dangerous technologies has been over for many years. Technologies, often dual-use, circulate easily in our globalized economy, as do the scientific personnel who design and use them . . . We assess that some of the countries that are still pursuing WMD programs will continue to try to improve their capabilities and level of self-sufficiency over the next decade.[1]

As the statement implies, proliferation is an evolutionary and developmental process. It derives from both political will, embodying a desire to improve military capabilities (and thereby reflects qualitative as much as quantitative desires for the states concerned), and from a diffusion of scientific expertise and technology, part of the industrialization of the developing world that cannot be easily arrested. Where the statement of McConnell differs from many previous statements is in its level of generality and lack of precision about how many states were engaged in the process. In the 1980s and '90s, when US administrations first sounded the tocsin over chemical proliferation beyond the Soviet Union, they were more emphatic. In statements and briefings spokesmen described a rapidly growing phenomenon from about five or seven states possessing or seeking to possess chemical weapons in the early 1960s to about 20 by 1989.[2] They also named various states engaged in the process, many of whom were in the Middle East, north Africa and Asia. Amplified in the popular press, these charges provoked predictable denials from many of the states concerned and fuelled propaganda disputes.[3] Similar statements on BW proliferation appeared more slowly, possibly reflecting the difficulty of determining the intent of clandestine programmes, but by 9 February 1989, Dr Barry J. Erlick, a BW weapons analyst for the US Army, asserted that 'The number of nations having or suspected of having offensive biological and toxin warfare programs has increased from 4 to 10 since 1972.' In the same hearings Judge William Webster, then Director of the CIA, claimed that 'at least 10 countries are working to produce previously known and futuristic biological weapons'. He added that 'at least 15 developing countries will be producing their own ballistic missiles' by 2000, and that 'one of the causes for alarm here . . . is not only the proliferation of chemical and biological weapons, but the development of new means of delivering them, particularly ground-to-ground missiles.'[4]

The Proliferation Debate

Just as the 'yellow rain' controversy provoked a vigorous debate, the proliferation charges aroused scepticism among certain scientists and political opponents. Critics neither denied that proliferation had occurred (as was evident in the Iran–Iraq War, see chapter Five) nor denied that it was potentially serious, but they chided officials over the way in which they presented their findings. As secret intelligence is not normally released into the public domain, whether in published statements or in off-the-record briefings, some suspected ulterior motives. S. J. Lundin, Julian Perry Robinson and Ralph Trapp suggested that these aims might have included boosting support for the expanding market in chemical protective equipment or mobilizing support for binary rearmament.[5] Such suspicions not only lacked substantive evidence but more importantly seemed less perceptive as official warnings about proliferation continued long after the demise of the binary programme.

Gordon Burck and Charles Floweree, co-authors of a substantial work on chemical proliferation, worried about the quality of information released to the public. The summaries of intelligence reports, they feared, might give only the conclusions of the authors and not the 'nuances and qualifications' that underpinned their analyses. Even the latter might be inherently limited if the 'bulk' of the information was derived from National Technical Means (NTMs), that is, surveillance systems that can monitor the least concealable facets of a CW programme – anti-chemical equipment, exercises and delivery systems. The latter, they argued, might not indicate an offensive programme, and NTMs would prove much less useful in determining the intent of an R&D programme or the products of some production facilities. Where the proliferation claims involved unverifiable allegations of chemical attacks in civil wars or in inter-state conflicts, they also suspected that the allegations might serve diverse propaganda purposes. Yet verifying circumstantial evidence was inherently difficult. On 12 June 1992 a UN mission reported on its investigation of the alleged use of chemical weapons within Mozambique. It had found effects on soldiers 'consistent with the use of an atropine-like chemical warfare agent and also with severe heat stress', and could not be more precise because a 'considerable delay' had elapsed between the alleged attack and the investigation.[6]

Compounding this element of uncertainty was a bewildering array of assertions about the scale and rate of proliferation. Initially officials, in 'on the record' briefings, refrained from identifying the specific countries and simply quantified the numbers involved. However these numbers, deriving from the differing estimates of various intelligence agencies, varied from briefing to briefing. On 1 March 1988 the Director of Naval Intelligence, Rear Admiral William O. Studeman, revealed that 'Worldwide, some ten countries possess a chemical warfare capability. As many are known or thought to be actively seeking it'; eight days later, Dr Thomas Welch, Deputy Assistant to the Secretary of Defense, maintained that 'at least 16 countries have an offensive chemical warfare capability'.[7] Pressed by several commentators to provide more detailed briefings with states listed under categories such as 'known CW states', 'probable CW states', 'seeking to possess CW states' and 'doubtful cw states', officials presented increasingly candid and specific reports. On 24 January 1989 Major-General William Burns, then director of the Arms Control and Disarmament Agency, distinguished between a capacity to produce chemical weapons (as possessed by some twenty states, including the two superpowers) and stockpiles of chemical weapons (as retained by 'a handful, five or six' besides the two superpowers).[8]

Julian Perry Robinson, though, was still not satisfied. In several articles he belaboured us and British spokesmen for their use of 'muddy language'. He asked what was meant by 'possession', when officials distinguished between states that possessed such weapons or were 'actively seeking to acquire' them. Similarly he wondered whether the term 'chemical-capable' meant anything more than having an industry capable of producing these weapons, or even what was meant by the term 'chemical weapon' as this could include obsolete munitions or a 'research tool for assessing chemical threats or for developing antichemical protection' or chemical agents that were not usable as weapons.[9] Ultimately he envisaged the introduction of a Chemical Weapons Convention as a potential remedy and a remedy that was within reach.[10]

In answering the critics, Judge Webster confirmed that intelligence agencies rarely favour public disclosure. 'Much of the information', he affirmed, 'that is currently being developed is quite sensitive and could readily be attributed to a limited number of discrete [sic] sources . . .'. Public disclosure, moreover, could lead to a 'slippery slope' whereby once an accusation is made, 'more proof is called for, and then people who have been entrusted with the information are sometimes not as discrete [sic] as they might be.'[11] Doug Feith, a Deputy Assistant Secretary of Defense (Negotiations Policy), had anticipated many of the criticisms from within the scientific community. In June 1984, he had argued that the likelihood of cw proliferation and increased cw use was 'symptomatic of the contempt in which international legal norms are held', and that it was unrealistic to respond to 'apparent and proven treaty violations' by demanding absolute standards of proof.[12] Nevertheless, the debate proved productive inasmuch as the official reports became increasingly specific and informative. In August 1993, the us Office of Technology Assessment published a voluminous report on the *Proliferation of Weapons of Mass Destruction: Assessing the Risks*. In 1996 and 1997, the Office of the Secretary of Defense issued reports on *Proliferation: Threat and Response*, with accounts of proliferation developments in various regions and the Pentagon's response.

During the 1990s, the Clinton administration began to evaluate the phenomenon in light of the dissolution of the former Soviet Union, and the possibility of so-called 'rogue regimes' acquiring sensitive equipment, weapons, materials or expertise from the former Soviet Union. Identifying certain states as 'rogues' because they purportedly had scant commitment to the existing international order was bound to be controversial but, in the wake of the Gulf War (1990–91), in which Iraq had defied the UN Security Council, it highlighted problems in the post-Cold War era. Iraq was not the only regime intent on acquiring weapons of mass destruction, whose behaviour was hard to predict and difficult to deter. Iraq had also been a party to various disarmament regimes, and a target of international bodies seeking to control the export of sensitive materials and dual-purpose equipment, and yet had made considerable progress with its WMD developments (see chapter Five).

Although the Chemical Weapons Convention had entered into force in 1997, it did not remove the threat of chemical warfare recurring. The convention has enabled states like Russia, the United States, India, South Korea, Albania and, after considerable pressure, Libya to declare their CW stocks for destruction and another twelve states to report CW production facilities, but it has not been implemented rigorously. In the absence of any challenge inspections suspicions remain, as reflected in a report to Congress (20 February 2008) that several countries may still be developing or producing chemical weapons. They included some signatories (China and Iran), as well as several countries that had not ratified the convention (Egypt, Israel, Syria and North Korea). On 26 October 2002, Russia also revealed that its special forces retained undisclosed gases when they employed a fentanyl-based gas to end the hostage siege at the Palace of Culture in Moscow. The gas accounted for all but five of the 129 fatalities and injured many more.[13]

Finally, several states remain listed in unclassified sources as possessing a BW capability. Just as the Soviet Union and Iraq denied possessing such a capability, none of the states concerned have admitted possession but the possible possessors include China, Cuba, Egypt, Iran, Israel, North Korea, Russia, Syria and Taiwan. Some of these suspicions dated from reports in the 1990s when Libya and Iraq were also listed among potential BW proliferators but, upon subsequent inspection, neither Libya nor Iraq was found to possess an active BW programme. The BW allegations, therefore, have to be treated with reserve, and the vagueness of McConnell's report in 2008 reflects the caution induced by recent intelligence failures.[14]

Proliferation Motivations

Underpinning any acquisition of chemical or biological weapons is the relative ease and cheapness of their production. Proliferation is a derivative of industrial development, particularly the diffusion of scientific competence and the requisite technology from the richer to the less developed parts of the world. As many of the requisite chemicals and manufacturing equipment are dual-use, and have perfectly legitimate applications in commercial production, the expansion of petrochemical, fertilizer, pesticide and pharmaceutical industries enhanced the feasibility of proliferation. Some industrial chemicals, like phosgene and hydrogen cyanide, could serve directly as CW agents as they did in the First World War. Other widely used chemicals could be used as precursors, like thiodiglycol in the production of mustard gas or phosphorus oxychloride in the production of tabun. As these agents were deliverable from various munitions, including artillery shells, rockets, aerial spray tanks, gravity bombs and surface-to-surface missiles, they could prove effective against an enemy lacking in protective equipment or poorly trained in how to use its kit. Moreover, if the enemy was highly vulnerable, say a small insurgent force operating in a localized area, massive quantities of chemical agent might not be necessary. As Gordon Vachon argued, the production of nerve agents is not 'beyond the reach of certain developing states', and the dissemination of these agents by available delivery systems is 'well documented in the open literature'.[15]

In any case, large quantities of biological and toxin agents could be produced rapidly by the process of fermentation. Anthrax bacteria can be produced from seed culture in 96 hours, and, with new computerized systems, the process can produce greater yields and higher quality products than in the past. As the relevant materials can be obtained from natural sources, such as infected wild animals, soil or infected food, and as most of the essential production materials and equipment can be acquired legitimately for vaccine development on the open market, concealment is eminently possible. 'The ultimate objective,' asserted Erlick, 'be it vaccine or weapon, depends on the intent of the user. Most production facilities utilizing micro-organisms, including pharmaceutical plants and even breweries, can be converted to produce biological or toxin agents in a matter of hours, with modest prior provision.'[16] Compared with the development and production costs of nuclear weapons or a mass chemical warfare arsenal, the basic R&D and production costs of an effective BW capability (on account of its relative potency on a weight-for-weight basis and potential area coverage) are likely to be far less expensive.[17]

Chemical or biological weapons have often been described in populist commentary as the 'poor man's atomic bomb'. The terminology reflects not merely the tendency to describe nuclear, chemical and biological weapons collectively as weapons of mass destruction (WMD) but also the relative differential between the costs and difficulty of producing CBW and those of acquiring fissile material and manufacturing nuclear weapons. Developing a chemical or biological weapons capability may serve as a deterrent in its own right (as chemical weapons did for the major belligerents during the Second World War) or as a stepping-stone towards the acquisition of a nuclear weapons capability. Once a state has the latter it might be willing to jettison chemical weapons (as in the case of Britain in the 1950s) or biological weapons (as in the case of the United States in 1968). Even if a state was about to demonstrate that it possessed a nuclear weapons capability (as in the case of India in 1998), it might still reckon that it could derive some political benefits from declaring its CW programme in June 1997 after joining the Chemical Weapons Convention, without sacrificing its deterrent. Alternatively, if lacking a nuclear weapons option, states as in the Middle East and Iran might still link nuclear, chemical and biological weapons, arguing that they needed such weapons to deter local adversaries, or that they could not disarm in one category unless their adversaries disarmed in all these categories too.[18]

More fundamentally, developing countries might simply be impressed by the military utility of chemical or biological weapons, regarding them as potential 'force multipliers' to offset the more powerful or larger conventional forces of an adversary. Taiwan, facing a formidable threat from the People's Liberation Army, may have considered this option,[19] and Iraq almost certainly made similar calculations when faced with Iran's human wave attacks (see chapter Five). Underpinning this potential was the linkage between states thought to be seeking chemical or biological weapons and those known to be building, acquiring and/or testing surface-to-surface ballistic missiles. Even if the missiles had ranges of less than 1,000 kilometres, they might still serve as highly attractive delivery systems on account of their speed, range and ability to penetrate an enemy's defences. In the context of historic inter-state rivalries, whether on the Korean peninsula or in parts of the Middle East, relatively short-range missiles might seem perfectly adequate, especially if an enemy's capital city or other high-value targets lay within range. Moreover, in coupling chemical warheads with ballistic missile systems, states may be able to construct an infrastructure upon which it could, with suitable refinements, subsequently develop a nuclear weapons delivery system. Even if this is not the aim, it might affect enemy perceptions and so act as deterrent (or encourage an adversary to develop anti-tactical ballistic missile defences, develop a capacity to threaten retaliation-in-kind, or, as Israel has done, launch pre-emptive strikes, most recently against a suspected nuclear site in Syria on 6 September 2007).[20]

Finally, states may desire chemical or biological weapons to counter insurgency operations. Employing chemical or biological agents against internal insurgents may seem cost-effective as the operations carry no risk of retaliation, economize on the use of manpower (particularly against guerrillas located in remote and inaccessible strongholds), and may inflict heavy casualties upon unprotected fighters, their families and civilian supporters. The delayed and insidious effects of a covert BW operation, especially if it involved the use of an agent that was indigenous to the area attacked, would lend itself to deniability by the perpetrator. The South African CBW programme of the 1980s reflects some of these assumptions. Launched initially with the aim of protecting the South African Defence Force as it engaged the Soviet-backed forces of the MPLA (Popular Movement for the Liberation of Angola), and their Cuban allies, it evolved into the development of crowd control and covert assassination weapons for use against the enemies of the state. Dr Wouter Basson of the 7th South African Military Health Service Medical Battalion took charge of the programme known as Project Coast, which involved the development, testing and production of chemical agents at the military front company, Delta G. Scientific, and BW products at Roodeplaat Research Laboratories (RRL). Evidence and documents presented to the South African Truth and Reconciliation Commission (1998), and at a subsequent trial of Dr Basson (1999–2002), in which he was acquitted on all counts of complicity to murder, fraud and dealing in drugs, indicates that his team was working on a range of chemical and biological agents. Although Delta G. Scientific had produced chemical agents on a fairly large scale, RRL had neither devised any weaponization plans for its BW agents nor conducted aerosol tests.

For the South African military and police requirements of the 1980s, natural vectors appeared to be adequate, namely water, food, alcohol and similar products. Among the bio-weapons provided were beer contaminated by botulinum toxin; coffee- or peppermint-flavoured chocolate laced with anthrax and botulinum toxin; salmonella hidden in paraquat bleach, whisky and sugar; thallium-contaminated whisky; and Camel cigarettes with anthrax-spiked filters. Supposedly designed for training purposes, some commentators believe that they were used against activists of the African National Congress or the bases of the South West African People's Organization in Namibia. There were also plans to develop an anti-fertility vaccine for South Africa's black population but the vaccine was never produced. What is unclear from the surviving evidence is how effective these weapons were, if they were used as various commentators allege.[21]

Similar uncertainties bedevil any assessment of the chemical and biological warfare waged during the Rhodesian civil war (1975–8) by the embattled regime of Ian Smith. Facing a protracted guerrilla war with chronic shortages of men and matériel, the regime approved a small, clandestine CBW operation. This improvised with readily available agricultural pesticides and rodenticides, such as parathion and thallium, biological agents including *Vibrio cholerae* (the causative agent of cholera) and *Bacillus anthracis* (the causative agent of anthrax), and toxins such as ricin and botulinum. The aims were to kill enemy guerrillas, divide these fighters from the villagers that supported them and drive rebels into more easily targeted killing zones by poisoning food and contaminating water supplies along known infiltration routes. These tactics probably accounted for several hundred, even a few thousand, enemy fighters, quite apart from the unprecedented number of deaths caused by an unexplained outbreak of anthrax in one region (1978–80), but the rebels under Robert Mugabe were able to replace their losses and sustain the struggle. When the Smith regime lost its international support, none of its military tactics could preserve it.[22]

Implications of Proliferation

When Western governments first sounded the alarm about the growth and extent of the proliferation of chemical and biological weapons, they did so at least in part because these weapons remained potentially useful, not least in the developing world. Even if the states in question had been the victims of cbw attacks in the past, their leaders might not share the reservations forged and shaped by historical or cultural memories of the chemical conflicts in the First World War. They might actually resent Western strictures on such matters as examples of selective morality after the Western states failed to curb the spread of nuclear weapons within parts of the developing world.[23] Moreover, the issue of battlefield predictability might matter much less in some of these theatres than it did in central Europe during the height of the Cold War. Any one-sided use of chemical or biological weapons might not encounter any significant anti-chemical defences, still less civil defences (other than in a state like Israel), and, depending upon the context, it might not risk any nuclear escalation either. An appropriate choice of agents and modes of dispersal would have to allow for topographical and meteorological factors, and in some operations the effects of these weapons could be magnified by psychological fears and civic disruption. Even if these weapons did not always function as instruments of mass destruction, they might function effectively as weapons of terror.

As both chemical weapons and ballistic missiles had been used in the Iran–Iraq War (see chapter Five), there was understandable concern about the ability of some states to combine chemical or biological warheads with ballistic missiles. In his careful study of these options, and comparisons with nuclear and conventional warheads, Steve Fetter argued that chemical warheads could not constitute a 'poor man's atom bomb' in actual effects but that biological weapons 'could approach nuclear weapons in lethality'. Conversely, ballistic missiles armed with chemical or some biological warheads were likely to prove more deadly than missiles armed with conventional warheads. Chemical warheads 'may be 50 times more deadly if civil defense is ineffective *or* weather conditions are favourable, and 500 times more deadly than conventional warheads when used against unprepared populations under favourable weather conditions'. Whereas some biological agents would not be suitable to delivery by air (as they decay rapidly in the sunlight), Fetter reckoned that 'bacillus anthracis, the bacteria that causes anthrax, seems especially well suited' because it forms 'spores that can survive violent dissemination methods and exposure to sun, air, and rain'.[24]

If such calculations seemed largely theoretical in the early 1990s, they seemed less speculative by July 2008 as Iran renewed the test-firing of its improved version of Shahab-3, a medium-range ballistic missile capable of striking targets 1,250 miles from its launch sites. Like Syria, Iran is thought to have advanced chemical and biological weapons programmes, as well as a missile delivery capability. By these tests, argued Major-General Paul E. Valley, former deputy commanding general of the us Army Forces Pacific, the Iranians were

> fine-tuning their systems to include perfecting command-and-control, launching, tracking, trajectory, those kinds of things. They've yet to perfect putting a warhead on the Shahab but they're working towards full capability, including nuclear, biological, and chemical.[25]

Fifteen Western industrialized countries had hoped that this would not happen. Faced with evidence that chemical weapons had been used in the Iran–Iraq War, they had formed the Australia (Suppliers) Group in 1985. After an initial meeting in the Australian embassy in Brussels, the informal forum began to meet twice yearly in the Australian embassy in Paris. Operating by consensus, it sought to harmonize the export controls of participants and the European Community (later the European Union) in the hope of ensuring that their exports did not contribute to the proliferation of chemical weapons. Accordingly, the group shared information on proliferation and devised increasingly comprehensive lists of precursor chemicals that required controls (those originally placed on a 'core list' for worldwide control and others on a 'warning list'). By May 1989, they had identified 50 chemicals that warranted controls, and, by May 1991, they agreed that industries would require export licences for all 50 precursor chemicals from the end of December 1991, effectively merging the 'core' and 'warning' lists. In December 1992 the group expanded its remit to agree measures of control over the export of human and animal pathogens, ten toxins, associated genetically modified items, and dual-use equipment that could be used in producing biological weapons.

Whether the group attained a limited measure of 'success', as some of its diplomats claimed – success being measured in impeding and adding to the costs of proliferation – is difficult to assess. Despite the movement towards the signing and implementation of the Chemical Weapons Convention (cwc) in the mid-1990s, the Australia Group continued its meetings, sharing information about proliferation and maintaining discriminatory export controls. As these controls applied to trade with some of the states that had become parties to the cwc, and were already parties to the btwc, they cast doubt on the effective functioning of both conventions. While the group maintained that national export controls enabled its members to uphold the objectives of both conventions more fully, they seemed at variance with obligations under both conventions not to impair the economic and technological development of other states parties.[26] Developing states have recurrently protested that the group has become a 'suppliers' club', with beneficial internal trading relationships, hence its attraction for new members. By 2007 the Australia Group had 41 members, including all 27 members of the European Union.

This expansion of membership hardly obscured the shortcomings of a group that operated by consensus and lacked any sanctions over its membership. As the members imposed export controls in different ways (and with differing definitions of 'worldwide' initially), their activities never stemmed the growing number of states reported as possessing or seeking to possess chemical and biological weapons. Proliferation also flourished because there were alternative sources of supply beyond members of the Australia Group, including the option of indigenous production. Even worse, it required bilateral action in the form of diplomatic demarches and public exposure by the Reagan administration before a member of the group, West Germany, took action over its own industrialists who were involved in the construction and equipping of a chemical weapons production plant at Rabta in Libya.[27] Aside from this celebrated episode, and the voluminous trade that sustained the development of weapons of mass destruction by Iraq (see chapter Five), export controls were always battling against the commercial pressures that were driving the trade in chemical and biological materials and equipment. As us licences for the export of micro-organisms and toxins grew from 90 in 1991 to 531 in 1994, only one export-application was denied in 1991 and four in 1994.[28] Legitimate exports could be retransferred to embargoed countries, and even where customs officials intervened, acting within the scope of domestic legislation, successful prosecutions did not always follow. In 2006 hm Customs and Revenue admitted that it had secured only five successful prosecutions since 2000. As the department explained in an internal memorandum, prosecutions could be hampered by the complexity of the process, particularly the need to provide sufficient evidence, the requirement to disprove the defence, and the difficulty of disclosing all relevant evidence to the defence: 'far more cases', it admitted, 'are carefully considered for prosecution and rejected, than are taken forward'. Despite the disrupting of another trafficking operation by 25 May 2006, officials conceded that their efforts had not resulted in any individuals being retained in custody.[29]

The chequered history of export controls, and the limited impact of multilateral arms control treaties, failed to impress the us administration of George W. Bush. Like its predecessor, the Bush administration never requested any challenge inspections under the cwc and preferred a more proactive approach through the Proliferation Security Initiative (psi). Announced by President Bush in Krakow on 31 May 2003, and codified by eleven founding participants in Paris on 4 September 2003, the psi represented a commitment to interdict wmd-related cargoes, whether by sea, land or air. Though hailed as an innovative counter-proliferation initiative, it had an unfortunate precedent in 1993 when American inspectors searched the Chinese freighter *Hin Ye*, fruitlessly for a cargo of chemicals to manufacture nerve gas.[30] Undeterred by the abject apology that the Clinton administration had to proffer, the Bush administration acted upon more accurate intelligence to interdict centrifuge technology bound for Libya on board the bbc *China* in the Italian port of Taranto (October 2003). This seemed a success as Libya, already suffering from international isolation and diplomatic pressure from Britain and the United States, offered to abandon its wmd programmes.[31] Over 70 states adhered to the psi within a period of three years. By April 2006, Stephen G. Rademaker, a State Department official, described the psi as 'not a treaty-based organization, but rather . . . an active security cooperation partnership to deter, disrupt and prevent wmd proliferation'.[32]

Conclusion

Whatever counter-proliferation policies are pursued in the aftermath of the Bush administration, the policies will need to evolve and adapt to changing circumstances. In 1994 Kathleen Bailey perceptively warned the us Senate that 'Just because our own leaders do not view chemical weapons as usable or necessary does not mean that the leaders of other countries view them similarly.'[33] This warning certainly applies to biological weapons, too. Neither the efforts of multilateral export control groups nor the norms upheld by the disarmament regimes have arrested all the pressures driving the process of proliferation. If states like South Africa and Libya have succumbed to external sanctions, and sought international rehabilitation through abandoning, or offering to abandon,[34] their WMD programmes, others have not, and it is very unlikely that the form of counter-proliferation applied in another case, Iraq (see chapter Five), will ever be replicated.

5

Iraq's Chemical and Biological Warfare Programmes

Military modernization was a longstanding objective of the Iraqi state. Saddam Hussein, who was originally second-in-command after the Ba'ath party's putsch of July 1968, had become all too aware of the country's military shortcomings. The belated and derisory contribution to the Yom Kippur War (1973) – a division that arrived on the Golan front ten days after the war began only to be ambushed by the Israelis at a cost of some 100 tanks – underscored Iraq's military weakness. Faced with a Kurdish insurgency in the following year, and an Iranian incursion into Iraq on behalf of the Kurds (January 1975), Iraq had to make territorial concessions to Iran along the Shatt al-Arab waterway in the Algiers Agreement (13 June 1975). The events of 1979, both Saddam's seizure of the presidency of Iraq and the Iranian revolution that overthrew the Shah, emboldened Saddam to attack Iran in September 1980. Localized victories in Iran were soon eclipsed when Israel bombed Iraq's nuclear reactor at Osiraq on 7 June 1981. Acquiring enhanced conventional armaments, ballistic missiles, and nuclear, chemical and biological weapons became crucial to securing Saddam's regime and fulfilling its foreign policy agenda. Nuclear weapons, as his biographers argue, had now become 'a personal obsession. A symbol of Iraq's technological prowess, a prerequisite for regional hegemony, the triumphal achievement of the self-styled Nebuchadnezzar . . . [and] the ultimate guarantee of absolute security.'[1] Following this massive setback to his nuclear ambitions, and the failure to secure a decisive victory over Iran, Saddam invested heavily in his chemical and biological warfare programmes.

Iraq's Chemical Warfare Programme

In the 1960s Iraq had launched its chemical and biological warfare programmes by sending officers for training to the Soviet Union. These officers later formed the nucleus of the Iraqi Chemical Corps.

Learning from foreign experience, including Egypt's use of gas in the Yemen (1963–7), the Iraqi corps sought authorization in 1971 to synthesize small amounts of CW agents in laboratories at al-Rashad near Baghdad for training purposes and to set up training facilities in Iraq. The US Defense Intelligence Agency reckoned that Iraq had established some fifteen CBR (chemical, biological and radiological) obstacle courses, whereby soldiers could be trained to operate in contaminated environments, wearing protective kit and performing contamination avoidance drills. Each Iraqi division acquired an organic chemical company 'equipped primarily with Soviet-manufactured materiel such as the truck-mounted ARS12 and DDA53 decontamination apparatus'.[2]

In the 1970s Iraq also approached various Western industrial companies with requests for dual-use equipment and large quantities of pesticides for a production plant capable of manufacturing up to 1,000 tons a year of organic phosphorus compounds. Although several companies rejected the lucrative contracts, and alerted Western intelligence agencies, the West German firm Karl Kolb through its affiliate, Pilot Plant, and many others proved willing to co-operate. They assisted in the building and equipping of a production facility 80 kilometres north-west of Baghdad and 50 kilometres south-west of Samarra. Later known as the Al Muthanna State Establishment (MSE), the plant spread over 170 square kilometres and encompassed five large research laboratories, an administrative building, the first production buildings, and munitions filling and storage facilities including eight large underground bunkers. Described as a 'general multi-purpose pilot plant' for purposes of external deniability by Iraq and its suppliers, the pilot production line began producing chemical warfare agents in the early 1980s: 150 tons of mustard in 1983 and 60 tons of tabun as well as pilot-scale production of sarin in 1984. It subsequently undertook research on other nerve agents, soman and VX, and produced GF, a semi-persistent nerve agent, which it used with sarin in a binary weapon. The MSE also conducted pesticide R&D at this site to expand its knowledge of organophosphorus production.[3]

Initially, Iraq relied upon the importation of machinery, equipment, technical expertise and precursor chemicals. The Hamburg-based firm Water Engineering Trading (WET) sold Iraq over $11 million worth of machinery, equipment and tons of chemicals, including phosphorus trichloride, a dual-purpose chemical with legitimate industrial uses as well as a precursor for nerve agents. The company continued trading with Iraq over the period 1984–7 despite the efforts of the Australia Group and the export controls of the Federal Republic. It assisted Iraq when the latter sought to reduce its dependence upon foreign suppliers and began constructing three plants for the production of precursor chemicals near Fallujah (also known as the Habbaniyah facilities) between 1986 and 1988. WET supplied the design for one of the plants as well as technical expertise to supervise the construction and installation of the production lines. Among the highly toxic chemicals produced were phosphorus trichloride and phosphorus oxychloride, both precursors for nerve agent.[4]

Chemical Weapons in the Iran–Iraq War

Underpinning the development and expansion of Iraq's chemical warfare programme were the critical course of events in the Iran–Iraq War (1980–88). Launched in September 1980 at a seemingly propitious time, when the revolutionary regime in Tehran had alienated the United States, its former supplier of military equipment and training through the hostage crisis, Iraq sought to reassert its rights in the disputed Shatt al-Arab region. It also sought to curb the propaganda onslaught and political interference of the Iranian regime that was dedicated to the overthrow of the Iraqi Ba'ath party. After the initial incursions in the oil-rich southern regions of Iran, Iraq retained its captured territory over the period October 1980–May 1981 before the Iranians began to mount massive counter-attacks, involving surprise night attacks by armoured units, followed up with 'human wave' assaults. By mid-July 1982, as the Iranians launched an assault upon Basra, Iran claimed that Iraqi artillery fired shells filled with riot-control agents to break up advancing infantry. Given the reports of Iranian soldiers fleeing in terror, possibly in fear of lethal chemical attacks, these reports have some credibility, but the artillery were only an ancillary element in an operation involving heavy air and mechanized units.[5]

Iraq's initial success encouraged further usage of chemical weapons, including mustard gas, but it was still in a fairly limited and sporadic manner. Facing attacks along the entire 650-mile front in the summer and autumn of 1983, the Iraqis had to compensate for the dispersion of their forces and increasingly employed aerial bombs to deliver their limited stocks of chemical weapons. Although the Iranians tried to exploit the propaganda benefits by denouncing Iraqi 'war crimes', and distributing pamphlets depicting Iranian chemical casualties in Tehran hospitals, there was little international response. This would change as the Iranians seized parts of the oil-rich Majnoon Islands in February 1984, and the Iraqis battled desperately to recover them, employing mustard gas and tabun against the entrenched Iranian forces. Better protected than formerly, the Iranian regular troops were able to hold on. Nevertheless, Iran asserted that 1,700 troops had been killed or wounded by chemical weapons and soon began sending its casualties for treatment to hospitals in London, Vienna, Stockholm and Tokyo. Confirmation that these soldiers were victims of chemical weapons prompted the UN Secretary-General Javier Pérez de Cuellar to send a team of specialists to Iran to investigate the evidence of chemical attacks. In a report published on 26 March 1984, the UN team confirmed that chemical weapons in the form of aerial bombs had been used in the areas inspected, and that types of mustard gas and tabun had been employed.[6]

Confronted with proof that nerve agent had been used for the first time in war, Britain, the United States, France and Japan banned the export of chemicals used to manufacture mustard and nerve agent to Iraq and Iran. Iraq nonetheless continued to employ chemical weapons in a fairly circumscribed fashion over the next few years. Massively outnumbered and forced to defend vital sectors, such as the approaches to Basra (where the soft and muddy terrain thwarted the movement of armoured vehicles and artillery), Iraqi commanders felt compelled to employ weapons of area denial. Flooding canals, building earthworks and laying minefields on dry patches of ground, with machine guns sited on islets around the marshes, proved of some assistance, but so did the gassing of slow-moving, infantry assaults concentrated in relatively small areas. The aim was to delay the enemy while mobile combined-arms units reinforced the imperilled sectors and launched counter-attacks. After the defeat of a major offensive in March 1985, the Iranians attributed the outcome to the Iraqi receipt of US satellite intelligence and the extensive use of chemical weapons. At this time such claims were probably exaggerated to excuse the Iranian defeat. The Iraqi forces, handicapped by limited stocks of chemical agent and munitions, were still learning how to use these weapons effectively. While Iraqi gunners struggled to determine the most potent mix and dispersal of chemical warheads, pilots found that they could not inflict mass casualties in single-aircraft attacks. Moreover, bombing at low level required the use of time-delayed fuses that sometimes proved unreliable. Irrespective of the mode of delivery, it was often difficult to build up concentrations of gases amidst the capricious winds and the high temperatures in which mustard gas tended to volatilize rapidly.[7]

As the Iraqis acquired larger stocks of chemical agent, they refined their tactics and employed gas more extensively in the defence of Faw (1986) and Basra (1987). By relying increasingly upon high-altitude bombing with impact fuses, they delivered more effective aerial bombardments. They used rapid-acting nerve agents to break up front-line Iranian assaults and more persistent agents, particularly mustard gas, to deny terrain and bombard rear-area targets. Once on the offensive in the spring of 1988, Iraqi forces demonstrated that they had incorporated chemical weapons into their operational plans. Iraqi gunners pounded enemy command posts, artillery and supply points, using non-persistent agents to kill and disable them but leave them free of chemicals by the time attacking Iraqi forces reached them. They also exploited local conditions as Iranian soldiers struggled to wear protective suits and masks for any length of time in the searing temperatures. In describing an attack on Koushk and the Majnoon Islands (25 June 1988), the Iranian Chief of Medical Services of the Ahvaz military region observed that it began with an artillery barrage

> using chemical ammunition and lasted for approximately two hours. Later, aeroplanes and helicopters had joined the attack . . . the frontline had been attacked with cyanide and organophosphorous compounds. Logistic units, command posts and reserves had also been attacked but with mustard gas . . . the use of nerve gas was limited to the frontline, as its effects dissipated quickly and facilitated the advance of attacking troops. On the other hand . . . mustard gas was being used against rear echelons near Hamid to disrupt possible counter-attacks, because of its lasting effects on troops, equipment and environmental conditions.[8]

Iraqi forces were now able to employ gas systematically in every sector of the front, including the mountainous regions in the north, where mustard and nerve agent impeded movement through critical routes. Iraqi gas attacks not only assisted in driving back Iranian assaults but also supported combined-arms units in their recapture of territory that had been lost in earlier years. Belatedly Iran began to retaliate-in-kind but its gas capabilities were far inferior to those of Iraq, relying upon short-range mortar grenades to inflict minimal casualties at Sulaimaniya (1 July 1988). The Pentagon suspected that both belligerents had engaged in the chemical attacks upon the Kurdish town of Halabja (16–17 March 1988), where about 10,000 unprotected civilians may have been injured and some 4,000 killed. More recent research based upon thousands of Iraqi secret police documents, coupled with interviews with Kurdish survivors, senior Iraqi defectors and retired US intelligence officials, attributes the attacks solely to the Iraqi forces then operating in northern Iraq under the command of Saddam's cousin, Ali Hasan al-Majid (nicknamed 'Chemical Ali'). The attacks were carried out by about twenty Iraqi MIG and Mirage aircraft and involved the delivery of mustard gas and nerve agents. The traces of cyanide found on victims, which inspired the charges of Iranian involvement, since Iraq did not possess hydrogen cyanide in its stock of chemical warfare agents, were probably by-products from the use of impure tabun.[9]

At the time Iran insisted that this was solely an Iraqi atrocity and distributed photographic images at home and abroad of women, children and animals lying dead in the streets. Ironically this propaganda, coupled with new alert signals on Iranian radio in the case of chemical attack, demoralized Iranian citizens already suffering from ballistic-missile attacks in the 'war of the cities'. Although each side had fired conventionally armed missiles at the other's cities since 1982, Iraq had extended the range of its missiles (known as al-Hussein missiles) by adding an extra ton of rocket fuel to each missile and reducing the payload from 800 kilograms to 190 kilograms. It compensated for these smaller warheads by firing more than twice as many at Iran (up to 200 compared with 77 SCUDS fired by Iran) in the period from February to April 1988. When the war-weary residents of Tehran, the principal target of Iraqi attacks, became increasingly fearful lest the incoming missiles were going to carry chemical warheads, many of them fled from the capital. As this collapse of domestic morale coincided with the Iraqi recapture of the Faw peninsula and the oil-rich land near Basra, as well as serious naval losses to the Americans in the Persian Gulf, Iran accepted the truce brokered by the United Nations on 18 July, which came into effect on 20 August 1988. In short Iraq's ballistic missiles, coupled with the panic caused by the propaganda about chemical weapons, had had a political and psychological impact out of all proportion to any physical damage inflicted.[10]

The effectiveness of Iraqi chemical weapons and their contribution to its recovery and eventual successes in the war remains a matter of debate. Some early assessments, reflecting upon the usage of poison gas in 1983 and 1984, or even through to 1986, cast doubt on their battlefield impact. Perry Robinson was then quoted as regarding them as 'a propaganda weapon, not a firepower weapon' in a futile attempt to break Iranian morale; Efraim Karsh argued that they had had 'a negligible impact on the course of the war, inasmuch as they had caused only about 2 per cent of Iranian casualties up to 1984'; and Burck and Floweree dismissed the chemical warfare as merely involving 'low-level, sporadic use of chemical weapons'.[11] By 1988, Iraqi use of gas was much more substantial, systematic and sustained. At a time when Iranian morale, both military and civilian, was sagging, when Iraqi commanders had a decisive advantage in the air/land battle, and when they were able to employ gas in unprecedented amounts at the outset of every major offensive, chemical weapons undoubtedly contributed to operations that recovered vital areas of territory: in effect, they enabled Saddam Hussein to secure many of his strategic objectives.

Internally, they helped to suppress the Kurdish insurgency not only at Halabja but also reportedly in the bombardments of the Kurds in August 1988. Launched on 25 August and sustained over several days, Iraqi aerial attacks precipitated the flight of Kurdish civilians and Pesh Merga fighters from the northern border region across the mountains into Turkey. By 5 September 1988 some 65,000 Kurds had gathered in five separate Turkish locations, and despite denials from the Iraqi News Agency and statements from the Turkish authorities that their doctors had not found evidence of chemical wounds (contradicting earlier press reports), the refugees testified to widespread chemical bombing. An investigatory team of staff from the US Senate Foreign Relations Committee reported 'overwhelming evidence' of Iraqi chemical attacks gathered from the statements by 200 refugees in different camps (12–15 September), and the absence of any alternative explanation, including bullet wounds, for the sudden mass exodus of Kurds. They quoted from eyewitnesses, including Bechet Naif of the Bekule village:

At 6 a.m. on August 25, eight planes flew over our village. All eight dropped weapons. They dropped 32 chemical bombs. We counted them later. When they dropped the bombs, a big sound did not come out – just a yellowish color and a kind of garlic smell. The people woke up, and some of them fainted. Those who poured water on themselves lived: those who could not reach the water, died.[12]

A medical mission by Physicians for Human Rights confirmed these findings from interviews, questionnaires and the physical examination of certain refugees (7–16 October 1988). The refugees reported the deaths of animals and people with blackened skin and blood oozing from their mouths and noses near the sites of the bombing, and survivors described classic symptoms of mustard-gas poisoning (eye pain, shortness of breath, skin blistering and vomiting). Although neither team gained access to the bomb sites in Kurdistan, and could not determine the exact agents employed (with the rapid deaths possibly indicating the use of nerve agent as well as mustard gas), journalists reported that Iraqi troops were subsequently seen operating in the attacked areas, wearing respirators. A British journalist, Gwynne Roberts, undertook a clandestine visit to some of the sites twelve weeks after the reported attacks to gather soil samples and exploded bomb fragments, which were later found through analysis at Porton Down to contain degradation products of sulphur mustard. Even allowing for the absence of an independent on-site investigation, and the unrepresentative sample of the refugees (all of whom came from the narrow border region and were not among those most severely affected), the evidence seemed consistent with Iraqi attempts to destroy the Kurdish insurgency by depopulating villages and towns in Kurdistan, and either deporting Kurds outside Kurdistan or relocating them in more controllable settlements. Just as Iranian soldiers and Kurdish refugees testified to the terror caused by poison gas, so many commentators maintained that chemical weapons had contributed to the Iraqi military successes of 1988.[13]

The Iraq Survey Group has confirmed that the Iraqi use of chemical weapons was prodigious, involving about 1,800 tons of mustard gas, 140 tons of tabun and over 600 tons of sarin dispersed by some 100,000 chemical munitions (almost 19,500 chemical bombs, over 54,000 chemical artillery shells and 27,000 short-range chemical rockets). By Iraqi estimates, these weapons inflicted over 30,000 Iranian casualties, a relatively low number in this war, but once again CW agents did not have to kill vast numbers to prove effective: 'demoralizing the enemy force and degrading its units' capabilities', as Al Mauroni argued, 'was enough to tip the battle to the attacker's favor [*sic*]'. Saddam Hussein appeared to agree; he persevered with chemical operations despite diplomatic protests and belated censure by the UN Security Council (26 August 1988) because they had helped to preserve his regime without incurring any political penalty. As the Survey Group observed, he perceived that Iraq's 'WMD capabilities had played a central role in the winning of the Iran–Iraq war and were vital to Iraq's national security strategy'.[14] Reflected in this perception was the drive to enhance the CW programme after the end of the hostilities. By the invasion of Kuwait (2 August 1990), Iraq had completed the testing and filling of 50 nerve-agent warheads for the al-Hussein missile, the filling of 1,000 bombs with 'binary' nerve agent (a mix before-flight system), the accumulation of thousands of short-range chemical rockets, artillery shells and bombs, and hundreds of tons of bulk agent, and the acquisition of 750 tons of precursor chemicals for its VX nerve agent production programme.

Iraq's Biological Warfare Programme

The Iran–Iraq War had also led to a revival of Iraq's biological warfare programme, which began in the 1960s when Iraq sent officers overseas for CBW training. After the abortive attempt of army officers to embark on a BW research programme in the late 1960s, the regime of President Ahmad Hasan Al Bakr founded the Al Hazen Ibn Al Haithem Research Institute in 1974, which was a front for clandestine research on chemical weapons, biological weapons, electronics and optics. It trained, developed, and sometimes sponsored scientists for overseas study and established several research laboratories, including the Ibn-Sina Centre, masquerading as 'The Centre for Medical Agriculture'. Initially only nine scientists conducted research into bacteria, toxins and viruses, focusing upon production, pathogenicity, dissemination and the storage of agents. Although the institute foundered amid allegations of fraud and embezzlement in 1978, and the BW research programme was shut down on 16 January 1979, Iraq rebuilt the infrastructure for BW research over the next six years. A Technical Research Centre, part of the State Security Apparatus, replaced Al Hazen; scientists conducted small-scale research at Al Salman; and a militarily relevant BW programme resumed at Al Muthanna in 1983. Lieutenant-General Nizar Al Attar, director general of Al Muthanna, and a former student of CBW at Fort McClellan, Alabama in the 1960s, authorized the programme. He informed Dr Rihab Taha, who came to lead the BW research programme in 1984, that he 'did not want research to put on a shelf. He wanted applied research to put in a bomb.'[15]

A wartime initiative, this revival of the BW programme derived from the major strategic concerns of Iraq: Iran and Israel. Brigadier Dr Mahmud Farraj Bilal, who led the BW weaponization programme, claimed that Iraq's success with chemical weapons served as a catalyst for the revival of Iraq's BW effort: 'if the Iran war lasted beyond 1988', he thought that 'Saddam would have used BW'. Less speculative was Bilal's contention that Iraq needed a strategic counterbalance to Israel, and that in the wake of the setback to Iraq's nuclear programme caused by the Osiraq bombing (1981), biological warfare seemed a strategic option capable of achieving surprise. Iraq, though, lacked an effective delivery system.[16] The revived programme, nonetheless, made rapid progress under Dr Rihab, who ordered reference strains of several pathogenic organisms from a variety of foreign sources in 1985 and began research on candidate BW agents, including *Clostridium perfringens* (gas gangrene) and botulinum toxin. In the following year the regime required her group to embark upon a plan that would lead to the weaponization of biological weapons within five years. Dr Rihab facilitated the ensuing research by securing multiple isolates of pathogens, such as *Bacillus anthracis*, from the American Type Culture Collection, supposedly for work at Baghdad University. In 1987 the group recruited more staff, broadened its range of research, and moved from Al Muthanna to Al Salman, where research was already underway on the anti-plant agent wheat cover smut. At the end of the year orders were placed for large quantities of bacterial growth media (eventually 39 tons). In 1988 Iraq opened a production plant at Al Hakam, enabling the production of anthrax and botulinum toxin to begin in the spring of 1989 and the production of *Clostridium perfringens* in August 1990. It had other production facilities at Al Taji, Al Fudhaliyah and at the Foot and Mouth Disease Vaccine plant at Al Daura (later renamed Al Manal), where it conducted viral research on haemorrhagic conjunctivitis, human rotavirus and camel pox, but this research remained in its infancy at the outbreak of Desert Storm.

Conducted in strict secrecy under the guise of legitimate scientific research, the programme struggled to import dual-use equipment from overseas. Unable to import three 5-cubic-metre fermentation vessels, it overcame this by requisitioning fermentation vessels from an Iraqi veterinary vaccine plant, but it could not surmount the failure to import spray dryers and other processing equipment for drying anthrax safely before Desert Storm. In spite of the laboratory progress and diversification to include research on ricin, wheat cover smut and fungal toxins (trichothecene mycotoxins and later aflatoxin) with animal experimentation and field tests, the weapon tests were less successful. After the failure of a crude dissemination device in February 1988, Iraq conducted trials of R-400 aerial bombs using anthrax simulants in March 1988. It accelerated these efforts after the speech of Saddam Hussein on 2 April 1990, where he boasted that Iraq possessed binary chemical weapons and threatened to retaliate against any Israeli strike by making 'the fire eat half of Israel'.[17]

Saddam's son-in-law, Hussein Kamel Hassan, then minister of defence and director of the Military Industrial Commission, pressed for BW weaponization. In November 1989, further weaponization trials were held at the Muhammadiyat test range at Al Muthanna, employing the anthrax simulant *Bacillus subtilis*, botulinum toxin and aflatoxin fired from 122 mm multi-barrel rocket launchers. Deemed a success, more field trials with 122 mm rockets and the same agents followed in May 1990, and trials with R-400 aerial bombs in August 1990. In the following December, a BW spray tank underwent testing based on a modified aircraft drop tank but neither this test nor another in January 1991, using a spray tank and a remotely piloted vehicle, proved successful. Nevertheless, three additional drop tanks were modified and stored, ready for use. By the outbreak of Desert Storm, Iraq had produced at least 19,000 litres of concentrated botulinum toxin (some 10,000 litres in munitions), 8,500 litres of concentrated anthrax (nearly 6,500 litres in munitions) and 2,200 litres of concentrated aflatoxin (1,580 litres in munitions). In addition Iraq had produced 340 litres of concentrated perfringens and ten litres of ricin. It had also filled 100 R-400 bombs with botulinum toxin, 50 with anthrax and sixteen with aflatoxin and 25 Al Hussein warheads (thirteen with botulinum toxin, ten with anthrax and two with aflatoxin). These weapons were then deployed at four locations where they remained throughout the Gulf War.[18]

Within a mere five years, the Iraqi BW programme had developed a comprehensive range of agents and munitions. It was innovative, developing agents not normally considered as candidate BW agents such as aflatoxin (a toxin commonly associated with food grains and known for the induction of liver cancers) and wheat cover smut, an anti-plant agent for purposes of economic warfare. It developed lethal agents (anthrax, botulinum toxin and ricin) and incapacitating agents (aflatoxin and mycotoxins), and discerned the potential of several viruses (haemorrhagic conjunctivitis and rotavirus). The Iraqi Intelligence Service also saw the possibilities of ricin as an assassination weapon. The programme moved rapidly from R&D through field trials and large-scale production to weapon trials, whereupon the Iraqis sought to cover the entire range from battlefield weapons (122 mm rockets and artillery shells) to strategic ordnance (aerial bombs and Al-Hussein missiles). Compared with the nuclear and chemical warfare programmes, the BW programme depended upon the individual expertise of relatively few scientists, whose achievements over five years were described by the UN inspectors as 'remarkable'. They added that

> The programme appears to have a degree of balance suggesting a high level of management and planning that envisioned the inclusion of all aspects of a biological weapons programme, from research to weaponization . . . detailed thought must have been given to the doctrine of operational use for these weapons of mass destruction.[19]

The Gulf War (1990–91)

The Gulf War was another conflict in which recourse to chemical and biological warfare was expected but never materialized. After the invasion of Kuwait (2 August 1990), which triggered the imposition of UN sanctions, and Operation Desert Shield (a five-month period in which the United States deployed air, sea and land forces in the Persian Gulf region and organized diplomatic, economic and military support internationally within the remit of UN Security Council resolutions), Iraqi chemical weapons and ballistic missiles attracted most attention. Having used these weapons and missiles extensively in the Iran–Iraq War, the Iraqi forces had unrivalled experience in the employment of diverse chemical agents, particularly mustard gas and nerve agent. Iraq now had the option of using these weapons either tactically on the battlefield or strategically in missile attacks upon Saudi Arabia and Israel.

The American-led coalition sought to deter, degrade and limit any damage from Iraqi chemical and biological weapons. Although the Bush administration had resolved not to retaliate with nuclear or chemical weapons if the coalition forces were attacked with chemical weapons, it sought to maximize Iraqi uncertainty by threatening to retaliate, if so attacked, with 'overwhelming' and 'devastating' force. In meeting Tariq Aziz, Iraq's foreign minister, us Secretary of State James Baker deliberately 'left the impression that the use of chemical or biological agents by Iraq could invite tactical nuclear retaliation'. Just as Baker thought that this ambiguous threat might have been part of the reason for the non-use of chemical weapons, Tariq Aziz later informed Ambassador Rolf Ekéus that 'the Iraqi side took it for granted that it meant the use of maybe nuclear weapons against Baghdad, or something like that. And that threat was decisive for them not to use the [chemical and biological] weapons.'[20]

Coalition military commanders could not assume that this would be the case. They planned to degrade Iraq's CBW capabilities by aerial operations throughout Iraq, aiming to neutralize Iraq's command, control and communications, destroy its NBC production facilities (or at least those identified as such by allied intelligence), disrupt logistic supplies, suppress aerial delivery capabilities, and pound Iraqi artillery in the Kuwaiti Theatre of Operations (KTO). The coalition forces also sought to counter any residual chemical strikes by protecting air bases with surface-to-air missiles and by mounting highly mobile ground operations. They brought with them CB defensive kit, including alarm systems, detectors, protective suits and masks, decontamination apparatus and medical support. Far from being a source of reassurance, though, much of the American kit was found to be deficient in quality and quantity, and few us military units had practised CB defence sufficiently for them to be able to operate effectively in a chemically contaminated environment. Accordingly, Pentagon spokesmen touted the virtues of their equipment, hoping to bluff the enemy and buy time while American forces undertook training in their full Mission-Oriented Protective Posture (MOPP) in Saudi conditions.

After the war the Pentagon was much more candid. It reported criticisms of the 30-year-old M17 mask, the weight of us protective clothing, the lack of collective protection for the medical facilities, inadequate stocks of drugs and vaccines, the lack of rapid detection systems for biological weapons, and many problems with the water-based decontamination apparatus. It was doubtless embarrassed that it had to acquire 1,300 chemical agent monitors from the British and 60 Fuchs (renamed Fox) NBC reconnaissance vehicles from the Germans.

In these circumstances General H. Norman Schwarzkopf, commander of Central Command, prudently planned for 10,000 to 20,000 casualties: 'The possibility of mass casualties from chemical weapons', he wrote, 'was the main reason we had sixty-three hospitals, two hospital ships, and eighteen thousand beds ready in the war zone.'[21]

When Operation Desert Storm began (17 January 1991), it was first and foremost an air war that lasted for 38 days. If the air war achieved most of its objectives – incapacitating Iraq's command, control and communications, achieving air supremacy (without losing a single aircraft in air-to-air combat) and degrading and isolating Iraqi forces in the KTO – it had less success in destroying Iraq's NBC capabilities or in suppressing Iraq's ballistic missiles. US bombing damaged most of the CW infrastructure, including buildings at Al Muthanna involved in the production, processing and filling of chemical munitions; all three precursor chemical facilities at Habbaniyah; and the BW research laboratories at Al Salman and the munitions-filling station at Al Muthanna. The opening bombardment of 17 January also destroyed the only aircraft and spray tank ready for BW use. Although American commanders made extravagant claims during and immediately after the war about their destruction of Iraq's NBC facilities, including a baby milk factory erroneously bombed as a covert BW plant, the Pentagon subsequently admitted that it had 'an incomplete target set' caused by 'shortfalls in US knowledge of the extent and disposition of Iraqi nuclear research and chemical and biological weapons facilities'. This shortfall included the BW production plant at Al Hakam that was left untouched by the bombing.[22] Moreover, Iraq had utilized the four months of Desert Shield to disperse and conceal much of its CBW agent and munitions, preserving 30 chemical (and 25 biological) Al Hussein warheads, 1,024 R-400 bombs with chemical payloads (and 157 with BW agents), 38,537 filled and empty chemical munitions, 690 tons of chemical agent, over 3,000 tons of precursor chemicals, and an indeterminate amount of bulk BW agent at a succession of locations around the periphery of Baghdad. As Iraq subsequently declared this agent, BW equipment and the Al Hakam production plant to the UN inspectors, and the Iraq Survey Group, this confirmed the limitations of pre-war US intelligence and the successes of Iraqi wartime concealment.[23]

Wars, though, are not won by concealing weapons. In response to the coalition aerial assault, Iraq fired SCUD missiles at Saudi Arabia, Bahrain and Israel, hoping to drag the Jewish state into the war and split the UN coalition. Once again early coalition claims to have negated the missile threat by striking the fixed-launch sites, bombing the missile production sites and suppressing the mobile launchers proved unfounded. The Iraqis had removed key equipment and components from the production sites, and post-war reports by the Gulf War Air Power Survey cast doubt on the likelihood that a single mobile launcher had been hit. The vast diversion of allied air power (and the insertion of special forces on the ground) to counter the SCUD launches reduced the rate of attacks but Iraq kept firing SCUDs from 18 January to 26 February 1991. Nor did the hasty deployment of Patriot surface-to-air missile systems (six batteries in Israel and twenty in Saudi Arabia and Bahrain) prove an effective means of intercepting these relatively primitive incoming missiles. In Israel, which had undertaken an extensive if controversial distribution of gas masks to its citizens, the Patriots provided only a measure of political and psychological reassurance. The thirteen SCUDs that landed on Israel before the Patriot deployments did far less damage, and injured and killed fewer people, than the 26 fired after these deployments. Yet the physical damage inflicted by the SCUDs was of less moment (despite the fact that a SCUD killed 28 US troops and injured another 98 at Dhahran air base, the highest death toll against coalition forces of any Iraqi action during the war)[24] than the fear that the next incoming strike might be carrying a chemical warhead. 'We were not concerned about the accuracy', recalled Schwarzkopf, 'The biggest concern was a chemical warhead threat . . . each time they launched . . . the question was, is this going to be a chemical missile. That was what you were concerned about.'[25]

Similarly, when Schwarzkopf launched his 'hail Mary' – a rapid ground offensive that would drive the Iraqis out of the KTO in only 100 hours – he admitted that

one of my biggest concerns from the outset was the psychological impact of the initial use of chemical weapons on the troops. If they fight through it, then it is no longer ever going to be a problem. But if it stops them dead in their tracks and scares them to death, that is a continuing problem. And that was one of the concerns we had all along.[26]

When pressed after the war about why the Iraqis had not used gas, Schwarzkopf admitted that he didn't know. He thought that the extensive destruction of Iraqi artillery and the suppression of the Iraqi air force might have been contributing factors but he added, 'I just thank God they didn't.' Other military sources in Riyadh noted that the prevailing winds came from the southwest during much of the attack, so any short-range release of chemical agent may have blown back over the Iraqi forces in Kuwait.[27]

In retrospective testimony, Iraqi sources confirmed that Saddam had deployed chemical weapons and delegated authority to use them to field commanders during the conflict. This dispersal included the 75 'special warheads' for Al Hussein missiles, which were deployed at four sites with the warheads and missiles stored separately. In a recorded 'closed-door meeting' in January 1991, Saddam ordered that biological weapons should be prepared for counter-city bombardments, especially agent that was 'long term, the many years kind'. For targets, he specified, 'Riyadh and Jeddah, which are the biggest Saudi cities with all the decision makers, and the Saudi rulers live there. This is for the germ and chemical weapons . . . Also the Israeli cities, all of them. Of course you should concentrate on Tel Aviv, since it is their center.' He also envisaged using his chemical weapons if the coalition attacked Baghdad with unconventional weapons. As he announced on the eve of the ground campaign, the Al Hussein missile was 'capable of carrying nuclear, chemical and biological warheads' and that Iraq 'will use weapons that will match the weapons used against us by the enemy, but in any case, under no circumstances will we ever relinquish Iraq'. When asked by an American interviewer in 2004 why he had not used WMD during Desert Storm, Saddam reportedly replied, 'Do you think we are mad? What would the world have thought of us? We would have discredited those who had supported us.'[28]

The implications of Iraq's non-use of chemical and biological weapons were debated extensively after the war. As already stated (see chapter Two), some commentators asserted that the non-use merely confirmed the ineffectiveness of these weapons against modern conventional ordnance, and that the wartime precedent should accelerate the drive to conclude a Chemical Weapons Convention. Others were more prudent, arguing that 'Saddam's supine strategy and feckless tactics revealed little or nothing about the combat effectiveness of any of the weapons at his disposal (conventional or unconventional)', and that it proved nothing about the value of these weapons as 'force multipliers' in wars between developing states or in civil wars.[29] The Pentagon cautiously observed that 'potential adversaries' would study the war as closely as the United States. While some might be deterred by the punishment meted out to Saddam's forces, others might want to avoid his mistakes and wonder

> if the outcome would have been different if Iraq had acquired nuclear weapons first, or struck sooner at Saudi Arabia, or possessed a larger arsenal of more sophisticated ballistic missiles, or used chemical or biological weapons.[30]

UN Inspections

Following the operational ceasefire on 28 February 1991, the UN Security Council passed a definitive ceasefire resolution on 3 April 1991. Entitled SCR 687 (1991), it created the UN Special Commission (UNSCOM) and required Iraq to accept unconditionally the destruction, removal or the rendering harmless, under international supervision, of its chemical and biological weapons and all ballistic missiles with a range greater than 150 km. The International Atomic Energy Agency (IAEA) was also charged with the elimination of Iraq's nuclear weapons programme. Iraq was required to submit a declaration of the locations, amounts and types of such weapons within fifteen days, and UN sanctions were to remain in place until UNSCOM and IAEA reported that they had accomplished their missions.

Faced with misleading declarations, concealment and acts of obstruction by the Iraqis, the UNSCOM inspectors persevered over seven years, surveying 1,015 sites and carrying out 272 inspections. Largely composed of specialist staff seconded from over twenty supporting governments, as well as professional and support staff from the UN, the UNSCOM staff operated out of headquarters in New York, in Bahrain, and later in the Baghdad Ongoing Monitoring and Verification Centre. They benefited from a clear mandate, unprecedented rights of access, the ability to mount zero-notice inspections, unlimited rights of surveillance whether by U2 aircraft or by helicopters, the right to bring in inspection equipment without prior notice or Iraqi approval, unlimited sampling authority, and the right to operate open and encrypted communications without restrictions. All these inspection arrangements flowed from the coerced ceasefire, accompanied by the continued imposition of sanctions on Iraq and the resolute support of the Security Council in the early years. The activities of UNSCOM, in other words, are hardly a model for challenge or routine inspections under the Chemical Weapons Convention.[31]

This in no way detracts from the achievements of the UNSCOM inspectors, particularly their dedication in the face of blatant obstruction and intimidation, and their innovative use of information, technology and new methodologies in pursuit of Iraq's disarmament. In explaining the 'success' of UNSCOM, Tim Trevan, who served as an inspector, praised the quality of the staff 'bound by a strong culture of achievement through innovation and attention to detail', and attributed its problems to growing political divisions within the Security Council (1997–8), which Iraq sought to exploit by suspending all co-operation with UNSCOM on 31 October 1998.[32] The commission, though, was compromised when another of its unique features, namely the coupling of national intelligence with an international inspectorate, began to unravel. Once it was confirmed that intelligence gathered by UNSCOM inspectors had been passed onto the CIA, and thence to the Pentagon to assist in its targeting for Operation Desert Fox (the bombing of Iraq, 16–19 December 1998), this damaged the credibility of Richard Butler, the head of UNSCOM, exacerbated relations within the Security Council, and handed Saddam a propaganda triumph.[33]

UNSCOM may have destroyed more of Iraq's weapons of mass destruction than the entire aerial bombing campaign of Desert Storm, but as Hans Blix, director general of the IAEA, noted, very few weapons or little nuclear material were found at undeclared sites. It was largely inadequate accounting on the Iraqi side, and its history of cheating and concealment, that prevented UNSCOM or its successor, the UN Monitoring, Verification and Inspection Commission (UNMOVIC) from ever declaring that Iraq was in 100 per cent compliance.[34] In fact, as the Iraq Survey Group found after the abortive search for Iraq's WMD following Operation Iraqi Freedom (2003), Iraq had destroyed its weapons unilaterally in July 1991. This was only a tactical move by a regime that valued its WMD highly and had employed chemical weapons in quelling the Shi'a revolt in March 1991. Allowed to retain helicopters under the terms of the ceasefire, Iraq flew these machines out of Tamuz air base, dropping sarin-filled R-400 bombs on the insurgents. When these bombs proved ineffectual (they had been designed for release from high-speed aircraft flying at higher altitudes), the MI-8 helicopters dropped larger aerial bombs filled with CS in areas around Karbala, Najaf, Nasariyah and Basra.

Having reluctantly accepted the terms of SCR 687 (1991), Saddam only declared part of Iraq's chemical warfare and ballistic missile programmes – the most visible elements of Iraq's NBC capabilities – but not the nuclear or biological warfare programmes. He still regarded these weapons, or at least the threat of them, as vital for Iraq's security vis-à-vis Iran, especially as the Security Council never fulfilled the objective of establishing a nuclear-weapon free zone in the Middle East, as stipulated in SCR 687. Accordingly, the Technical Research Centre and the Al Muthanna State Establishment dispersed chemical and biological bombs and missile warheads in concealed sites until July 1991. Iraq also hid missiles, launchers, uranium enrichment equipment, strategic materials, missile-manufacturing equipment and large amounts of documentation. The regime, as the Survey Group reported, 'attempted to balance competing desires to appear to cooperate with the UN and have sanctions lifted, and to preserve the ability to eventually reconstitute its weapons of mass destruction'.[35]

This strategy foundered in only the second inspection of a suspected nuclear facility (28 June 1991) where the Iraqis, having blocked access to David Kay's team of inspectors, were then caught on film removing bomb-making equipment from the site. Faced with such resourceful inspectors, Saddam ordered the unilateral destruction of large numbers of undeclared weapons and materials in the following month to conceal the extent of Iraq's WMD capabilities. As Iraq retained a cadre of skilled scientists that could resume the WMD programmes whenever sanctions were lifted, Iraqi officials recall that Saddam instructed the directors general of Iraqi state companies and other state entities to keep these scientists fully employed and to prevent them from leaving the country.[36] Meanwhile Iraq had to deal with the inspectors, who continued to press for documentation to verify the unilateral destruction of chemical weapons, materials, missiles, warheads and launchers. Some inspectors also remained doubtful about the declaration that Iraq had only undertaken biological research for defensive purposes. Pressed for an accounting of the vast amount of imported growth media, which exceeded the stated requirements for hospital use, Iraq eventually admitted that it had produced BW agent in bulk quantities but denied weaponization (1 July 1995). However, after the unexpected flight of Hussein Kamel Hassan to Jordan, Iraq released long-concealed WMD documentation, including extensive details about the BW and VX programmes by means of planting this information in Hussein Kamel's 'chicken yard' and directing the inspectors to it. After four years of abortive searching, UNSCOM could now reveal the extent of Iraq's BW programme[37] and approve the destruction of biological weapons production equipment and the facilities at Al Hakam (May–June 1996). Far from being a triumph for UNSCOM, this decisive breakthrough derived from an entirely fortuitous defection.

Relations between Iraq and UNSCOM remained tense, with the inspectors testing Iraq's concealment policies and probing gaps in the accounting and documentation (and there were gaps in the latter, as Iraqi officials had spent two days burning about a quarter of the information before revealing the remainder in the 'chicken yard').[38] Despite the efforts of UN Secretary-General Kofi Annan to ease the dispute by establishing criteria for presidential site visits, and the decision of the Security Council to review the status of sanctions every 60 days, the tensions came to a climax in mid-1998. When the inspectors claimed that they had detected traces of vx-related compounds on ballistic missile fragments and discovered another document describing the use of special weapons by the Iraqi Air Force, Iraq protested that the vx allegations were further evidence of collusion between the United States and UNSCOM. Whereas an American laboratory confirmed the original findings, the results from French and Swiss laboratories proved inconclusive, and Iraq maintained that the results could not have been accurate since the vx production run had failed and the nerve agent had not been used in munitions. Convinced that UNSCOM would never find Iraq in compliance, and that sanctions would not be lifted, Iraq suspended co-operation and expelled the inspectors.

Intelligence Blunders and Operation Iraqi Freedom (2003)

The loss of intelligence from the UNSCOM inspectors forced the US intelligence community to rely upon less reliable and less detailed sources of information. It was by no means alone in assuming that Iraq, on account of its previous use of chemical weapons, its covert programmes to develop nuclear and biological weapons, and its record of deceiving the UN inspectors, wanted to resume its WMD programmes. Indeed, it assumed that Iraq had something to conceal, including chemical and biological weapons and their means of delivery, as well as an inclination to exploit the UN's 'Oil for Food' programme to reconstitute dual-use facilities. Allied intelligence agencies evinced similar views, vindicating the sceptical remark of the French President Jacques Chirac that these agencies sometimes 'intoxicate each other'.[39] Chirac, though, did not believe that Iraq had retained any weapons; both Bush and Britain's prime minister, Tony Blair, did and they used published intelligence reports to justify the resumption of hostilities with Iraq, and to remove the regime of Saddam Hussein, without UN endorsement. In America's case the National Intelligence Estimate (NIE), and a declassified version also published in October 2002, provided crucial judgements on Iraq's WMD (and has since been severely criticized by the Senate's Select Committee on Intelligence and a WMD commission). In Britain's case a government dossier, *Iraq's Weapons of Mass Destruction* of 24 September 2002, based on the findings of the Joint Intelligence Committee (JIC), has been reviewed critically by a committee of Privy Councillors, chaired by Lord Butler.

None of the allied agencies had access to reliable sources of information. The American intelligence community lacked any sources inside Iraq, gained only limited insights from signals intelligence, and relied primarily upon ambiguous satellite imagery in respect of Iraq's chemical weapons capability. It also insisted that Iraq possessed mobile biological production facilities mounted on three tractor-trailers, a sensational claim derived from a single Iraqi defector, interrogated by German intelligence, to whom American intelligence never had direct access. Known as 'Curveball', this Iraqi engineer passed on a mixture of fantasy and fact through German briefings, and its significance was magnified by American and British intelligence agencies: it formed a core element of the NIE, Blair's dossier and the address of Secretary of State Colin Powell to the United Nations on 5 February 2003. As Bob Drogin observed, 'If Curveball fused fact and fiction, others twisted and magnified his account in grotesque ways. His marginal story took on an importance it did not deserve. Senior intelligence officials irresponsibly hyped his claims and accepted unconfirmed reports.'[40]

The assertions of 'Curveball' assumed such importance because the intelligence community had become the victim of a form of 'groupthink' whereby they looked for evidence of an expanding WMD programme once the inspectors had left Iraq, and analysts interpreted ambiguous data as evidence of the expanded programme they expected to see. Their judgements suffered from a 'layering' effect whereby assessments were built upon previous judgements without carrying forward the uncertainties of the original judgements.

Accordingly, when the NIE estimated that Iraq had up to 500 tons of chemical weapons, this was based largely upon accounting discrepancies and production capacity rather than any new evidence. As analysts became increasingly confident on account of the revelations of 'Curveball' that Iraq was producing and hiding biological weapons, they assumed that Iraq must have been doing likewise with its chemical weapons.[41]

Operating within this collective mind-set, the American intelligence community tended to ignore or minimize evidence that contradicted their preconceptions. They discounted the negative findings of the UNMOVIC inspectors, who had resumed inspections in Iraq carrying out 731 inspections at 411 sites from 27 November 2002 to 18 March 2003, as reflecting the relative inexperience of the UNMOVIC personnel and the success of Iraq's campaign of denial and deception. Even worse in composing their case, they presented judgements in an emphatic manner, stripped of any caveats or uncertainties, a tendency that was magnified in the declassified version, *Iraq's Weapons of Mass Destruction Programs* (4 October 2002). This led to overstatements of what was known and, in respect of reconstructed dual-use facilities, to deductions about what Iraq was doing rather than what Iraq might do. The failings of analysis and presentation, argued the Senate Intelligence Committee, stemmed from 'a combination of systemic weaknesses, primarily in analytic trade craft, compounded by a lack of information sharing, poor management, and inadequate intelligence collection'.[42]

The British dossier, an unprecedented publication in British political history, was compiled in a mere three weeks. Like the US publications, it was conspicuous for its lack of caveats, qualifications, or warnings about the limited intelligence base. The British Secret Intelligence Service (MI6) had information from five human intelligence sources, but the material derived from three of them that helped to underpin the assessments of the JIC was later found to be unreliable. That would have mattered less had the published document retained the cautious and qualified prose of previous secret briefings (for example, that of 15 March 2002) but elements of uncertainty were swept aside to state that Iraq has 'continued to produce chemical and biological weapons', and that 'some of these weapons are deployable within 45 minutes'. As the Butler report observed, this 'eye-catching' phrase was left in the document without any contextual reference or any precision about what munitions might be involved.[43]

Supposedly the published intelligence reports were intended to inform debate rather than advocate policy, and many of their assumptions were widely held, if open to differing interpretations. Even Robin Cook, who resigned from the British cabinet on the eve of the war, accepted that Iraq probably had 'biological toxins and battlefield chemical munitions' but disputed that these could be classed as weapons of mass destruction since they could not be delivered against a strategic city target. Opposed to war without UN sanction or before the inspectors had completed their task, he did not believe that the Iraqi forces, known to be weak, demoralized and poorly equipped, posed 'a clear and present danger to Britain' as the prime minister alleged.[44] Ironically Paul Wolfowitz, the US deputy defense secretary, broadly agreed. He, too, thought that Iraq possessed chemical and biological weapons but judged the regime to be so weak that it would break easily; in other words, a war aimed at regime change in Baghdad 'was doable'.[45] This view would be vindicated in the ensuing Operation Iraqi Freedom, a 43-day war (17 March–1 May 2003) in which US-led forces swept into Baghdad, exploiting complete air supremacy, heavy use of precision-guided munitions and rapid speed in the movement of armoured forces, mechanized infantry and logistic support. In an abject defence of Iraq, Saddam neither fired any missiles nor employed chemical and biological weapons, nor even made any preparations to employ such weapons.

The great shock after the war was the inability of US forces to find any weapons of mass destruction. After exhaustive searches the Iraq Survey Group conceded that Iraq had destroyed large numbers of chemical and biological weapons in July 1991, and that Iraq was correct in claiming that the tractor-trailers, believed to be producing biological agent, were in fact producing hydrogen. David Kay returned from Iraq to admit 'we were almost all wrong' and to speculate that the former Iraqi leader had not revealed evidence of this unilateral act because 'He did not want to appear to the rest of the Arab world as having caved in to the US and the UN'. Such 'creative ambiguity', argued Kay, may have been useful in Iraq's foreign relations, and internally, as Saddam had used chemical weapons against the Kurds and Shi'a. By creating the impression that Iraq retained these weapons, Saddam may have preserved some 'leverage' over these dissident groups.[46]

Chemical warfare, though, recurred in the Iraqi context during the protracted insurgency that erupted during the occupation that followed the Second Gulf War. On 28 January 2007 suicide bombers detonated a truck laden with explosives and a chlorine tank in the town of Ramadi in the al-Anbar province. Having killed sixteen people with this improvised explosive device (IED), insurgents mounted nearly a dozen vehicle-borne IEDs, designed to release chlorine gas on detonation, over the next four months. As chlorine was employed extensively in water treatment, or supplies could be secured from Jordan, the attacks were easy to mount, using a diverse array of tanker trucks, dump trucks and ordinary cars. Although the casualty levels from blast and gas were unpredictable (ranging from quite ineffectual when the gas was burnt off or blown away to causing as many as 350 casualties and eight deaths in a double bombing at Fallujah on 16 March 2007), the attacks proved excellent instruments of propaganda and intimidation, not least as the chlorine gas was visible to its intended victims, causing increased fear. Denunciation by the new UN Secretary-General, Ban Ki-Moon (19 March 2007)[47] proved of no avail. Militants in Tal Afar circulated leaflets, threatening further chemical attacks against local Sunnis and the police, and proceeded to implement their threats.

US forces responded by raiding various warehouses in Baghdad and al-Anbar province where they found stores of lethal chemicals, propane tanks, and vehicles being prepared as car bombs. The Iraqi authorities organized armed guards for convoys of trucks transporting chlorine and ensured that trucks carrying chlorine from Jordan were escorted safely from the border checkpoints to their destinations. They also imposed bans upon vehicle traffic in Tal Afar. There were reports, too, that the Iraqi government considered imposing drastic limitations upon the use of chlorine in water treatment.[48]

Chemical and biological warfare, in short, retained its potential to evolve and to challenge civil and military authorities. Its research, development and production in Iraq had exposed the limitations of Western intelligence monitoring and the difficulties of on-site inspection. Both the intelligence agencies and the UN inspectors had developed collective mindsets, whereby they could not accept that Iraq had destroyed all the weapons that they had used so effectively in the Iran–Iraq War and had retained as a challenge to the US-led UN coalition during the First Gulf War. The subsequent employment of chlorine during the US-led occupation demonstrated that gas had not lost its potential as a weapon of terror.

6

Chemical and Biological Terrorism

The prospect of terrorists employing toxic chemical or biological agents as weapons has aroused considerable speculation and debate. The speculation derives from the crucial differences between terrorism and war, with the former being defined by the US Department of State as 'premeditated, politically motivated violence perpetrated against noncombatant targets by subnational groups or clandestine agents, usually intended to influence an audience'.[1] As terrorists can choose when, where and how to attack their targets, they avoid many of the uncertainties that have bedevilled the military use of chemical and biological weapons. By maximizing the element of surprise, they can attack targets with low or non-existent levels of protection; by careful choice of target environment, especially an enclosed facility, they need not wait upon optimal meteorological conditions; by attacking highly vulnerable areas, they may use a less than optimal mode of delivery; and by making a chemical or biological assault, they may expect to capture media attention and cause widespread panic.[2] Their purposes may range from assassination (notably the murder of Georgi Markov with a ricin-tipped umbrella in September 1978), economic terrorism (particularly attempts to poison or threaten to poison crops, livestock or produce), sabotage, social disruption and mass murder. Yet even within a broad definition of terrorism, the number of incidents involving chemical or biological agents is relatively small. This has prompted debate about the likelihood of terrorists employing these weapons; divergent analyses of the major case studies and of reflections upon the so-called 'new terrorism', including al-Qaeda in the aftermath of the 9/11 atrocities; and reflections upon counterterrorism including the 'War on Terror'.

Debate on CBW Terrorism

The use of chemical and biological agents by non-state actors is quite diverse in scope, if limited in number. A 1994 survey, using a very broad definition of terrorism, identified 244 such incidents since the First World War in 26 countries. Of these incidents only 60 per cent involved actual use (the rest were threats to use or acquisition), and only 25 per cent reflected political motives, with the remainder being perpetrated by criminals (often intent on extortion), by psychotics and hostile employees, among others.[3] Placing such analysis in a broader context, the CIA found that the 22 terrorist incidents involving 'exotic pollutants' around the world from 1968 to 1980 represented only one half of one per cent of all terrorist incidents in that period. None of these involved weapons per se, and the most notable incidents involved the injection of mercury into Israeli and Spanish citrus fruits in 1978.[4]

In a volume on chemical and biological terrorism, edited by Brad Roberts, several commentators attribute this limited usage to enduring technological and political barriers. Joseph Pilat, a strategic analyst at Los Alamos, argued that any recourse to chemical, biological (and nuclear) terrorism involves costs compared with 'the simpler, less expensive, and more predictable results of conventional explosives'.[5] Although terrorists could acquire the requisite materials and produce chemical or biological agents in small facilities, without distinguishing features, they would have to do so safely and in sufficient quantity to achieve lethal or incapacitating dosages with their chosen means of dissemination. Chemical agents are easier to synthesize than biological agents but need to be produced in sufficient quantities and purities if the aim is to cause a large number of casualties. Producing a biological agent poses more difficult, if not insuperable, challenges, especially the conversion of liquid slurry into particles of the requisite size and density for effective delivery as an aerosol. An aerosol can be delivered as a wet mist or dry powder but the latter is easier to transport and generally travels further on the wind, thereby enhancing the potential to inflict casualties over a wider area. Delivering agent in a dry form, though, requires the drying of pathogens into a solid cake and then milling the latter into a fine powder – technically challenging tasks that might require state-sponsorship or the recruitment of experienced scientists from the former Soviet Union, South Africa or some other country that had an advanced BW programme. Karl Lowe, an analyst at the Institute for Defense Analyses, reckoned that there are only 'a relatively small number of biological agents that can be produced, refined, weaponized, and effectively disseminated by clandestine means unless a country with a biological warfare program is involved'.[6]

Whether a state-sponsored or independent terrorist organization would wish to pursue this option is moot. Ron Purver, a Canadian intelligence analyst who has examined the vast literature of chemical and biological terrorism, identified a dozen or so factors that may have inhibited recourse to such weapons in the past. Much depends, as he admits, upon the nature of the terrorist organization and its political objectives. For those groups seeking discreet political objectives, or planning to attack a specific target with discriminate effects, chemical or biological weapons might seem too unpredictable and potentially indiscriminate in their impact. Operationally, these weapons could prove problematic, especially for those fearful of their own safety during production or use, or fearful of employing weapons deemed illegitimate in inter-state warfare. Such fears could erode group cohesion and provoke defections. Employing these weapons, moreover, might prove counterproductive, alienating followers or potential followers and inviting severe reprisals from the state attacked. A state sponsor might wish to avoid association with such an act, and the consequent retaliation. Finally, terrorists might prefer simpler technology that was cheaper and easier to obtain, attracted less attention, and could be employed by operatives requiring minimal expertise and training. This links with the famous observation of Brian Jenkins that 'terrorists want a lot of people *watching*, not a lot of people *dead*'.[7]

Admittedly Purver found evidence in the open literature that contradicted most of his own points, including claims that nearly all the technical and political constraints were steadily eroding, that groups such as Aum Shinrikyo might relish employing chemical and biological agents, and that the taboos against the terrorist use of CB agents were largely illusory. The balance of the argument was shifting with the proliferation of chemical and biological weapons in the 1990s, the diffusion of precursor chemicals and dual-use technologies, and the potential spread of expertise after the collapse of the Soviet Union and of information through the Internet. Terrorism appeared to be changing, too, involving individuals willing to die for their cause (suicide bombers), recourse to indiscriminate mass killing (the bombing of the US embassies in Nairobi and Dar es-Salaam) and the capacity of a charismatic, if paranoid, leader, Shoko Asahara, to attract sufficient funding, recruit able if not expert scientific participation, and maintain group cohesion over several years of trying to develop and use chemical and biological weapons. 'A sufficient number of countervailing trends', argued Purver, had undermined 'important past constraints, lending support to the widespread consensus among analysts that the likelihood of terrorist use of CB agents in the future' was 'both real and growing'.[8]

In anticipating this development various commentators, including directors of the CIA, had often highlighted the potential attraction of chemical and biological weapons for terrorist operations. Compared with nuclear weapons, chemical and biological weapons were easier and cheaper to acquire, and, as instruments of destruction, they could be 'very small and easily concealed, and utilized in places like the ventilation system of a key building'. The precursor chemicals, as Judge Webster added, 'are not all that rare or hard to come by', and the agent could be produced in a relatively small, clandestine facility with few distinguishing features for external detection. As the problems of handling chemicals were hardly trivial, terrorists would need containers that resisted the corrosive effects of the chemicals and be able to develop 'maximum purity to prolong the shelf life . . . once these chemicals are placed in weapons'. But, as he concluded, 'no one has a corner on the knowledge anymore'.[9] Testifying six years later, in 1995, CIA Director John Deutch confirmed the agency's view: 'For a terrorist group, I think the judgment of all experts would be chemical first, biological second, nuclear third.' Chemicals would be the 'weapon of choice' partly because of ease of acquisition, partly because biological materials required greater care in the handling until they were used.[10]

Robert H. Kupperman, a senior advisor of the Center for Strategic and International Studies and an authority on chemical and biological terrorism, has long sounded warnings over this phenomenon. He has argued that CB terror might be used to threaten industrial and economic disruption as much as 'killing on a grand scale' and need not involve classical nerve agents since potent insecticides, such as TEPP or parathion, are 'commercially available . . . [and] are almost as toxic as their military counterparts'. Moreover, cultures of anthrax could be found in most areas of the world: in the soil of cattle country or in sheep's wool as well as in medical research laboratories. Producing anthrax, Kupperman argued, would be easier than preparing it for dissemination as spores, but the

> aerosol dispersal technology is easy to obtain from open literature and commercial sources, and equipment to aerosolize biological agents is available as virtually off-the-shelf systems produced for legitimate industrial, medical, and agricultural applications. With access to a standard machine shop, it would not be difficult to fabricate aerosol generators and integrate components to produce reliable systems for dispersing micro-organisms or toxins.[11]

Quite apart from the availability of materials and dual-use equipment, most urban populations are highly vulnerable to chemical or biological attacks. Lacking real-time warning, exposed civilians would also lack protective equipment and medical treatment services could be stretched by a massive number of casualties. Large-scale decontamination is conspicuous by its absence in most countries. In these circumstances, democratic states rely primarily upon their intelligence services, surveillance facilities and law-enforcement agencies to intercept terrorist groups before they can launch their attacks. Faced with the power of the state, bolstered by conventional military force, terrorists may seek to counter these strengths asymmetrically. Although most terrorists will prefer cheap conventional weapons, and the use of proven tactics, some may wish to exploit the terrifying impact of CB weaponry as an instrument of psychological warfare. As Harvey McGeorge has observed, 'The odious and insidious nature of chemical and biological agents suggest that they are potentially the most powerful and effective instruments of terror available.'[12]

Case Studies and their Lessons

Despite the potential feasibility and possible attractions of chemical and biological weapons as instruments of terror, recourse to this option has been relatively rare. Only 24 biological attacks occurred in the United States between 1970 and 2013.[13] In *Toxic Terror*, Jonathan B. Tucker examined twelve groups or individuals who sought to acquire or use CBW agents over the period from 1945 to 1998. Whatever the value of his chosen methodology, and Tucker admits that his case-study approach has 'drawbacks', it highlights the range of motivations involved, the variety of techniques employed, the apocryphal nature of some reported cases, and the mistakes exploited by law enforcement agencies to foil many, though not all, of these individuals and groups. Setting aside the apocryphal cases, several terrorists were apprehended or foiled before they could use CBW agents, notably the radical eco-terrorists RISE (1972), who had to abort their attempt to poison water supplies with microbial pathogens; the Alphabet Bomber (1974), who was arrested before he could develop the nerve agent for an attack on the US Capitol; and two groups penetrated by the FBI before they could mount their CBW attacks: the Covenant, the Sword and the Arm of the Lord (1986) and the Minnesota Patriots Council (1991). More successful groups included a small team of Jewish Holocaust survivors, known as DIN or 'Avenging Israel's Blood', who poisoned 2,283 German prisoners of war with an arsenic mixture in Stalag 13 (April 1946). The Rajneesh cult also dispersed Salmonella bacteria in Oregon (August and September 1984), sickening 751 people, including local commissioners hostile to the group, and citizens in a town called The Dallas, in order to affect the outcome of a local election. Whether the perpetrators of the World Trade Center bombing (26 February 1993) incorporated hydrogen cyanide gas into their 1,500-pound urea-nitrate bomb, as stated by Judge Kevin T. Duffy in sentencing four of the convicted bombers (24 May 1994), is less clear but they certainly wanted to do so and had acquired a bottle of sodium cyanide.[14]

If none of these cases gained the notoriety of the Aum cult, the groups had distinctive characteristics as bodies willing to employ CBW agents. The DIN was a small, radicalized group representing a 'heavily brutalized' community. Having dehumanized their enemy, they believed that all Germans bore collective guilt for the Holocaust. Desperate for revenge, they were willing to die, if necessary, in the course of poisoning the dark rye bread provided for the German prisoners. The Rajneeshees, dominated by a charismatic leader, were a cult isolated from the rest of society in rural Oregon. Increasingly at odds with their neighbours, and contemptuous of them, they sought to take over Wasco County and to exploit their scientific expertise by developing a BW option. Having considered several biological agents, they prepared Salmonella typhimurium as a less traceable option than S. typhi, bacteria that cause typhoid fever. In launching the first large-scale use of biological terrorism on American soil, the Rajneeshees demonstrated the ease with which they could order pathogens and produce biological agents in clandestine facilities. The World Trade Center plotters also demonstrated a visceral hatred of their enemies (both the United States and Israel), a capacity to exploit some chemical expertise, and a readiness to kill as many people as possible.[15]

Case Studies: Aum Cult

Aum Shinrikyo ('Aum Supreme Truth') achieved worldwide notoriety after its attack with the nerve agent sarin upon commuters travelling on five trains towards Kasumigaseki station on the Tokyo underground (20 March 1995). Twelve people died from the gas and over 1,000 (out of the 5,500 who sought hospital treatment) were injured in an attack that had a precedent, namely a previous incident in Matsumoto on 27 June 1994 that killed seven and injured 144.[16] Despite the arrest of many members of the cult, including its partially blind, charismatic leader, Shoko Asahara, widespread panic and disruption followed threats of further attacks. On 5 May and 4 July 1995, there were another two less successful attempts, involving the release of hydrogen cyanide on the Tokyo subway. When police raided the premises of the cult, they found vast quantities of precursor chemicals, including 500 drums of phosphorus trichloride, 160 barrels of peptone (for cultivating biological spores), large amounts of equipment for manufacturing chemical and biological agents, an extensive library and a four-storey concrete laboratory under construction, equipped with a clean room, an air lock and a filtration system for removing contaminants.[17]

The sect was a remarkable body. Its theology included teachings from Tibetan Buddhism and yoga, the book of Revelation and the prophecies of Nostradamus, and involved the worshipping of Shiva, the Hindu god of destruction. Asahara predicted an imminent Armageddon, in which Japan would be laid waste by an American-led attack, and foretold salvation at the end of Armageddon for those who adopted the Aum faith. Membership grew rapidly from a score of members in 1984 to over 40,000 members (and some estimates reckoned in excess of 50,000) by 1995, including graduates with degrees in medicine, biochemistry, biology and genetic engineering. Aside from a membership in excess of 10,000 in Japan, the cult attracted 30,000 followers in Russia and had members scattered across the United States, Germany, Taiwan and several other countries. By 1995, it had some 1,400 devotees, who had renounced the outside world, donated all their earthly possessions to the cult and lived at the Aum facilities. From the members and numerous moneymaking ventures – some legal (noodle shops), some illegal (extortion and drug manufacture) – the cult amassed assets in excess of $1 billion or some 100 billion yen by 1995. It had over 30 branches in six countries, including a major compound at the base of Mount Fuji about 100 kilometres from Tokyo, and ran a trading company in Taiwan, a tea plantation in Sri Lanka, an engineering company in Okamura Tekko in the Ishikawa prefecture (which enabled the cult to purchase technical equipment) and a ranch in Australia (where it experimented with sarin on sheep). It also purchased a helicopter from Russia in June 1994, from which it had planned to disperse cw agent.[18]

Obsessed with the impending apocalypse, and the prospect of an American attack on Japan with nuclear weapons, it sought to acquire a diverse arsenal of weapons, ranging from assault rifles, pistols and knives to laser and microwave devices. In seeking to alert the populace to the dangers that Asahara foretold, Aum also wished to punish Japanese voters on account of its defeat in the elections of February 1990, rival religious organizations, and lawyers campaigning against the cult. As early as 1990, Aum began the production of biological weapons, initially botulinum toxin, in an effort led by a young microbiologist, Seiichi Endo. Truck-mounted attempts to spray the poison across central Tokyo, the American naval bases at Yokahama and Yokosuka, and the central airport at Narita (April 1990) all failed. Three years later the cult tried again, pumping a slurry of liquid anthrax into a sprayer on the roof of an Aum building in Tokyo and trying to create a lethal cloud. Failure on this occasion (June 1993) prompted further attempts to spray from buildings and trucks but the clogged sprayers and a relatively harmless strain of anthrax thwarted all these efforts. Despite failing in at least nine biological attacks, Aum tried to obtain the Ebola virus from Zaire and to produce Q-fever, but the guru had already switched priorities from biological to chemical weapons.[19]

From the spring of 1993, Aum began its preparations for chemical operations by procuring extensive quantities of precursor chemicals, laboratory and industrial equipment, and other materials. Its scientists investigated several nerve agents – sarin, soman, tabun and vx – before choosing sarin initially, for which the precursor chemicals were readily available. Production was relatively easy in the facility known as Satyam No. 7 within the Kamikuishiki compound.

Aum mounted three ineffectual attacks with sarin in 1993, injuring only one person, before the major attack at Matsumoto (27 June 1994). It also used vx to kill one person and injure two more in three assassination attempts (1994–5). Faced with impending police probes of its facilities, Aum launched another abortive attempt to spray botulinum toxin on the Tokyo subway (15 March 1995), and then produced sarin rapidly for the subway attack on 20 March. Five cult members carried the sarin in small nylon bags, wrapped in newspapers, onto the five trains, and released the gas by puncturing the bags with umbrellas possessing sharpened tips. Neither this mode of dissemination nor the relatively impure sarin maximized the level of casualties but understandably Senator Sam Nunn warned that 'The cult known as Aum Shinrikyo, thus gained the distinction of becoming the first group, other than a nation during wartime, to use chemical weapons on a major scale. I believe this attack signals the world has entered into a new era.'[20]

Case Studies: Anthrax Letters

In 5 October 2001, within a month of the 9/11 atrocities, Robert Stevens, a Florida-based photograph editor, became the first fatality of a letter containing spores of high-quality, weapons-grade *Bacillus anthracis*, later identified as the Ames strain held at the us Army Medical Research Institute of Infectious Diseases at Fort Detrick. It was soon revealed that several letters containing these finely powdered spores had been sent to addresses in New York, Connecticut, and Washington, DC, including the offices of Democratic Senators Tom Daschle of South Dakota and Patrick J. Leahy of Vermont. The attacks resulted in at least 22 cases of anthrax, involving five fatalities. Following so soon after 9/11, the letters caused massive panic and chaos across the United States at a time when 680 million letters a day were passing through the us Postal Service. Some 30,000 people in Washington, DC, took prophylactic antibiotics and thousands more were traumatized. Two branches of the federal government, specifically parts of the us Congress and the Supreme Court, had to be closed for several days, and the Hart Senate Office Building required extensive decontamination, costing some $200 million. The Postal Service spent nearly $200 million cleaning up the facilities at Trenton, New Jersey, and Brentwood, where two employees died, and the Brentwood office was not reopened for 26 months. The massive costs multiplied as the FBI, assisted by postal inspectors, interviewed over 10,000 people in six months, conducted 67 searches and issued over 6,000 subpoenas.

The effects of this case derived from five (possibly eight) letters, containing about ten grams of dry, powdered anthrax, demonstrated that bioterrorism can cause massive shock, colossal economic damage, immense containment and decontamination problems, and pose all manner of difficulties and embarrassments for law-enforcement agencies. The FBI's erroneous targeting of Dr Steven J. Hatfill, a former scientist at Fort Detrick, led to a lawsuit against the US government with a settlement of $5.8 million for damaging his reputation and career. Even when the FBI pronounced the case closed after the suicide of another scientist at Fort Detrick, Dr Bruce E. Ivins (on 29 July 2008), many questions remained about the largely circumstantial evidence against him. Unable to prove that Ivins had prepared or posted these letters, or that he had a motive in doing so, the FBI could only indicate that the strains of *Bacillus anthracis* were similar to those used in a RMR-1029 flask in the Army's biodefence laboratory, which Ivins (and another 100 researchers) had access to, and that Ivins had engaged in some unusual late-night activities prior to the postings. In 2008 the FBI asked the National Academy of Sciences (NAS) to review the scientific aspects of the investigations, and to its chagrin, the NAS reported in 2011 that it was 'impossible to reach a definitive conclusion about the origins of the *B. Anthracis* in the mailings, based on the available scientific evidence alone'.[21]

Case Studies: Lessons

These case studies have provoked a vigorous debate. Initially the Aum revelations provoked anxiety about the onset of the 'new terrorism'. Bruce Hoffman, then at the Centre for the Study of Terrorism and Political Violence at St Andrews University, reckoned that 'We've definitely crossed a threshold. This is the cutting edge of high-tech terrorism for the year 2000 and beyond.' John Sopko, who quoted Hoffman in his extensive staff statement on the Aum cult for a Senate committee, asserted that the terrorist actors had changed, that they now had access to technological expertise, materials, equipment and new methods of delivery, and that their motivation was mass murder. Japanese police authorities confirmed many of these findings after their seizure of large quantities of culture media, equipment and other materials, an extensive scientific library, and the discovery of a production plant that had a sophisticated, computerized control system. Despite a series of accidents and failures in the later stages of production, the plant had produced ten tons of precursor chemicals for sarin.[22]

Many commentators took comfort from the failures of Aum, particularly their failure to obtain virulent strains of biological agents or to weaponize and disseminate biological weapons effectively, their chaotic development programmes, recurring accidents, and their inability to produce sarin that was more than 30 per cent pure. Larry C. Johnson, a former deputy director, Office of Counterterrorism, State Department, summarized the outcome of the five-year effort, involving millions of dollars, the employment of several PhD scientists and the construction of several laboratories designed and equipped to make CBW agents:

> They tried twice unsuccessfully to produce and use Botulinus Toxin A (one of the deadliest biological agents). They had a similar failure with anthrax. They successfully produced the nerve agent sarin, but it lacked the purity and effectiveness associated with military-grade weapons. Their attack on the Tokyo subway system injured five thousand (*sic*) people and killed 12. Despite the attack the subways were back in operation the same day.[23]

Aum, argued Ian Reader, displayed 'a remarkable degree of incompetence' and their efforts, far from serving as a precedent, simply ensured that the Japanese police tightened their surveillance and intelligence gathering over religious groups. The state also imposed financial and import controls thereafter, impeding other groups from the clandestine acquisition and development of chemical and biological weapons.[24]

Yet the diluted sarin attack of 20 March 1995, involving a primitive dispersal mechanism, was only a hastily conceived operation prepared over a weekend and intended to divert the police from an imminent raid on Aum premises. It caused massive panic on the day of the attack, and similar fears resurfaced after a more sophisticated attack was planned for Shinjuku Station, Tokyo, on 5 May 1995. Aum, nonetheless, had failed to acquire potent strains of biological agents and had never mastered the techniques of aerosolization. If intent upon causing mass casualties, terrorists would need to disperse BW agents as dry, milled particles of the proper size for aerosol dissemination. Compared with the liquid slurry used by Aum, dry agent is more easily handled and transported (and a smaller volume could inflict casualties over larger areas). Drying bacteria, though, into a solid cake and then milling it into a fine powder of the requisite size are challenging tasks that Aum failed to master.[25]

Does this mean that Aum, as several commentators claimed, was an aberration, a terrorist group unusual in the lavishness of its funding, in the scale of its facilities, and in its ability to procure the requisite materials and equipment for chemical and biological terrorism during the early 1990s without interference by the authorities? Claims that Aum broke a taboo against the non-use of chemical and biological weapons, and hence that other groups would follow suit, lack substantive evidence (other than in the anthrax case). Perry Robinson even depicted the subsequent 'footling terrorist attempts to acquire CBW' as little more than a 'localized nuisance'.[26] Moreover, as the Mumbai massacre (26–28 November 2008) demonstrated, terrorists can still employ conventional explosives to achieve immediate, dramatic effects; inflict significant numbers of casualties; and gain publicity through acts of physical destruction. Far less dramatic, the dispersal of chemical or biological materials would be much less predictable, losing much of the agent by dilution in the atmosphere. The degree of dilution would depend upon the local micro-meteorology, so reducing any certainty about the likelihood of achieving a harmful concentration in the target area. Finally, the effects of a chemical or biological attack would involve a delay of minutes to hours or days before an effect became apparent, hence the use of CB materials, as Graham Pearson argued, might be 'regarded by terrorists as less predictable and less reliable and overall much more chancy and less attractive than high explosives'.[27] The overwhelming majority of terrorist outrages since Aum have involved the use of conventional ordnance.

Drawing too much reassurance from these examples, though, would seem unwise. On the one hand, the relevant technology, especially the techniques of biotechnology, is evolving rapidly, becoming much more widely understood and opening up new possibilities in the acquisition or refinement of chemical and biological agents (see Conclusion). On the other hand, the nature of terrorism has changed, with many more groups ready to inflict mass casualties. As Walter Laqueur, the doyen of terrorism studies, argues, the danger of CBW terrorism has increased because of the confluence of two trends: the increasing accessibility of mass-casualty weapons and the emergence of more ruthless forms of religious and ideological fanaticism.[28] There is abundant evidence that many of these groups, including al-Qaeda, want to acquire these weapons and every reason to assume that they will be ready to cross the threshold and employ chemical and biological weapons whenever they can do so with maximum effect. In the vanguard of the 'new terrorism' are extremist fundamentalist organizations and apocalypse-inspired sects that are much less discriminating in their use of violence than the old terrorist movements. Engaged in what they perceive as a life-or-death struggle with a 'satanic' enemy, these 'new' terrorists may envisage mass-casualty violence as not only a strategic riposte to this enemy but also as a symbolic act and a means of waging asymmetric warfare that would reverse past humiliations and punish the target population. Within this mind-set chemical weapons might be the weapon of choice for some, easier to develop than biological weapons and capable, if disseminated effectively, of inflicting heavy casualties and causing panic within confined spaces, but biological weapons could prove the consummate instrument of CBW terrorism.

Biological agents are much more potent on a weight-for-weight basis than any of the most deadly chemical agents. In some scenarios their delay in the onset of symptoms may enable the terrorists to flee the scene or even the country concerned. The 'signature' left by the materials may prove difficult, if not necessarily impossible, to trace (as the FBI discovered in their lengthy investigation of the anthrax attacks), and their effects upon a target population could prove extremely hard to counter. Above all, as living micro-organisms with a capacity to grow and mutate, they could cause mass panic. Paradoxically the unpredictability of biological agents, notably the anthrax used in the United States, coupled with their intrinsic characteristics as 'silent, stealthy, invisible and slow-acting' weapons, means that they could induce 'levels of anxiety approaching hysteria'. When the staffs of 43 Capitol Hill offices were surveyed seven months after the attacks, about one in three people who had had no contact with the contaminated office believed that they had been exposed to anthrax and feared that they might die from it.[29]

Agricultural Terrorism

All the case studies of CBW terrorism exemplify the crucial point that terrorism never follows an utterly predictable pattern, and that entirely different cases could arise in the future, including the possibility of agricultural terrorism. There are precedents in the poisoning of Israeli oranges by Palestinian terrorists in 1979, and the reported lacing of Chilean grapes with cyanide in 1989 that caused an estimated loss of $210 million. Historically, too, the ancient tactic of biological sabotage recurred during the First World War, with more elaborate preparations following in the Second World War (see chapter Two). Between 1951 and 1969, the United States invested heavily in the stockpiling of anti-crop agents, and the Soviets followed suit, developing anti-plant, anti-animal and zoonotic pathogens that affect animals and man. Iraq concentrated its efforts on wheat cover smut, doubtless with the intention of targeting the valuable wheat crop of Iran.[30]

If these programmes reflected the feasibility of these weapon systems, the huge economic, social and (sometimes political) costs of naturally occurring diseases and infestations testified to their potential effects. FMDV outbreaks cost Taiwan $7 billion in 1997, and Britain at least £8.5 billion in the slaughtering of between six and a half million and ten million animals, the ruin of many farms and rural businesses, and massive losses for UK tourism.[31] The immensely profitable agricultural sectors of North America and parts of Europe are vital to the economies of their respective countries (agriculture represented some 13 per cent of the US gross domestic product and 17 per cent of employment in 2003). In poorer countries, heavily dependent on a staple crop, even slight reductions in the harvest can raise food prices and fuel food riots among the urban poor. Agricultural sectors are also extremely vulnerable, being impossible to protect (in a military sense) and difficult to monitor on account of the areas involved (American soybeans, for example, are grown over 31 million hectares, representing 50 per cent of the world's crop in 1997 and then worth $16 billion). Animals are even more vulnerable inasmuch as they tend to be reared in large numbers in close quarters (some American feedlots contain from 50,000 to 800,000 animals or in poultry-raising operations up to a million birds).[32]

In such circumstances, bioterrorism could thrive upon the ease of acquiring, moving and dispersing pathogens. Terrorists could find anti-plant pathogens in nature or by purchasing cultures of pathogens from commercial companies (though some of these tend to be less virulent than agents found in nature) or by obtaining animal disease pathogens from sick or dead animals. Once terrorists possessed an anti-animal pathogen, they could, as Michael Dunn of the US Department of Agriculture (USDA) argued, inject the 'pathogen into livestock to amplify it, draw blood from the animal, and produce a deadly serum'. They could then disperse the pathogen through an aerosol spray either by a crop duster or hand-held equipment or by inserting the agent into a ventilation system of an animal enclosure. As many serious, communicable diseases are spread by contact with animal hosts, insects and tainted food or water, a disease such as soybean rust that occurs in Southeast Asia could be spread in the United States by 'placing spores into seed supplies or directly onto fields of production', with the windborne spores capable of travelling 'hundreds of miles in a short period of time, thus infecting vast areas'.[33]

In planning such terrorism the terrorist could handle anti-plant pathogens without personal risk and would not require the skills to 'weaponize' a germ for anti-personnel purposes. 'Plant viruses, bacteria and fungi', as Debora MacKenzie argued, 'are already adept at seeking out and destroying victims that don't move.'[34] Only tiny amounts would be needed as even a limited contamination could take an entire crop off the export market and cause massive economic damage. The pathogens could be released locally by disgruntled individuals, and domestic terrorists, or dispersed over long distances across a border or from offshore. They could also be smuggled across borders where customs officials, however vigilant in detecting the unapproved products of law-abiding passengers or insects in plants, meat products and packing crates, cannot inspect everything (as reflected in the importation of large volumes of illegal drugs). Any undetected vectors could then be dispersed over a single area near a port of entry, so resembling the pattern of a natural outbreak caused by an accidental import.

The long time lag between the introduction of a pathogen and the discovery of the resulting disease that diminished the appeal of these agents for general-war purposes may suit the agenda of terrorists. The time lag may increase the area of the contamination either through the movement of infected livestock, the distances travelled by windborne viruses or the dispersal and breeding of insect vectors. It would also enable the perpetrator to flee the original site of infection and enhance the difficulty of detection, as a biological attack might resemble a natural outbreak, depending on the pathogen selected and its mode of introduction. Indeed the target government, struggling to cope with the effects of the outbreak and any ensuing social dislocation, panic and media attention, may not wish to admit that the outbreak had been intentionally caused. As Dunn observed, 'while biological attacks on agriculture may seem to be less direct, they can be just as insidious and every bit as deadly'.[35]

Whether al-Qaeda had a preference in its choice of weaponry is unclear but it undoubtedly wished to employ CB weapons. As Osama bin Laden once declared, 'We don't consider it a crime if we tried to have nuclear, chemical, biological weapons', and, in the wake of Operation Enduring Freedom (2001), US forces and CNN journalists found evidence that al-Qaeda was far more advanced in its search for WMD than pre-9/11 intelligence had indicated. Computer files and videos found in Kabul confirmed that the organization had begun its research and development on chemical and biological weapons. In a memorandum written in April 1999, Dr Ayman al-Zawahiri complained that the movement had been slow to develop weapons that had a destructive power 'no less than that of nuclear weapons'. Al-Qaeda had apparently earmarked between $2,000 and $4,000 in 'start-up' costs for the programme, code-named al-Zabadi (Arabic for curdled milk). It had begun experiments with toxic agents on dogs and rabbits at a camp near Jalalabad, issued instructions to begin building a laboratory, and acquired both biological agents and commercial equipment for work on 'Agent X' (thought to be anthrax). A progress report complained that the use of non-specialists had 'resulted in a waste of effort and money', and that the recruitment of experts was the 'fastest, safest and cheapest' route to follow.[36]

Prior to the American bombing of al-Qaeda's headquarters and training camps in late 2001, an Egyptian engineer, Abu Khabab, whose real name was Midhat Mursi al-Sayid Umar, had been training Western recruits in how to mount chemical attacks in Europe and possibly the United States at the Darunta complex in the Tora Bora region. Undoubtedly displacement from Afghanistan, and the loss of protection by the Taliban government, undermined the R&D programme, denying al-Qaeda access to large-scale and secure encampments in which they could begin their R&D activities. US intelligence officials, though, were convinced that al-Qaeda sought to reconstitute this programme in other countries wherein they sought refuge. Abu Khabab reportedly worked on 'contact poisons' that could be rubbed on doorknobs, and, in December 2002, was allegedly involved in a plot to deploy a device called a *mubtakkar*, with the aim of dispersing cyanide gas within New York subways. *Mubtakkar*, which means 'invention' in Arabic, is a canister with two interior compartments – one of which contains sodium cyanide and the other hydrogen – and by using a fuse that can be activated remotely, the internal seal can be broken making and then releasing the gas. Zawahiri apparently scuttled the plot, claiming that 'We have something better in mind.'[37]

Just as the CIA released information about this aborted plot, so intelligence sources continued to highlight fragments of evidence, reflecting al-Qaeda's continued interest in developing weapons of mass destruction. Whereas US intelligence had lacked human intelligence sources from within the movement prior to 9/11, it gathered information from at least one inside source by 2003 as well as from captured reports, training manuals, material posted on jihadist websites and apprehended al-Qaeda operatives. There were reports that al-Qaeda had recruited 'competent' scientists and a Pakistani microbiologist, Abdur Rauf; that materials had been gathered to manufacture botulinum toxin and salmonella as well as cyanide gas; that Yazid Sufaat, a biology graduate from Sacramento State University, had been leading al-Qaeda's BW programme in Malaysia before his arrest in late 2001; and that eight al-Qaeda-linked militants (out of thirteen arrested) had been convicted in Jordan of plotting to launch a chemical attack against the US embassy, the prime minister's office and the headquarters of the Jordanian intelligence service in Amman. Reportedly these men were associates of the slain, former leader of al-Qaeda in Iraq, Abu Musab al-Zarqawi.[38]

How much substance there is to these charges is difficult to determine. Intelligence agencies, law-enforcement bodies and judges have erred in previous allegations or in their commentary upon the actions of terrorists. The claims of Judge Kevin T. Duffy that the World Trade Center bombers of 1993 had incorporated sodium cyanide into their bombs have been vigorously disputed, if not the intent of the terrorists then the 'technical, logistical and financial obstacles' confronting them. There have also been highly contentious assertions at lower levels. When nine North Africans were arrested in north and east London in January 2003 on the charge of conspiracy to spread poisons, including ricin, the case resulted in just one conviction (and not specifically on poisons) two years later.

Another blunder occurred in East London on 2 June 2006, when 250 police apprehended two Asians, shooting one of them, on 'specific intelligence' that they were planning to use a chemical bomb but then failed to find any evidence of the bomb in an operation costing £2.2 million.[39] The task of gathering and analysing intelligence correctly on groups of non-state actors remains notoriously demanding but ignoring public warnings by the heads of Western intelligence agencies seems imprudent. Henry Crumpton, when appointed head of counter-terrorism at the State Department, warned of 'micro targets such as al-Qa'eda which, when combined with WMD, have a macro impact'. Like intelligence directors John Negroponte, and his successor J. Mitchell McConnell, Crumpton was reflecting upon the full spectrum of WMD threats, including nuclear or at least radiological weapons, and alluding to the sustained efforts of terrorist groups and their growing expertise in these areas. Dame Eliza Manningham-Buller, when director-general of MI5, agreed that it would be 'reckless' to underestimate the 'capability and intent' of terrorist groups such as al-Qaeda, and that they probably had a capability to make an 'unconventional weapon'.[40]

War on Terror

Understandably, in the wake of the 9/11 attacks the Bush administration took the lead in shaping the international response. Al-Qaeda's assault upon the continental United States was not only the most costly terrorist attack ever in loss of life, economic destruction and psychological shock but it also exposed the vulnerability of the United States and challenged its sense of exceptionalism. The subsequent war in Afghanistan led to a swift overthrow of the Taliban regime that had harboured al-Qaeda and the discovery of evidence confirming the latter's programme to develop WMD. Thereupon President Bush made a series of speeches adumbrating the assumptions and rationale underpinning his 'War on Terror'.

In his State of the Union message (29 January 2002), President Bush seized upon the findings in Afghanistan to claim that the depth of al-Qaeda's 'hatred' was only equalled by 'the madness of the destruction they design'. The evidence, he argued, 'confirms that, far from ending there, our war against terror is only beginning'. Tens of thousands of terrorists, he affirmed, were still at large, viewing the entire world as their battlefield and 'we must pursue them wherever they are.' US objectives were twofold: 'First, we will shut down terrorist camps, disrupt terrorist plans, and bring terrorists to justice. And, second, we must prevent the terrorists and regimes who seek chemical, biological or nuclear weapons from threatening the United States and the world.' In denouncing the so-called 'axis of evil' – North Korea, Iraq and Iran – he claimed that

> By seeking weapons of mass destruction, these regimes pose a grave and growing danger. They could provide these weapons to terrorists, giving them the means to match their hatred . . . We will work closely with our coalition to deny terrorists and their state sponsors the materials, technology, and expertise to make and deliver weapons of mass destruction.[41]

In a subsequent speech before the graduates of West Point (1 June 2002), Bush explained the aims and approach of US counter-terrorism. 'For much of the last century', he declared,

> America's defense relied on Cold War doctrines of deterrence and containment. In some cases, these strategies still apply. But new threats also require new thinking. Deterrence – the promise of massive retaliation against nations – means nothing against shadowy terrorist networks with no nation or citizens to defend. Containment is not possible when un-balanced dictators with weapons of mass destruction can deliver those weapons on missiles or secretly provide them to terrorist allies.

While homeland security, involving the co-location of 22 separate federal agencies under the new Department of Homeland Security (DHS), and missile defence became part of a stronger security posture, the war on terror, argued Bush, would 'not be won on the defensive': Americans must be 'forward-looking and resolute . . . ready for pre-emptive action when necessary to defend our liberty and to defend our lives'.[42]

These priorities found reflection in the *National Security Strategy* issued in September 2002 and reissued, in a slightly modified form, in March 2006. Although the latter admitted scope for a degree of 'tailored deterrence of both state and non-state threats', including the employment of WMD, it reiterated the assertion of the first document that

The greater the threat, the greater the risk of inaction – and the more compelling the case for taking anticipatory action to defend ourselves, even if uncertainty remains as to the time and place of the enemy's attack. There are few greater threats than a terrorist attack with WMD [with the last sentence added in the 2006 report].[43]

Taking action involved more than merely the overthrow of the Taliban regime (November 2001), and the continuing attacks upon the Taliban and al-Qaeda in Afghanistan and north-west Pakistan (including missile strikes launched by the CIA from Predator unmanned aerial vehicles, one of which reportedly killed Abu Khabab on 28 July 2008).[44] If these actions disrupted al-Qaeda's operations and denied it safe havens, they complemented other counter-terrorism measures, notably the efforts of the US Treasury Department to detect and disrupt terrorist financing, money laundering and the financial and other support networks. Launched on 24 September 2001, this was one of the earliest initiatives in the war on terror and one that recognized the need for multilateral assistance, as terrorists had limited investments in the United States. Accordingly, the Bush administration promoted UN Resolution 1373 (28 September 2001), requiring states to criminalize the financing of terrorism and to deny terrorists safe havens, and launched a G-8 Global Partnership Against the Spread of Weapons and Materials of Mass Destruction (Kananskis summit, June 2002). The latter built upon a decade of US non-proliferation assistance for former Soviet states, derived from the Co-operative Threat Reduction programme, sometimes known as the Nunn-Lugar (after its two sponsoring senators) programme of Fiscal Year 1992. By 2005, the United States had invested over $9 billion in the programme, which not only involved nuclear weapons and materials, but also included enhanced security at 35 per cent of Russia's chemical weapon facilities, funding a nerve-agent destruction facility, improving security at four former biological weapon sites, and conducting peaceful, joint US-Russian research at 49 former BW facilities. All these initiatives, including the Proliferation Security Initiative (see chapter Four), reflected a preference for active security co-operation instead of relying upon treaty-based, multilateral disarmament regimes. Having incurred a major terrorist attack on the continental United States, and observed the panic caused by the anthrax letters, the Bush administration felt that it had to pursue an active counter-terrorist programme.[45]

The United States also secured the adoption of UN Security Council Resolution 1540 (28 April 2004) with its pronounced anti-terrorism message. In professing grave concern about 'the threat of terrorism', and the risk of non-state actors obtaining nuclear, biological and chemical weapons and their means of delivery, the Security Council – for only the second time in its history – invoked its Chapter VII powers and required states to act in response to a general rather than a specific threat to international peace and security. It urged all states to criminalize the manufacture, acquisition, development, transport, transfer or use of these weapons, and their means of delivery by non-state actors. It required states to institute effective export controls and enhance security for nuclear, biological and chemical materials. It also established a Security Council Committee to monitor reports from states on their implementation measures but, in spite of an injunction requiring states to report within six months, 62 states had not reported to the Committee by 19 April 2006.[46] Finally, the United States co-operated with partner nations and the World Health Organization (WHO) to strengthen global bio-surveillance capabilities for the early detection of suspicious outbreaks of disease. By revising its International Health Regulations in 2007, WHO required member states to notify the agency within 24 hours of any threat to public health that could affect more than one country.

International action, though necessary and useful, was never going to suffice after 9/11 for an administration that understandably regarded domestic security as its prime concern. Accordingly, it sought to counter the threat of bioterrorism by enhancing bio-security in the United States, specifically the capacity to detect and respond to biological attacks, to secure dangerous pathogens, and to restrict the spread of materials useful in the production of biological weapons. It requested, and largely secured from Congress, massive increases in funding for basic and applied research on diseases of bioterrorism concern, accelerating the purchase and stockpiling of antibiotics and vaccines to combat anthrax, smallpox, and other agents of bioterror, deploying air-sampling detection systems at various sites, and developing rapid diagnostic tools and enhanced medical countermeasures. Similarly, it invested in improving chemical detection and other anti-chemical capabilities at home and abroad, including enhancing the training and equipment of the military forces and emergency responders so that they could manage the consequences of an attack with chemical weapons.

By the end of 2008, the United States had spent some $48 billion on biodefence measures since 9/11. With expenditure on civilian biodefence by the DHS and several other departmental agencies, including Health and Human Services, Agriculture and State, as well as the Environmental Protection Agency and the National Science Foundation, growing from $690 million in FY2001 to $5.4 billion in FY2008 (quite apart from the $5.6 billion earmarked for Project Bio-Shield (July 2004) over ten years), this had all the appurtenances of a crash programme. Counter-terrorism was not the sole concern. The federal expenditure was intended to counter major deficiencies in the American public health infrastructure and to counter both the threats from natural emerging infections, such as pandemic influenza as well as from biological weapons. It also sought to repair critical weaknesses exposed by the anthrax letters: inadequate detection systems at key sites, inadequate stocks of drugs and vaccines to treat victims of known biological weapons, deficiencies in the US laboratory, forensic and diagnostic capabilities, inadequate plans for the distribution of medication and the provision of treatment for mass casualties, and shortcomings in establishing a clear chain of command for incident response and of managing comprehensive communications strategies during crises.[47]

The federal expenditure has multiplied the number of research laboratories working on 'select' agents. By 2007, USDA and the Centers for Disease Control and Prevention (CDC) had registered 13,506 public and private Biosafety Level (BSL)-3 laboratories (to handle agents such as anthrax and tularemia for which a vaccine or treatment exists), and fifteen BSL-4 laboratories, instead of the five registered with CDC and operational pre-9/11 (able to investigate agents with no vaccine or cure, such as Ebola virus and Lassa fever). As of February 2009, some 15,300 staff had active security risk assessment approvals and so had access to agents of bioterrorism concern. In 2003 the United States had also deployed a $1 billion detection system, called Bio-Watch, in 30 major cities to detect certain airborne biological threats, including anthrax, plague and smallpox. On 30 September 2008, it established the National Biosurveillance Center to provide early warning of a BW attack (and other natural epidemics) by linking local, state, federal and private sector surveillance across food, agriculture, public health and the environment. The administration also expanded the Strategic National Stockpile, launched during the Clinton administration. This repository of drugs and vaccines, stored at sites across the United States, now includes over 300 million vaccine doses for smallpox (compared with 90,000 before 9/11), and the reported rates of delivering antibiotics have been cut from 2.5 weeks in 2001 to four days by 2008. The new National Biodefense Analysis and Counter-measures Center, a 160,000 square-foot facility, costing $150 million, opened at Fort Detrick, Maryland, in 2009. Containing a large BSL-4 laboratory, it assesses emerging biological threats to people and agri-culture, and establishes a new national capability for performing forensic analysis of bioterror events.[48]

Whether this massive expenditure has transformed the bio-secu-rity of the United States is debated fiercely. Timely detection remains an issue as the first generation of BioWatch detectors are only deployed in a few cities, may not detect pathogens released indoors, under-ground, on planes, buses or in most subways, and may not provide real-time information for first responders. The General Accountability Office has confirmed that the filters of these devices have to be col-lected manually and then tested in state and local laboratories, producing results within ten to 34 hours. The process is both cost- and labour-intensive, generating false alarms and quality-control prob-lems. New detectors known as Generation 3.0 were intended to replace the existing technology, beginning in 2010 with the replacement com-pleted by 2013. These systems were expected to provide an automated analysis of air samples that could reduce the elapsed time between sampling and testing to four to six hours, and detect a much broader range of identified biological agents. Before acquiring and deploying 100 of these new detectors, each costing $120,000 per unit, with annual maintenance costs of $65,000 to $72,000 per unit, decisions have to be taken on whether to deploy an interim automated system. This, too, is costly (about $100,000 per unit) and would only detect the same range of agents as the current sensors. While the authori-ties of New York City have campaigned for the deployment of the interim units, federal officials have cast doubt on their reliability.[49]

Rather than invest so heavily in large-scale technological responses, some sceptics advocate more investment in improved diagnostic tests at hospitals (and on-the-spot detection and diagnostic devices that can be used in rapid response to any suspected animal disease outbreak), in the training of physicians to diagnose anthrax, botulism, plague and smallpox, and in preparing hospitals with the requisite staff and facilities to cope with large-scale casualties. In June 2006 Grotto and Tucker argued that

Only fifteen states and/or cities currently have the capability to administer stockpiled vaccines and other drugs on a large scale. More than 50% of Americans today live in states that do not have plans to deal with a large number of casualties in the event of a bioterrorist attack, and 20% live in states where hospitals lack medical equipment that would be required in a major emergency.[50]

This continuing vulnerability reflects the fact that the early planning in the wake of the anthrax letters assumed a strictly limited role for the federal government. By devolving homeland security duties to local level, and cutting general-purpose grants for local agencies, the Bush administration sought urgent improvements in counter-terrorism. Apart from building up stocks of NBC suits, mobile command posts, other equipment, and conducting periodic exercises to test the emergency services, most major cities and states formed 'fusion centres' to share intelligence among the military, federal, state agencies, local sheriffs and police departments. This information-sharing model was so successful that it even prompted emulation by the Israelis. Yet major terrorist incidents in the United States, like natural disasters, remained extremely rare, and the abject response to Hurricane Katrina was a timely revelation: as one official admitted,

We initially thought that because all crises are local, our states and high-value-target cities would be able to manage a serious or sustained attack if they received enough federal dollars to help them prepare . . . We now know, as Hurricane Katrina demonstrated, that the federal government would have to take the lead in a true bioterror emergency.[51]

Conclusion

Managing such a vast federal responsibility has not been easy and it testifies to the immense costs that the threat of chemical and biological terrorism can impose. The United States may be peculiar in the vast size of the country, the complexity of the political authority split between federal, state, city and/or local authorities, the vulnerability of so many targets at home and in embassies, bases and facilities overseas and the impossibility of providing complete security against terrorists that could strike whenever they choose. At best the complex layers of detection, containment, rapid response to any incident involving people, animals or plants, emergency medical provision, and decontamination may raise the threshold for a potential attack, and if coupled with the fear of massive retaliation, may provide a limited deterrent. Even if the United States after the war on terror adopts a posture of routine vigilance, investment in co-ordinated intelligence, law enforcement and security operations will remain essential. Faced with external (and in some cases) internal terrorists, and from organizations with a global 'reach', the co-ordination requires an international dimension with allied agencies, monitoring, tracking and intercepting terrorists where possible before they can mount their attacks.

7

The Recurrence of Chemical Warfare in the Middle East

The recurrence of chemical warfare in the second decade of the twenty-first century confounded predictions that the use of chemical weapons could be banned from 'the face of the earth', and claims that it could be inhibited by a moral 'taboo'.[1] The revived usage first by the Syrian regime of Bashar al-Assad, and later by the insurgents of ISIS (the Islamic State in Iraq and Syria), reflected the contextual pressures and opportunities within the Syrian and Iraqi civil wars. Allegations of a Syrian chemical (and biological) warfare capability had a lengthy pedigree and undoubtedly influenced the decision of President Obama to lay down his 'red line' on 20 August 2012 over CW operations in the Syrian civil war. The controversy over the abortive application of the 'red line', the subsequent disarmament efforts of the OPCW and the recurrence of chemical warfare thereafter, coupled with the response of President Donald Trump, warrant further analysis.

The Origins of Syria's Chemical and Biological Weapons Capability

When Judge Webster, as director of the CIA, testified on 9 February 1989 that 'Syria began producing chemical warfare agents and munitions in the mid-1980s, and currently has a chemical warfare production facility',[2] he was merely confirming evidence that the US intelligence agencies had leaked several years previously. Using sources from the Pentagon, the CIA and the State Department, Jack Anderson and Dale Van Atta had revealed that Syria had been in receipt of 'chemical weapons assistance' from the Soviet Union and Czechoslovakia at least since 1973, including 'chemical agents, delivery systems and training'. Only in the midst of the Iran–Iraq War, they added, when Iraq employed chemical agents with impunity, and Iran pleaded for assistance from Damascus, did the lack of an indigenous capability become significant. As the Soviet Union was assisting Iraq's chemical warfare activities, the Syrians sought supplies of precursors, equipment and training from companies in Western Europe. Building an indigenous capability confirmed Syria's reputation as 'the most advanced chemical-warfare capability in the Arab world, with the possible exception of Egypt'.[3] Capable of producing mustard gas and nerve agents in two production sites – one just north of Damascus and the other near Homs[4] – Syria caused even more alarm among US and Israeli sources on account of its delivery capabilities. No longer dependent upon delivering chemical munitions by artillery shells and aerial bombs from Egypt, Syria acquired modernized delivery systems, particularly the highly accurate, short-range ss-21 missiles as well as longer-range Scud missiles.[5]

Coupled with reports about the widespread proliferation of cw capabilities (see chapter Four), Syrian capabilities came firmly into focus. Webster highlighted that Middle Eastern states sponsored terrorism or gave a high priority to covert weapon programmes. Those states, he argued, did not share the Western 'sense of outrage and horror' at the use of chemical weaponry; on the contrary, they viewed it as efficient, cheap and 'another weapon of destruction', a possible counter to a perceived 'nuclear presence in the Middle East'.[6] Although Syria served as an ally of the US-led UN forces that expelled Iraq from Kuwait in the Gulf War (1991), it only gained financially from the experience (several billion dollars from Saudi Arabia and other members of the coalition). Strategically, the regime of President Hafiz al-Assad had not assuaged its sense of insecurity after heavy defeats by Israel, the loss of the Golan Heights and the demonstration of US air power in crushing Iraq. Syria was thought increasingly dependent upon unconventional forms of weaponry to deter Israel, to fight tactically with chemical-armed artillery, aerial bombs and FROG-7 rockets and, *in extremis*, to threaten Israeli cities with chemical missiles. Rear Admiral Thomas Brooks, when Director of Naval Intelligence in 1991, added that this unconventional arsenal included 'an offensive BW capability', which Senator John McCain described as 'R&D and weapons stocks'.[7]

Given the secrecy shrouding these programmes, Syria's diplomacy aroused more suspicions, namely a refusal to ratify the Biological and Toxin Weapons Convention and to sign the Chemical Weapons Convention lest Syria be 'exposed to the nonconventional threat from Israel'.[8] Syria also centralized the control of its military research through the Scientific Studies and Research Centre (SSRC), often known as CERS after its French title, Centre d'Etude et Recherché Scientifique. Ostensibly a civilian enterprise, it worked covertly to establish the production of chemical munitions, beginning with the initial production, albeit on a small scale, of sarin. Importing chlorine-resistant pipes and vessels from a West German glass company facilitated the production of nerve agent. A US National Intelligence Estimate of 1991, now declassified, reported that Syria probably possessed 500-kilogram (1,100-pound) aerial bombs containing sarin. More important, though, in view of the superiority of the Israeli Air Force over its Syrian adversary, was the chemical filling of missile warheads, probably unitary warheads initially on elderly Scuds. Only ten years later, in 1997, Syria began filling bomblets with nerve agent in the cluster warheads of the SCUD-C missiles.[9]

Further refinements included the dispersal of chemical production sites beyond the original centres near Damascus and Homs, including missile complexes at Aleppo and Hama, with another facility in Latakia. Syria also employed various pharmaceutical plants and dummy companies to acquire dual-use chemicals and equipment, importing at least 800 kilograms of precursors in 1993 for the production of the persistent nerve agent VX. Despite the improvement in its indigenous capabilities, Syria still relied upon assistance from China, Iran, North Korea and Russia 'for advanced components and technologies'.[10]

After the open-air testing of a chemical bomb in 1999, Syria conducted a missile test in July 2001, which probably involved a simulated chemical warhead, and two long-range (600–700-kilometre) Scud missile tests in an airburst mode in May 2005. Amid the successful tests were several failures – a SCUD-D missile test in 2005, which fell apart over Turkey, and an explosion at a CW-agent storage facility near Aleppo on 26 July 2007 during the fitting of mustard-gas warheads. The latter caused several fatalities, including engineers from Iran and North Korea. Just as revealing were the deaths of ten North Korean scientists during the Israeli bombing of Syria's secret nuclear reactor at al-Kibar on 8 September 2007, a bombing that left Syria ever more dependent on its chemical, biological and missile capabilities.[11]

Of these capabilities, the chemical component was the most mature, with production sites, munitions, storage bunkers and diverse delivery systems dispersed and concealed across the country. By 2008 Anthony Cordesman, employing publicized findings of US and Israeli intelligence, reckoned that Syria had 'stockpiled 500 to 1,000 metric tons of chemical agents', including 'persistent (vx) and non-persistent nerve agents (sarin) as well as blister agents'. It was also able to deliver chemical agent by artillery shells, bombs and surface-to-surface missiles, probably 'between 100 and 200 Scud missiles fitted with sarin warheads'.[12] In effect, Syria possessed a deterrent against Israel, a capability that could survive, at least in part, an Israeli first strike and pose a potential threat to Israeli forces and cities.

Much less clear was the evidence of an emerging bw capability. Under the scientific direction of the ssrc, and the guise of legitimate 'defensive' research, Syria conducted its r&d in a dispersed array of laboratories and research wings. These were linked to pharmaceutical industries, medical and chemical facilities and veterinary institutes, all under the oversight of the Ministry of Defence. While Israeli sources claimed that Syria had weaponized anthrax, ricin and botulinum toxin in the 1990s, us defence and intelligence agencies insisted that Syria was only 'pursuing the development' of biological weapons before engaging in 'major weaponization or testing related to biological warfare'.[13] Even when John R. Bolton, as the State Department's Under Secretary for Arms Control and International Security, broke with diplomatic protocol and named violators of the btwc at Geneva on 19 November 2001, he merely claimed that Syria 'has an offensive bw program in the research and development stage, and it may be capable of producing small quantities of agent'.[14]

Differences in interpretation doubtless reflected the extreme secrecy that enveloped the bw programme, and the ambiguity of such terms as 'weaponization'. As Cordesman argued, weaponization simply involved the older types of biological weapon, using wet agents in bombs or unitary warheads. The potential effectiveness of these rudimentary weapons would be extremely limited. Were the Syrians able to produce pathogens in dried powders, milled to the appropriate size, microencapsulated and delivered slowly over a long line of flight, using helicopters, cruise missiles or unmanned aerial vehicles, then the effects could be altogether different. In ideal meteorological conditions, they could possibly achieve 'lethalities as high as 50–100 kiloton weapons'.[15] During an extensive interview in December 2007 Dr Jill Dekker, a nato consultant, claimed that Syria had worked on anthrax, plague, tularemia, botulinum, smallpox, aflatoxin, cholera, ricin and camelpox, making 'tremendous gains' from the assistance of the 'Soviets and more recently the Russians and

DPRK' (North Koreans). She asserted that Syria had 'mastered micro-encapsulation which is necessary for aerosol dispersal', experimented with 'parachute dispersal techniques' and undertaken 'field testing with the cooperation of Khartoum'. In making these claims, she criticized the 'US Intelligence Community' for underestimating and denying 'the sophistication of the Syrian biological weapons program'. Despite failing to provide any supporting evidence, Dekker's account is comprehensive in scope and detail,[16] reaching conclusions that James R. Clapper, as the US Director of National Intelligence, would move towards in his congressional briefing of 11 April 2013:

> Based on the duration of Syria's longstanding biological warfare (BW) program, we judge that some elements of the program may have advanced beyond the research and development stage and may be capable of limited agent production. Syria is not known to have successfully weaponized biological agents in an effective delivery system, but it possesses conventional and chemical weapon systems that could be modified for biological agent delivery.[17]

Syria's Civil War and Obama's 'Red Line'

The so-called 'Arab Spring', which began in Tunisia on 18 December 2010 and spread through the region in a wave of protests and uprisings, seeped into Syria in March 2011. As huge demonstrations erupted in the southern city of Deraa, President Bashar al-Assad responded in traditional manner with fierce repression. Defying calls from President Obama and European leaders to step down, and ignoring resignations from his government and army, Assad plunged Syria into a civil war that would eventually displace millions and injure and kill hundreds of thousands. Initially the regime refrained from using chemical weapons, but, in July 2012, US intelligence officials informed the *Wall Street Journal* that they believed Syria had moved chemical weapons out of their storage facilities 'either in preparation for use against the rebels or to safeguard the weapons against capture'.[18] Only ten days later, on 23 July 2012, Jihad Makdissi, a Syrian Foreign Ministry spokesman, declared in a live televised news conference in Damascus:

> Any stock of WMD or unconventional weapons that the Syrian Army possesses will never, never be used against the Syrian

people or civilians during this crisis, under any circumstances. These weapons are made to be used strictly and only in the event of external aggression against the Syrian Arab Republic.[19]

Faced with the virtual admission of a Syrian cw capability, and continuing concerns about its security, or potential use whether authorized or unauthorized, Barack Obama announced at an impromptu press conference on 20 August 2012:

> We have been very clear to the Assad regime, but also to other players on the ground, that a red line for us is that we start seeing a whole bunch of chemical weapons moving around or being utilized. That would change my calculus. That would change my equation.[20]

Although Secretary of State Hillary Clinton had also mentioned a red line in respect of cw use, the president's remarks were soon revealed as unprepared and off-the-cuff, a notable departure from his reputation for precise and cautious statements on foreign affairs. They surprised his advisers, gave false hope to Syrian rebels and contradicted us policy in the Middle East, which, as demonstrated in Libya (2011), gave priority to resolving matters in Iraq and Afghanistan before considering further interventions. Nevertheless, in response to more intelligence that Assad's regime was preparing to use chemical weapons, Obama declared in a speech to the National Defense University (3 December 2012) that 'the world is watching' Assad and those under his command, and that 'the use of chemical weapons is and would be totally unacceptable. And if you make the tragic mistake of using these weapons, there will be consequences and you will be held accountable.'[21]

If Obama hoped that this statement would deter the Assad regime, he was soon confounded. As early as 23 December 2012 his administration faced the first of a myriad of cw allegations. Some of these reports would seem plausible, others less so, as the quality of the evidence was highly variable, and the chain of custody regarding samples taken from alleged attack sites to foreign laboratories open to debate. Often the allegations were coupled with images of dead and/or distressed survivors, the testimony of defectors, anguished accounts by reporters, doctors and spokespersons from non-governmental organizations, the findings of allied governments and charges and counter-charges by the Syrian regime and its motley array of rebels. Much of the commentary sped round the globe on the Internet, on 24-hour news broadcasts and on social media, demanding instantaneous response.

The early allegations referred to attacks that were small in scale. Julian Perry Robinson analysed these allegations up to 26 June 2013, reckoning that they represented '20, perhaps 30, episodes of chemical warfare . . . in which a total of more than 95 people apparently died from poison, and at least 700 more were affected by it'. By that stage, as he rightly noted, the civil war had already claimed the lives of 'at least 93,000 people', while 'hundreds of thousands more have been injured, and a still greater number forced to flee'.[22] Several incidents involved bizarre descriptions of symptoms, and of chemical agents employed such as BZ-CS, an incapacitating and a harassing agent, in an early report from Homs (6 April 2012), all reflecting the 'incentives to spread falsehoods'.[23] Muddying the evidence further was the alleged attack on a regime-held suburb of Khan Al-Asal, near Aleppo (19 March 2013), which reportedly killed twenty individuals, mainly Syrian soldiers, and intoxicated 124 survivors. As both sides claimed that the other was responsible, the Syrian regime invited a UN mission to investigate the event. While the White House discounted use by Syrian rebels, implying that the incident was either an accident or an attempt to frame the rebels, the UN Secretary-General Ban Ki-Moon agreed to send a mission. Both France and Britain requested that its mandate should include the investigation of all CW allegations as well as the Khan Al-Asal incident. Professor Åke Sellström of Sweden would lead the investigation team.[24]

Even more embarrassing for the Obama administration, US allies continued to assert that chemical weapons had been employed. On 25 March 2013 both Britain and France informed the UN that the Syrian regime had used chemical weapons on several occasions since December, and copies of these confidential letters were leaked to the *New York Times*. At a conference in Tel Aviv on 23 April 2013 Brigadier Itai Brun, commander of the research division of the Israeli Defence Force Intelligence Directorate, declared that the Damascus regime 'has used deadly chemical weapons against armed rebels on a number of occasions in the past few months. Probably sarin.'[25] This forced the White House to publicize its own intelligence assessments in letters written by its Legislative Director, Miguel Rodriguez, to two US senators, John McCain and Carl Levin. 'Our intelligence community', wrote Rodriguez, assessed, 'with varying degrees of confidence, that the Syrian regime has used chemical weapons on a small scale in Syria, specifically, the chemical agent sarin'. However, he added that this knowledge 'doesn't tell us when they were used, how they were used . . . We have to act prudently. We have to make these assessments deliberately.'[26] As an exercise in prevarication, these letters bought scant relief, since on the same day the Foreign Office confirmed that scientists at Porton Down had found traces of sarin in soil samples brought back from the outskirts of Damascus. This confirmation was 'extremely serious', said the British prime minister David Cameron: 'this is a war crime.'[27]

Further allegations came from Turkey, where gas victims had been treated in hospital, and most importantly from France. Reporters from *Le Monde* had spent two months on the Jobar front on the outskirts of Damascus with the Free Syrian Army, and had brought biomedical and clothing samples back to the French CBW defence establishment at Le Bouchet. These tested positively for sarin (and confirmed the findings from blood samples sent from another alleged attack in Idlib province). The reporters asserted that Syrian forces had used gas repeatedly in the 'key battleground' of Jobar during April, in the 'areas of toughest fighting' with the encroaching rebels. They collected witness statements from rebel commanders about evacuating the wounded, 'while others were paralysed with fear', and from doctors, including photographs and videoed evidence of the victims. On 13 April a press photographer was present during an attack on a zone of the Jobar front, and had suffered blurred vision and respiratory difficulties for four days afterwards. Jean-Philippe Rémy speculated that the Syrian forces had been cautious in their use of gas, using mixtures of chemicals including tear gas to complicate subsequent analysis, and 'avoiding the kind of massive spread of toxic chemicals that would easily constitute irrefutable proof'. He believed, too, that the CW attacks on the outskirts of Damascus were intended to destabilize rebel units and test international reaction. In more distant fronts, like Adra and Otaiba, he reckoned that 'greater' quantities of gas had been used, judging by the numbers of hospital admissions.[28]

Even if the laboratory evidence, as revealed by French Ministry of Foreign Affairs spokesman Laurent Fabius on 4 June 2013, did not meet the highest standards of scientific proof (Åke Sellström would still require site visits to clarify concerns about the chain of custody),[29] it heaped pressure on the Obama administration. Fabius declared that France 'is now certain that sarin gas has been used in Syria several times and in a localised manner', and nine days later the US Deputy National Security Advisor Benjamin Rhodes had to concede:

> Following a deliberative review, our intelligence community assesses that the Assad regime has used chemical weapons, including the nerve agent sarin, on a small scale against the opposition multiple times in the last year. Our intelligence community has high confidence in that assessment given multiple, independent streams of information.[30]

Nevertheless, in a letter made public on 23 July 2013 to Senator Levin, chairman of the Senate Armed Services Committee, General Martin Dempsey, the chairman of the Joint Chiefs of Staff, unveiled all the costly and risky options of intervening in the Syrian conflict. Of the five options, the most complex involved controlling Syria's chemical weapons, which would require a no-fly zone, air and missile strikes, and inserting 'thousands of troops on the ground' at a cost of over $1 billion a month.[31]

On 21 August 2013, almost a year after Obama's 'red line' declaration and three days after the arrival of twenty UN inspectors in Damascus, American caution would be tested as never before. Early in the morning, after an onslaught of conventional ordnance upon rebel-held suburbs around the capital, CW rockets fell upon residential areas in Eastern Ghouta (2.30 a.m.) and later on areas of Western Ghouta (5.00 a.m.). A temperature inversion maximized the effects of the sarin, and soon thousands of victims, mainly civilians, sought medical treatment. Local activists claimed over 1,200 dead, and laid out scores of corpses, many of them children, for photographs and video evidence (over a hundred video clips could be seen on the Internet within 24 hours), and journalists recorded harrowing tales from first responders and doctors. Despite the limitations of visual evidence, the United States and its allies blamed the Syrian regime (even if a Syrian military commander may have launched the Ghouta attacks without explicit authorization), and pressed for the UN team to visit the sites.[32]

After five days Damascus approved an expansion of the UN team's mandate, and allowed the inspectors to visit Moadamiyah in Western Ghouta and Ein Tarma and Zamalka in Eastern Ghouta.

Having either doubted that this permission would be granted, or feared that the analysis would be much more difficult after a time delay, us allies professed support for punitive military action led by the United States, even without the approval of the un Security Council (where Russia continued to defend the Assad regime).[33] Intervention, though, proved problematic in both Britain and the United States, where memories of intelligence blunders in Iraq, and costly interventions in Iraq and Afghanistan, remained all too vivid. Opinion polls in both countries showed overwhelming majorities against intervention, some generals questioned what a limited strike would achieve, and several analysts questioned whether Assad's choice of weapons should determine us policy or whether action was justified, arguing it was a 'moral nonsense' to distinguish between 'one form of slaughter and another'.[34] Cameron's coalition government chose to place the issue before the House of Commons on 29 August 2013, where arguments couched in moral invective ('one of the most abhorrent uses of chemical weapons'), intelligence assessments about what had happened and who was responsible, and the purported duty of upholding the 'international taboo against the use of chemical weapons' fell upon stony ground. The government was defeated by 285 votes to 272 – the first such defeat of a British government over a war motion in 200 years.[35]

Both the United States and its 'oldest' ally, France, publicized their intelligence findings. While France concluded that the Ghouta attacks were beyond the capacities of the Syrian opposition,[36] the us revealed from 'streams of human, signals and geospatial intelligence' that regime forces, 'operating in the Damascus suburb of Adra', had made preparations for the chemical attack for three days prior to the assault, and that satellites corroborated rocket and artillery attacks on the morning in question. Less convincingly (in the absence of mass funerals) the us assessment claimed that 1,429 people had died, including 'at least 426 children'.[37] As Ralf Trapp, a chemical warfare analyst, prudently argued, the 'precise number of casualties' could neither be established nor verified: the casualty figures, he reckoned, 'ranged from 355 to more than 1,500 people killed, plus many more injured'.[38]

Prudence, though, was conspicuous by its absence when us Secretary of State John Kerry sought to rally American opinion around the strike option. In a series of speeches, interviews and congressional testimony, he declared that the 'staggering scale' of the Ghouta attacks should 'shock the conscience of the world', and that the 'international norm [against chemical warfare] cannot be violated without consequences'. President Obama, he affirmed, 'believes that there must be accountability for those who would use the world's most heinous weapons against the world's most vulnerable people'.[39] On 3 September 2013 he initiated the quest for congressional support by appearing alongside Defence Secretary Chuck Hagel and General Dempsey before the Senate Committee on Foreign Relations. He sought to reassure senators that the intelligence was far more convincing than in 2003, and that the objects of a punitive strike would be to deter and degrade Syria's cw capability, not to intervene in the civil war. Lapsing into sophistry, he claimed that this was not about Obama's 'red line' but 'about the world's red line, it's about humanity's red line, and . . . about Congress's own red line', since it had ratified adherence to the Chemical Weapons Convention. Inhibiting further recourse to chemical warfare would serve both the national security interests of the United States and the stability of the Middle East: this was 'not the time for armchair isolationism', he declared.[40]

The 10:7 split in the committee testified to, if it did not fully reflect, the scale of American disenchantment. At a time when opinion polls were registering barely 23 per cent (Reuters-Ipsos) or 29 per cent (Pew) in favour of a military strike,[41] opposition mounted steadily in both houses of congress. Obama was only able to avoid an embarrassing defeat by Russian intervention on 9 September 2013 after an apparent gaffe by Kerry in London, where he speculated that Syria could avoid a military strike if it handed over all its chemical weapons, which it was not about to do. Russian Foreign Minister Sergey Lavrov immediately suggested that these weapons could be put under international control in a process monitored by international observers, while Syria joined the Chemical Weapons Convention. On the following day Obama postponed the congressional vote, accepted Lavrov's proposal as well as Syria's agreement to join the cwc and thereby avoided any need to uphold his 'red line'. The president later claimed that he had decided not to authorize a strike as early as 30 August, in the wake of Cameron's debacle. A cruise-missile strike, he feared, might imperil the un inspectors, could not eliminate the chemical weapons, and represented a 'trap – one laid both by allies and adversaries' that could drag his administration into another Middle Eastern conflict.[42] If true, then Obama's declaration of a 'red line' was little more than an act of hubris and bluff, and its implementation a display of fecklessness that put American credibility at risk.

The UN Mission and OPCW Inspectors

The UN mission led by Sellström included experts from the World Health Organization and the OPCW. After the Ghouta attack, it had a twofold mandate: first to report on the alleged use of gas in Eastern and Western Ghouta, determining whether and to what extent chemical weapons had been used, not who used them; and second, to investigate another sixteen allegations of chemical warfare. Despite being fired upon by a sniper, the team entered the Ghouta suburbs, spending 26 August in Moadamiyah and 28–9 August in Ein Tarma and Zamalka. It inspected the impact sites, examined remnants of munitions and estimated their likely flight trajectories from the craters and embedded munition parts. It also interviewed over 50 survivors and other witnesses, medically examined 80 survivors and collected blood, hair and urine samples from 34 patients as well as 30 environmental samples. Subsequent analyses of the chemical, medical and environmental samples in OPCW-designated laboratories enabled the mission to issue its report on 13 September 2013. It concluded that chemical weapons had been used 'against civilians, including children, on a relatively large scale', and that there was 'clear and convincing evidence that surface-to-surface rockets containing the nerve agent sarin were used in Ein Tarma, Moadamiyah and Zamalka in the Ghouta area of Damascus'.[43]

The mission took longer to investigate the sixteen alleged gas attacks, each of which had been reported to the UN Secretary-General by Britain, France, the United States and the Syrian Arab Republic. Some of these attacks had been referred by more than one of the above governments. The mission resolved that it had neither sufficient nor credible preliminary evidence to investigate nine of the allegations, all brought by France, Britain and the United States. Risk assessments in the midst of the civil war restricted the mission to two site visits, at Jobar and Bahhariyeh, but the inspectors failed to find primary evidence at either site as each had been corrupted by mine-clearing activities. Nevertheless, the mission revealed additional findings from the analysis of environmental samples taken from Ghouta to confirm the relatively large-scale use of sarin in that incident. Otherwise it interviewed survivors, doctors and, where possible, first responders about the seven cases. It also collected blood samples for analysis and cross-checked the analytical results with medical records. On 12 December 2013 it reported that sarin had been employed in five of these alleged sites – Khan Al-Asal (19 March 2013), Ghouta (21 August 2013), Jobar (24 August 2013) and Ashrafiah Sahnaya (25 August 2013) – but failed to corroborate allegations about Sheik Maqsood (13 April 2013) and Bahhariyeh (22 August 2013). Although the mission could not determine who had employed chemical weapons in the proven cases, the Syrian regime had referred two of the five proven cases (Khan Al-Asal and Ashrafiah), stating that its soldiers were victims of these chemical attacks. Meanwhile the evidence alleged in the vast majority of cases by Western governments failed either to meet the requisite standards of proof or to include a custody chain that the mission could approve.[44]

Overshadowing the Sellström reports, and the debate over Obama's 'red line', was the audacious decision to dismantle Syria's declared chemical weapons programme in the midst of brutal civil war. The process built upon a framework agreement in Geneva between the Russian Federation and the United States of America to complete the elimination of this programme during the first half of 2014, and Syria's accession to the Chemical Weapons Convention, which came into force on 14 October 2013. By 27 September the Executive Council of the opcw had adopted a decision (EC-M-33/DEC.1) that converted the generalities of the framework agreement into a detailed plan of action, and, on the same day, the Security Council of the United Nations endorsed this decision by adopting resolution 2118 (2013).

As early as 1 October the first team of nineteen opcw inspectors arrived in Syria (and additional personnel followed on 10 October) to begin inspecting Syrian facilities and advising the regime on how to prepare for the destruction and removal operations. On 16 October 2013 the UN and opcw established a Joint Mission in Syria (JMIS) under a special coordinator, Sigrid Kaag, to implement and supervise the process. On the same day the Technical Secretariat requested voluntary financial contributions from the opcw states parties to support the destruction of Syria's chemical weapons (receiving €50.3 million by 24 August 2015), supplementing the in-kind contributions such as air transportation for the deployed teams, armoured vehicles for these teams and air transportation for the vehicles. The Secretariat had to report on a monthly basis to the Executive Council about progress in implementing its decision, with the opcw's Director-General, Ahmet Üzümcu, forwarding monthly reports to the Security Council.[45]

Syria had declared a total of 41 facilities at 23 sites, including eighteen CW production facilities, twelve storage facilities, eight mobile filling units and three CW-related facilities. Complementing this large infrastructure was the declaration of approximately 1,000 metric tons of category-1 chemicals, that is, chemicals listed in Schedule 1 of the CWC, largely binary CW precursors for sarin, VX and mustard gas; approximately 290 metric tons of category-2 chemicals; 1,230 unfilled chemical munitions; and two cylinders that did not belong to the regime's forces but were believed to contain chemical agent. Publicized in the Director-General's note of 25 October 2013, this declaration exceeded some external pre-war estimates. In the following month Syria marginally amended its declaration to include 1,260 munitions and provided receipts for chemicals and production equipment procured between 1982 and 2010.[46] At this time questioning the accuracy of the declaration was not the issue it would later become, as the Secretariat wanted to seize the unprecedented opportunity of undertaking a disarmament programme in wartime, and do so with a widespread degree of political support and goodwill.

By November 2013 the OPCW team had completed its inspections of all the declared weapon stocks and production sites. It had also delivered on the Executive Council's first requirement by monitoring the destruction of all the declared production and mixing and filling equipment, rendering it useless or inoperable by the target date of 1 November 2013. This was important, as Ralf Trapp argued, since the Syrian forces used a binary system for the safe storage, loading and movement of precursor chemicals before mixing the two precursors (methylphosphonyl difluoride (DF) and isopropanol) with hexamethylene tetramine to produce sarin shortly before using the agent. 'Once the mixing and filling equipment had been rendered inoperable, under the watchful eyes of the inspectors,' Trapp claimed, 'the Syrian army had lost its means of delivering sarin effectively.'[47] While inspectors continued to monitor and verify destruction activities at 22 of the 23 declared sites (one was inaccessible on account of safety and security reasons and key items were moved from it to other accessible sites), and used sealed GPS cameras to support the verification, the next phase involved the removal of Category-1 chemicals from Syria for destruction outside its territory. The UN and OPCW formed an Operational Planning Group (OPG), consisting of 30 experts from various backgrounds, to prepare a plan that would protect people and the environment throughout the process of transportation and destruction. Given the priority of removing the chemicals for destruction outside Syria (hitherto, under the cwc, all destruction of cw capabilities had occurred within host countries), states parties had to modify the legal and regulatory procedures of the cwc. Thereupon a diverse range of states engaged in supplying maritime and transportation assets, surveillance and medical support equipment, 260 shipping containers, cw emergency response capabilities, fire-fighting and self-defence units. The removal operation relied upon assistance from the United States, Britain, Russia, China, Denmark, Norway, Finland and the Cypriot port of Limassol, and access through the Syrian port of Latakia. The jmis team verified the process to confirm the removal and ensure the non-diversion of chemical agents. At the loading stage they used tags and seals, site visits, analysis of representative samples and remote video photography, and at Latakia, their personnel verified the inventories, inspected seals and took representative samples. Ban Ki-Moon described the Joint Mission as 'working to achieve unprecedented objectives in a uniquely challenging environment, and in an extremely short period of time'.[48]

However, the opcw's plans to destroy these chemicals by hydrolysis in field-deployable cw destruction facilities that the United States would commission, and airlift to a country in the vicinity of Syria, proved abortive. A succession of states from Norway to Albania found a host of regulatory, legal and technical reasons for refusing to do so. This display of '"not-in-my-backyard" politics' forced the enterprise to rely upon us technological ingenuity and a planning process that involved departments across the Pentagon, and between the Pentagon and other agencies of the us government.[49] By reconfiguring two field-deployable facilities so that they could be installed aboard the 35,000-ton us maritime vessel *Cape Ray*, the us planned to neutralize the most dangerous chemicals (DF and sulphur mustard) aboard ship in the international waters of the Mediterranean Sea. Italy later agreed to provide a container port, Gioia Tauro, where these chemicals could be trans-loaded from Danish/Norwegian transport ships onto the *Cape Ray*. Other binary weapon components would be taken to the uk, the United States and Finland for destruction. Following the hydrolysis operations, the *Cape Ray* would take the chemically altered effluent in 269 international standard organization containers to Finland and Germany to be disposed of as industrial toxic waste.[50]

Yet the difficult security circumstances in Syria delayed the packaging, loading and transportation of hazardous materials from the twelve storage sites. As the first shipload left Latakia only on 7 January 2014, several of the original deadlines, both intermediate ones and the final completion of the process by 30 June 2014, would be missed. The removal process, nonetheless, proceeded in a desultory fashion until the final shipments of 22 and 23 June 2014, after the last eighteen containers had left the one remaining storage facility 'to which access had not been possible for several months'.[51] In addition Syrian authorities destroyed all their declared stocks of isopropanol, all chemical munitions and containers that previously held mustard gas. The one outstanding issue concerned the destruction of seven aircraft hangars and five underground structures at twelve cw production sites. While negotiations on these matters continued (and the final hangar was not destroyed until 23 June 2018), the opcw reported that *Cape Ray* had destroyed 600 metric tons of dangerous chemicals well ahead of schedule on 18 August 2014. Within a year of beginning its remarkable endeavour the opcw had destroyed 97 per cent of Syria's declared chemical weapons capacity, and its director-general had accepted the 2013 Nobel Peace Prize on behalf of his organization.[52]

Recurrence of Chemical Warfare in Syria and Iraq

However laudable the destruction programme of the opcw, which inclusive of in-kind support may have cost 'at least a quarter of a billion dollars [£150 million] – maybe more',[53] it did not quench the desire to use chemical weapons within the region. Even in the midst of the removal and destruction programme, doubts surfaced about the completeness of Syria's declaration, and reports circulated about new cw incidents, involving the use of chlorine gas. In its monthly reports to the opcw's Executive Council, Syria revealed two canisters of sarin as abandoned weapons found in rebel-held territory (25 July 2014), and three previously undeclared facilities, including an R&D facility and a production plant at Al-Maliha for ricin (14 July 2014). Although Syria agreed to destroy the Al-Maliha plant (26 November 2014), the ricin revelations merely underscored that Syria's bw programme had never been part of the opcw's mandate. Nevertheless, the opcw probed Syria's declaration through a Declaration Assessment Team that made fifteen visits to Syria in two years, collecting samples and discussing unresolved issues with Syrian officials, including the reported discovery of traces of sarin and vx at an undeclared military facility.[54] Ultimately the OPCW's director-general reported on 6 July 2016 that outstanding issues with the Syrian Arab Republic had not been resolved. He complained about the 'lack of original documentation', new information that contradicted earlier narratives and a 'lack of access to and engagement with senior leadership within the Syrian chemical weapons programme'.[55]

Further reports indicated that the Assad regime was ready to resume its chemical attacks while the disarmament programme was underway. As early as 11 April 2014 its helicopters allegedly dropped barrel bombs of chlorine on Kafr Zeta, a small town north of Homs, and further chlorine attacks followed at Talmenes (21 and 24 April 2014) and Al Tamanah (on five reported occasions from 12 April to 25–26 May 2014). At the behest of the UN the OPCW created a fact-finding mission to establish the facts surrounding these allegations but not responsibility for alleged use. Although the mission tried to visit Kafr Zeta in May 2014, it came under fire and had to turn back. Forced to operate at a safe location outside Syria, it carried out witness interviews with victims, first responders, doctors and eyewitnesses and, after the publication of its first report in mid-June, was inundated with video, medical records and other evidence. By 10 September 2014 the mission reported 'compelling confirmation' that chlorine gas – a dual-use, industrial chemical not covered in Syria's declaration – had been used 'systematically and repeatedly' in attacks on all three sites in northern Syria. It repeated this conclusion with 'a high degree of confidence' in a voluminous report issued on 18 December 2014.[56]

Condemnation of the use of chlorine gas as a weapon by the UN Security Council in Resolution 2209 (2015), passed on 6 March 2015, was the only international response. The Obama administration was not about to intervene directly and, in the face of Russian opposition, could not muster a consensus on the OPCW's 41-state Executive Council to impose international sanctions upon those responsible. Even a subsequent Resolution 2235 (2015) of the UN Security Council, passed on 7 August 2015, which established an OPCW-UN Joint Investigative Mechanism (JIM) 'to identify to the greatest extent feasible individuals, entities, groups or governments that were perpetrators, organisers, sponsors, or otherwise involved in the use of chemicals as weapons, including chlorine or any other toxic chemical, in the Syrian Arab Republic', gave the JIM only a one-year mandate.[57] This mandate, though extended once, eventually fell victim to a Russian veto in the

UN Security Council on 24 October 2017, and it never endowed the JIM with judicial authority or the ability to make a formal judicial determination of criminal liability.

Even worse reports of chemical incidents proliferated at an alarming rate, including allegations that Islamic State had begun using mustard gas in their mortar attacks upon Kurdish soldiers and civilians in northern Iraq and Syria (June–August 2015). Having over-run Saddam's old chemical weapons complex at Al Muthanna, ISIS had demonstrated an interest in developing chemical weapons by using chlorine in improvised explosive devices against Iraqi police. The subsequent incidents in northern Iraq, where German troops on a training mission reported a chemical attack upon the town of Makhmour (11 August 2015), prompted an investigation by a Franco-American team. As early as 21 August 2015 the US issued preliminary confirmation that ISIS militants had used sulphur mustard.[58] OPCW inspectors also investigated an incident at Marea in the Aleppo gov-ernorate (21 August 2015), involving several artillery shells filled with sulphur mustard. They revealed that ISIS had manufactured sulphur mustard, possibly based on the work of Iraqi scientists in laboratories at the universities of Mosul and Tel Afar, before these were bombed and the research relocated to the residential suburbs of Mosul. The production revelation, as Ahmet Üzümcu claimed, 'proves that they [ISIS] have the technology, know-how and also access to the materi-als which might be used for the production of chemical weapons'.[59]

The three-member Leadership Panel of JIM eventually confirmed that ISIS was responsible for the Marea attack but, in taking over a year to do so (21 October 2016), demonstrated that the painstaking processes of the OPCW were not keeping pace with an intensifying civil war. JIM had reported on Marea as part of an investigation into nine cases, which the fact-finding mission determined had involved the use of chemical weapons. Yet it could not attribute responsibil-ity in five of these cases, affirming only that the helicopters of the Syrian Arab Armed Forces had dropped barrel bombs or other devices to spread chlorine 'or a chlorine derivative' at Talmenes (21 April 2014), Sarim (16 March 2015) and Qmenas (16 March 2015). Even in these cases, and at Marea, it could not identify any of the actors involved 'owing to inconsistencies' in the evidence. That evidence extended far beyond the voluminous information gathered by the fact-finding mission, and included 8,500 pages of documents, 200 interview transcripts, over 950 photographs and more than 450 videos, 330 pages of forensic material and 3,500 multimedia files, all of which the Leadership Panel and four research institutes analysed. As Virginia Gamba, head of the panel, explained, the in-depth investigation 'had to be done in an independent, impartial, objective, and very professional manner, because we were very much being looked [at] by everybody'.[60]

Meanwhile the chemical war continued apace, with rumours and allegations multiplying even faster than the credible reports. Broader surveys of the gas war differed in their understanding of the numbers, dates and notions of credibility. In a programme aired on 15 October 2018, BBC Panorama and BBC Arabic reviewed 164 reports of chemical attacks since September 2013. It discounted all those from one source or bereft of sufficient evidence and focused on the remaining 106. Barred from filming in Syria, it could not 'categorically verify' the evidence in these incidents but the 106 included 37 cases that the fact-finding mission and the disbanded JIM had confirmed, and another eighteen reported by the UN Human Rights Council's Independent International Commission of Inquiry on Syria. The Berlin-based Global Public Policy Institute (GPPi) also reviewed 498 reports of chemical incidents from 23 December 2012 to 7 April 2018, dismissing 162 but assessing 336 as 'credibly substantiated', 'confirmed' or 'comprehensively confirmed', with 111 in the final category (that is, either confirmed by competent international bodies or supported by at least three independent sources). Like the BBC, the GPPi relied upon 'open-source' information, both witness testimony and original interviews with victims, medical workers and 'political representatives and members of rebel groups'.[61]

Despite their methodological differences, the surveys agreed that the Syrian armed forces were responsible for nearly all these attacks, employing chemical weapons as force multipliers for their conventional operations. They employed chemicals tactically in defence of besieged sites, such as the beleaguered air base at Deir Ezzor (2015), operationally in clusters of attacks before rebel offensives as in Hama and Idlib (2014), and again in Idlib (2015), and then to achieve major strategic objectives, including the recapture of Aleppo at the end of 2016 and Eastern Ghouta in early 2018. Chlorine was the agent of choice: it was cheap, readily available and easily dispersed from improvised munitions (both short-range rockets fired in salvos against enemy trenches and 'barrel bombs' dropped by helicopters against civilian communities). Moreover, as Julian Tangaere, a former OPCW inspector, observed:

> If you go to a site where a chlorine attack has happened, it's almost impossible to get physical evidence from the environment – unless you're there within a very short period of time. In that sense, being able to use it leaving virtually no evidence behind, you can see why it has happened many, many times over.[62]

Most of the reported attacks from 2014 to 2018 occurred in rebel-held areas, both the northern provinces of Hama and Idlib and the Ghouta suburbs round Damascus. None were attributed, as the regime alleged, to rebel forces other than ISIS, and of the five cases attributed to Islamic State, JIM confirmed its responsibility for a second attack at Umm Hawsh on 16 September 2016.[63] Aerial delivery, usually at night or in the early morning, appeared the preferred mode of operation, lending credence to the presumed responsibility of the Syrian air force. Employing chlorine as an 'instrument of collective punishment against populations supporting or hosting insurgents' fulfilled the Syrian counterinsurgency strategy. This aimed to inflict such pain and terror upon civilian communities that they either withdrew their support from the insurgents or fled the locality. As the GPPi survey observed, even when the Syrian army was ceding territory before rebel offensives in 2014 and 2015, its air force pounded rear areas with conventional and chemical ordnance, demonstrating the inability of the rebels to protect their civilians: the regime, in effect, succeeded in its 'political goal of separating insurgents and civilian populations'.[64] Later, when the tide of battle changed, assisted by Russian aerial strikes, Iranian forces and Hezbollah militias, and forced rebels into ever smaller urban pockets in Aleppo and later Douma, chemical attacks served as part of the *coup de grâce*. Mass exoduses followed gas attacks in the recapture of Aleppo (22 December 2016) and the surrender of Douma (9 April 2018), two pivotal events in the civil war. As Dr Lina Khatib, head of the Middle East and North Africa programmes, Chatham House, asserted, 'there's nothing that scares people more than chemical weapons', and so in the final stages of government offensives, chemical weapons helped 'to make the local population flee'.[65] Tangaere agreed that chemical weapons had enabled the regime to achieve crucial outcomes at minimal risk, and so 'have subsequently been shown to be worth the risk'.[66]

Calculations of risk, though, changed with the election of Donald Trump as president of the United States (5 November 2016).

Superficially this may seem surprising; candidate Trump, campaigning on an 'America first' platform, had evinced little interest in foreign policy beyond criticizing the Middle Eastern interventions of the Bush and Obama administrations, and advocating the crushing of 'radical Islamic terrorism', specifically ISIS, a long-term enemy of the Assad regime. Yet the imagery of large numbers of dead and suffering after an aircraft dropped a chemical bomb upon Khan Shaykhun (4 April 2017) horrified Trump, especially pictures of dead and suffering babies reportedly placed before him by his daughter, Ivanka. Eager to punish Assad, and embarrass Obama, he chose from an array of strike options prepared by Defence Secretary James Mattis, a cruise-missile strike that with careful targeting, and a fifteen-minute advance warning, would minimize the likelihood of killing Russians. On 7 April 2017 USS *Porter* and USS *Ross* fired 60 cruise missiles, one of which fell into the Mediterranean Sea while the others hit Shayrat airfield. On the following day the president issued one of his characteristic tweets: 'If President Obama had crossed his stated Red Line in The Sand, the Syrian disaster would have ended long ago! Animal Assad would have been history!'[67]

Assad would not be imperilled by this action but Trump earned widespread plaudits for his resolute response. Britain and France approved a joint response with the United States in the event of another chemical attack in Syria, and the OPCW's fact-finding mission, and JIM in its final report, confirmed the use of sarin at Khan Shaykhun. JIM was confident 'that the Syrian Arab Republic' was 'responsible for the release of sarin'.[68] Syria incurred no further punishment, and reports of chemical attacks multiplied from July 2017 onwards, predominantly in Eastern Ghouta. They represented a very small proportion of the munitions expended, but as the rebels retreated steadily towards Douma, and refugees crowded into its basements, they became increasingly vulnerable to chlorine attacks. The decisive chlorine assault of 7 April 2018 reportedly killed at least 43 and injured hundreds. Once again Trump expressed outrage over the images from Douma and threatened the Assad regime with a punitive response. The governments of Britain and France proffered support without reference to their legislatures (where opposition to 'gesture bombing' was reportedly rife on both sides of the House of Commons).[69] French and US intelligence claimed that they had proof of the chemicals involved, including 'an unnamed nerve agent' in the US account, which would be contradicted subsequently by the painstaking analysis of the OPCW fact-finding mission. Traces of chlorinated organic chemicals were reported in both accounts.[70]

Lacking any authorization by the UN Security Council, where Russia even vetoed a US resolution to create an inquiry that could apportion blame for the chemical attacks in Syria (10 April 2018), the three allies launched their strike on 13 April 2018. It involved almost twice as many missiles as the previous attack, aimed at three sites in Syria: the Barzah research centre near Damascus, an alleged CW storage site at Him Shinshar and a command post at Him Shinshar, about 7 kilometres from the storage facility. Fifty-seven US Tomahawk cruise missiles and nineteen joint air-to-surface stand-off missiles destroyed the Barzah centre, which the OPCW had inspected from 26 February to 5 March 2017, failing to find 'any activities inconsistent with obligations under the [Chemical Weapons] Convention'.[71] The allies aimed another nine Tomahawk cruise missiles, eight British Storm Shadow missiles, five French naval cruise missiles and two SCALP cruise missiles at the storage site, and seven French SCALP missiles at the command post. While Trump blustered about 'mission accomplished', Lieutenant-General Kenneth F. McKenzie, director of the US joint staff, accepted that Syria probably retained a 'residual element' of its chemical weapons programme: 'I'm not going to say that they're going to be unable to continue to conduct a chemical attack in the future. I suspect, however, they'll think long and hard about it.'[72]

Although pundits differed in assessing the effects of the bombing, the Syrian CW programme suffered a further blow from the murder of Aziz Asber, the director of the SSRC, in a car bomb (4 August 2018), a killing claimed by the Abu Amara Brigade but blamed on Israel by the Syrian authorities.[73] As the civil war entered its ninth year, any overall evaluation of the chemical war might be premature. More than a year after the allied punitive aerial strike, another chlorine attack on the village of Kabana (19 May 2019)[74] reportedly occurred during the assault on Idlib province. Even if chemical weapons accounted for only a tiny proportion of the 560,000 fatalities (as recorded by the Syrian Observatory for Human Rights on 10 December 2018), they have been an integral component of Syria's counterinsurgency strategy. Used tactically, operationally and strategically, they spread fear and terror and multiplied the effects of conventional ordnance. They also embarrassed the United States through Obama's ill-considered 'red line' and overwhelmed the resources of the OPCW. However remarkable the destruction and removal of 1,300 tons of chemical weapons during a civil war, the coerced declaration by Syria did not mean, as John Kerry rashly claimed, 'We got 100 per cent of the chemical weapons out.'[75] The OPCW inspectors fastidiously investigated subsequent allegations, using permission to apportion blame accorded by a special session of the Conference of State Parties on 27 June 2018 after the Novichok revelations (see chapter Eight). However, the first report of the Investigation and Identification Team only appeared on 8 April 2020, and referred to attacks on Ltamenah (24, 25 and 30 March 2017), involving two sarin bombs and a cylinder containing chlorine, which affected at least 106 persons.[76] In sum, the OPCW found itself outpaced by events on the ground and in the air, not least the punitive air strikes ordered by President Trump. Ultimately the exercise of raw military power may be the only means of upholding the international convention against the development, production and use of chemical weapons, but even as a last resort this may have limited impact.

8

Political Assassination
by Poisoning

Political assassination with chemical, biological and radiological (CBR) weapons may be rare but the process has precedents and distinctive characteristics. Unlike assassination by revolvers (Indira Gandhi, 1984), rifles (John F. Kennedy, 1963), bombs (Airey Neave, 1979) or edged weapons (Hendrik Verwoerd, stabbed with a dagger, 1966), many of which have involved lone assassins, CBR killings have all been state-sponsored affairs. Such killings may be infrequent because several plans have been aborted, including the MI5 plan to kill Colonel Gamal Abdel Nasser with nerve agent and the CIA's proposed poisoning of President Patrice Lumumba of the Congo, while others have failed, including the CIA's many unsuccessful attempts to kill President Fidel Castro with a range of poisons.[1] Political assassination by poisoning has been a fraught and unpredictable affair, with outcomes not always as the perpetrators desired. In these cases, too, the instruments of assassination or attempted assassination, whenever revealed, have often triggered political outrage and occasionally international repercussions. The Novichok poisonings in the UK (2018) may have been relatively recent events, but the precedents set by the deaths of Georgi Markov (11 September 1978), Alexander Litvinenko (23 November 2006) and Kim Jong-nam (13 February 2017) all exposed the vulnerability of dissidents from certain countries living in foreign lands.

Poisoning Precedents

Russia, and the former Soviet Union, has a long history of eliminating 'enemies of the people', whether defectors living in exile, political adversaries or national leaders. The methods employed have ranged from the crude and opportunistic use of an ice pick driven into the skull of Leon Trotsky (20 August 1940) to the random burst of gunfire as special forces stormed the presidential palace in Kabul to kill

President Hafizullah Amin (27 December 1979) and the employment of two laser-guided missiles, triggered by the victim's use of a mobile phone, to destroy Chechen president Dzhokhar Dudayev (21 April 1996). Poison appealed periodically as the KGB (the Soviet security and intelligence service) offered nerve agents and other poisons to the intelligence services of other Soviet bloc countries. In 1957 the KGB tried to liquidate another defector, one of its former officers, Nikolai Khokhlov, with radioactive thallium, possibly its first experiment with a radioactive poison (and chosen in the hope that it would degrade and leave no trace in an autopsy).[2]

Initially poison in the form of a crushed cyanide ampoule fired in a jet from a spray gun proved more effective in eliminating two leading Ukrainian émigrés, Lev Rebet in October 1957 and Stephen Bandera in October 1959. However, the assassin, Bohdan Stashinsky, became disillusioned with these 'special tasks' and defected with his girlfriend to West Berlin just before the Wall was erected in August 1961. Stashinsky's subsequent trial in Karlsruhe (October 1962) generated so much adverse publicity that the Politburo decided to abandon assassination as a normal arm of policy outside the Soviet bloc, other than on rare occasions such as the murder of President Amin. The KGB, nonetheless, persisted with acts of sabotage, efforts to track down defectors, intimidation of exiles like Rudolf Nureyev and the use of terrorist groups as proxies in its war against the United States and its allies.

Some of its Warsaw Pact security and intelligence allies were much less cautious, notably the Bulgarian Durzhavna Sigurnost (DS). Having abducted Boris Arsov, an exile, from Denmark, who had criticized the regime of Todor Zhivkov, they also shot dead three exiles in Vienna in 1975 before being tasked with eliminating Georgi Markov. He had defected in 1968 and then used the BBC World Service, Deutsche Welle and Radio Free Europe to make sarcastic and withering criticisms of the Bulgarian regime. After the DS sought the assistance of the KGB's poison laboratory, the agencies agreed to experiment with an umbrella that could be employed as 'a silenced gun capable of firing a tiny pellet containing a lethal dose of ricin'.[3] This would be used on 7 September 1978 when Markov was waiting at a bus stop on Waterloo Bridge, London. He felt a sudden sting in his right thigh and turned around to see a man picking up the umbrella. The latter duly apologized and got into a taxi. Markov did not feel any immediate ill effects but succumbed the following day, entering hospital, and died on 11 September. An autopsy recovered the pellet but failed to find any ricin, as it had decomposed. Fortunately news of Markov's assassination alerted another Bulgarian émigré, Vladimir Kostov, about the significance of a similar incident he had experienced in the Paris Métro on 26 August 1978. On this occasion the shot had come from a small bag and not an umbrella. Nearly a month later, on 25 September, doctors removed an intact steel pellet from his back, which revealed that ricin had been the poison.[4]

Apart from silencing a well-known and charismatic critic of the Bulgarian regime on Zhivkov's birthday, and so doubtless intimidating other defectors, the umbrella weapon had proved effective in many other ways. The delayed action of the ricin enabled the perpetrator to escape, and the unusual poison and mode of delivery baffled both those trying to treat the victim and those who investigated the crime. While the micro-engineered pellet indicated the likelihood of a state sponsor, confirmation had to wait upon the defection of senior KGB officers, Oleg Kalugin and Oleg Gordievsky. In working with Bulgarian counterintelligence, the KGB laboratory, as Kalugin recollected, 'decided that the best way was by shooting Markov with a tiny poison pellet, no bigger than the head of a pin. The poison to be used was ricin.'[5] Despite these remarks, and the subsequent allegation of a Bulgarian journalist, Hristo Hristov, that Francesco Gullino, a Dane of Italian origin, was the sole agent of the Bulgarian security services working in London at the time of the murder, there was never enough evidence to press charges against him.[6] So the Markov murder remained one of the classic assassinations of the Cold War era.

Somewhat less successful – insofar as the poisoning caused an immense controversy, the alleged murderers were named and the whole incident became the subject of numerous books and a public inquiry – was the murder of Alexander Valterovich Litvinenko. A former member of the Russian Federal Security Service (FSB), he had fled to Britain in 2000, where he was granted asylum and continued to work as a writer, journalist and consultant for the British intelligence agencies. His sudden illness on the evening of 1 November 2006 led to hospitalization and later his death on 23 November from poisoning by radioactive polonium-210. The incident had immediate precedents as under Vladimir Putin, Russian spy agencies had apparently resumed their 'special tasks'. These included their probable involvement in the mysterious deaths of Lecha Ismailov, a Chechen guerrilla commander (2002), and Roman Tsepov, a former Putin bodyguard and founder of a private security firm (2004). They both fell ill after drinking tea with FSB agents and endured ghastly deaths: Ismailov suffered skin peeling off his head, hair loss and organ failure; Tsepov, vomiting, diarrhoea and a catastrophic fall in white blood cells. Poison may also have killed Amir Khattab, another Chechen militant, in 2002, and the Duma deputy, Yuri Shchekochikhin, in July 2003, and been the weapon in the attempted murder of Viktor Yushchenko, the pro-Western presidential candidate in Ukraine, in 2004. Poisoned with dioxin, Yushchenko's face became jaundiced and covered in blisters but he later made a full physical recovery.[7]

The FSB, like the KGB before it, had access to a covert poisons laboratory, the successor to the Kamera (or 'the Cell' in Russian) of the Stalinist era. Housed in a building erected near Moscow during the early 1980s, its formal title was Scientific Research Institute No. 2 (Nauchno-Issledovatelsky Institute No. 2 or NH-2). Even this body, though, required cooperation with other ministries, and probably the coordination of these agencies at the highest level, before it could plan the killing of someone with a rare nuclear isotope.[8]

The poisoning of Litvinenko, then 43 years of age and in excellent health, occurred on 1 November 2006 in the Pine Bar of the Millennium Hotel in London, which overlooked Grosvenor Square. Having taken three or four swallows of cold green tea, he began vomiting in the early hours of 2 November and was admitted to Barnet Hospital the following day, and later University College Hospital. By 20 November he had suffered hair loss, severe bone marrow failure and gut damage, followed by cardiac arrests. On 23 November, after the third cardiac arrest, he died at 9.21 p.m. On this occasion the delayed action hardly benefited the perpetrators, as Litvinenko spent his time in hospital protesting to family, fellow dissidents including the oligarch Boris Berezovsky, journalists and the police about being poisoned on the orders of Putin. On 21 November he approved the taking of a photograph of himself, bald, gaunt and beset with medical monitoring equipment – an iconic image that went round the world. He also signed a deathbed statement, declaring 'You may succeed in silencing one man but the howl of protest from around the world will reverberate, Mr Putin, in your ears for the rest of your life.'[9]

Poisoning by polonium-210, which was only detected from the analysis of urine samples at Atomic Weapons Establishment on 23 November, proved invaluable in tracing the movements of the two suspects, Andrei Lugovoi and Dmitri Kovtun. Contamination analyses, detecting alpha radiation, demonstrated that the two men had tried to murder Litvinenko during a previous visit to London over 16–18 October 2006, and that Lugovoi had carried the poison with him during a second visit over 25–28 October. The trail of contamination was found on aircraft seats (and lockers) and in bars, hotel rooms, toilets, cars, restaurants, offices, a night club, a block of seats at the Emirates Stadium (where the Lugovoi family watched CSK Moscow play Arsenal after the fatal poisoning) and a meeting room where drinks were left unconsumed on 17 October (but Litvinenko still vomited later that night just from being near the poison). The levels of primary contamination were particularly severe in hotel rooms, notably the U-bend of a bathroom used in a Best Western (16 October), in a bathroom bin and on towels in the Sheraton (25–27 October), and in the U-bend of a sink in the Millennium (1 November). After Kovtun visited Hamburg (28–31 October), contamination was found in several houses, cars and a bed used by him. 'A very expensive poison' was his memorable quote, and, as Luke Harding added, it 'had left a very detectable signature.'[10]

The form of poisoning had also highlighted state involvement. Litvinenko died because he ingested 26.5 micrograms or 4.4 gigabecquerels of polonium, a quantity that far exceeded survivability levels. Consequently, Professor Norman Dombey (University of Sussex) asserted that at least 50 micrograms must have been put into the teapot, and that the assassins had a considerably larger amount at their disposal over the period from 16 October to 1 November. Given the purity of polonium used to kill Litvinenko, Dombey reckoned that a supply reactor was the most likely source. The only surviving commercial producer of polonium-210 in the world was in Russia, namely the Mayak/Avangard facilities, and the requisite quantities could have been diverted from this source. However plausible the circumstances of the assassination, even Sir Robert Owen's public inquiry (2014–16) conceded that any powerful high flux reactor, as the Russians claimed, could have produced 50 micrograms of polonium-210 by irradiating bismuth-209. So the evidence, if not conclusive, certainly indicated a nuclear reactor source, and hence state control.[11]

Fortunately international relations are not bound entirely by legal niceties. Lugovoi and Kovtun had no personal motive in murdering Litvinenko but they were caught on camera together with their victim by the Millennium Hotel's closed-circuit television (CCTV), and were undoubtedly ordered to carry and administer the lethal poison. They may not have known the name and properties of polonium-210, treating it with reckless abandon, but Lugovoi was still sufficiently proud of his role to send a T-shirt to Boris Berezovsky in July 2010 bearing the slogan: 'CSKA Moscow Nuclear Death Is Knocking Your Door'.[12] Lugovoi was by no means the only former KGB and FSB operative who regarded Litvinenko's criticisms before and after he left Russia of the Russian state in general, and the FSB in particular, as treacherous. As a campaigner and commentator, Litvinenko had sought to expose the mass murders of the FSB as well as its corruption and collusion with organized crime. He had become a prominent associate of Boris Berezovsky and Akhmed Zakayev, both leading critics of the Putin regime, had accepted a consultancy with British intelligence, and had offered to expose the activities of the 'Russian mafia' in a Spanish court. As Owen concluded, 'members of the Putin administration, including the President himself and the FSB, had motives for taking action against Mr Litvinenko, including killing him, in late 2006.'[13] Putin defended the assassins from external charges, refused to extradite them, claiming that this would infringe the Russian constitution, and in 2015 honoured Lugovoi for services to the fatherland.

If the primary aim was to punish a traitor, the poisoning also served as a warning or a deterrent to like-minded exiles. This does not mean that the FSB was responsible for any or all fourteen of the suspicious deaths in the UK, including Berezovsky, found hanged in his bathroom (March 2013). Yet the pattern of accidents, suicides and natural deaths was remarkable, not least Alexander Perepilichnyy, a fit 43-year-old former Russian banker and whistleblower, found dead after jogging in Weybridge, Surrey (November 2012). The police verdict of death by cardiac arrest held for several years until further tests in 2015 found a rare Asiatic poison, *Gelsemium elegans*, in his stomach.[14] At the very least the UK had developed a chequered history as a place of refuge for Russian exiles, a reputation that Sergei Skripal and his daughter Yulia would soon test.

Meanwhile another extraordinary murder occurred in the departure lounge of Kuala Lumpur international airport on 13 February 2017. Kim Jong-nam, the half-brother of Kim Jong-un, was travelling under a pseudonym to his home in Macau when two women assaulted him by wiping a cloth laced with the nerve agent VX over his face. Kim Jong-nam, rubbing his eyes and complaining of dizziness, sought medical help but died en route to a hospital within fifteen to twenty minutes of the incident. Caught in the act on CCTV, Siti Aisyah, an Indonesian woman, and Doan Thi Huong, a Vietnamese, were charged with murder but neither had any motive to kill Kim. Paid to take part in pranks, wiping liquid on people at airports, hotels and shopping malls, they thought that this was another prank for a reality TV show. Four North Koreans, who promptly fled the country, had apparently arranged the event, paying Siti the equivalent of $90 and advising the women to wash their hands after the assault.[15]

Kim Jong-nam, once considered the heir apparent to the former North Korean leader Kim Jong-il, had embarrassed the regime by trying to visit Tokyo Disneyland with a false passport (May 2001). Having fallen out of favour, he moved into exile, where he advocated reform in his native country. South Korean intelligence services claimed that Kim Jong-un had issued a standing order to assassinate him, and that two earlier attempts had failed in 2006 and 2012.[16] Like other murders associated with the North Korean regime, this one demonstrated the priority attached to the regime's security and survival, the reach and ruthlessness of Pyongyang's special operations personnel, and the vulnerability of dissidents living abroad. By choosing VX as the instrument of murder, the regime demonstrated its possession of a highly sophisticated arsenal of chemical weapons. As John V. Parachini (RAND Corporation) testified before the House Foreign Affairs Committee on 17 January 2018, North Korea in its choice of poison may have sent a 'signal' that it possesses 'capabilities short of nuclear weapons and is prepared to use them'.[17]

More importantly, this state-sponsored assassination was an act of defiance by an isolated and embattled regime. It demonstrated a willingness to take great risks by employing untrained and uncommitted operatives in a mode of assault that could easily have gone awry. All manner of mishaps or mistakes might have happened on the public concourse, from identifying the wrong target to encountering resistance or the interception of the assailants. Had the planned use of VX been exposed in a bungled attack, it would have proved profoundly counter-productive. Conversely, the successful outcome from a North Korean perspective revealed the ability of its special operations personnel to track and intercept the target, and to conduct an audacious assault in a public space. It showed, too, an ability to deliver a precise strike with a nerve agent but without the vast collateral damage that occurred in Rangoon on 9 October 1983. On that occasion North

Korea was blamed for a premature bomb explosion that killed 21 people and wounded 46 others but not the principal target, the South Korean president Chun Doo-hwan, who was delayed in traffic. Finally, the successful extraction of the North Korean team from Kuala Lumpur left the criminal investigation foundering: Siti Aisyah was released on 11 March 2019 and Doan Thi Huong on 3 May 2019.[18] Any political repercussions were conspicuous by their absence.

Novichok Poisoning (2018)

Another attempted assassination occurred when Sergei Skripal, a 66-year-old former Russian military officer and double agent, and his 33-year-old daughter, Yulia, were poisoned in England. Yulia had flown in from Russia to visit her father the previous day, but at 4.15 p.m. on 4 March 2018 they were found slipping in and out of consciousness on a public bench in the centre of Salisbury. Both were in a critical condition, with Yulia ashen and foaming at the mouth: they were taken separately by ambulance and air ambulance to Salisbury District Hospital. Two police officers, suffering from twitchy eyes and wheezing, received treatment for their minor ailments, while Detective Sergeant Nick Bailey, the first investigator at Skripal's house, had to be hospitalized in a serious condition. All these victims eventually recovered sufficiently to be discharged from hospital: Bailey on 22 March; Yulia, who regained consciousness after three weeks, began to speak and was discharged on 9 April; and Sergei, unconscious for about four weeks, was eventually discharged on 18 May 2018.

Less fortunate were Charlie Rowley and Dawn Sturgess, who lived in Amesbury, 8 miles from Salisbury. Charlie, having found a discarded perfume bottle some days earlier, gave it to Dawn on 30 June 2018. She sprayed it on her wrists, fell ill within fifteen minutes and died on 8 July. Charlie required hospital treatment, too, but survived. The nerve agent involved in Salisbury and Amesbury, as detected from samples sent to nearby Porton Down, was Novichok, which was identified from information passed to Alexander Yakovenko, the Russian ambassador to the UK, as A-234.[19]

Contextual comparisons with the poisoning of Litvinenko easily followed, as in the statements of Prime Minister Theresa May before the House of Commons on 12 and 14 March 2018. Having reminded the House of the 'barbaric assault on Mr Litvinenko' in her first statement,[20] she deplored this 'unlawful use of force by the Russian State against the United Kingdom' in her second. She also promised 'a full and robust response – beyond the actions we have already taken since the murder of Mr Litvinenko'. In cautious legalistic terminology May described it as 'highly likely' that Russia was responsible for this 'reckless and despicable act', and conceded that the Russian state might have lost control of a 'military-grade nerve agent', allowing it to fall 'into the hands of others'. As the Putin government had spurned the opportunity to supply evidence in support of the second hypothesis, and simply protested Russia's non-involvement, May declared that

> There is no alternative conclusion other than that the Russian State was culpable for the attempted murder of Mr. Skripal and his daughter – and for threatening the lives of other British citizens in Salisbury, including Detective Sergeant Nick Bailey.[21]

Once again Russia had a motive, inasmuch as Skripal was a former colonel in Russia's Main Intelligence Directorate (GRU) but had worked as a double agent for the UK Secret Intelligence Service from 1995 until his arrest in Moscow in December 2004. Convicted of high treason in August 2006, he had reportedly blown 'the cover of 300 Russian agents' and was sentenced to thirteen years in a penal colony. In 2010 he was part of a spy swap when pardoned by President Dmitri Medvedev, and allowed to settle in England. For 'a limited period', Skripal resumed working for British and other Western intelligence agencies, activities that could have made him a target for assassination (an action given legal sanction by the Russian Parliament in 2006).[22] Moscow, nonetheless, denied involvement but Kirill Kleymenov, a television news presenter, mockingly warned 'traitors', and those who 'just hate your country . . . don't move to England', where such people die in 'industrial quantities'.[23] The Russian state or the GRU may have had a motive to kill Skripal and embarrass Britain, but the reason for the choice of Novichok as an instrument of assassination was not so clear.

Novichok

Vil S. Mirzayanov, an analytical chemist who worked in the Soviet and later Russian chemical weapons laboratory, known as the State Research Institute of Organic Chemistry and Technology, had revealed the origins of the Novichok programme in the 1990s. Alarmed by the toxic effects of the new nerve agents, and their potential damage to the environment, he became a whistleblower, writing articles in the Moscow press and giving interviews to Will Englund of the *Baltimore Sun*. Though supported in his claims by Vladimir Uglev, a Soviet chemical weapons engineer, Mirzayanov was arrested and arraigned before a closed trial on 24 January 1994. Under intense foreign pressure this case was abandoned and Mirzayanov allowed to travel to the United States. He later wrote his memoirs, *State Secrets: An Insider's Chronicle of the Russian Chemical Weapons Program* (2008).[24]

In his various disclosures, Mirayanov described how Novichok, meaning 'newcomer' in Russian, emerged from the secret *Foliant* programme launched in the 1970s. This programme had sought to develop weapons that could penetrate the defensive kit of NATO forces while being safer to handle than existing nerve agents and undetectable by contemporary equipment. Hitherto the Soviets had followed Western lines of research, developing Substance 33, also known as R-33, a unitary nerve agent that was very similar to VX but was later found to be much less stable in storage. After extensive research and development over the period 1971 to 1973, Petr Kirpichev and his assistants produced a new nerve agent, A-230, which was five to eight times more toxic than Substance 33. Following successful field tests at Nukus, Uzbekistan, the Soviet Army adopted A-230 for all its munitions in 1990.[25]

Kirpichev's team synthesized over a hundred structural variants of A-230, most of which were too unstable and lost their potency, before discovering A-232 and its ethoxy analogue, A-234. These were both phosphate compounds in which an oxygen atom linked the carbon and phosphorous atoms. By 1987 Soviet scientists had developed a binary form of A-232, and three years later they successfully tested a binary rocket containing Substance 33. This proved that binary weapons could be mass-produced, and that Novichok agents in this form would be safer to handle and could be synthesized en route to their target. Adopted by the Army in 1991 as Novichok-5, A-232 had precursors and breakdown products that could circumvent the list of chemicals likely to be controlled by the forthcoming Chemical Weapons Convention. As the latter focused upon classical nerve agents, with their 'signature' carbon-phosphorous bonds, it excluded phosphates, which had extensive use as agricultural chemicals (such as pesticides or herbicides). So Mirzayanov claimed that 'Since A-232 and A-234 were phosphates, they were ideal agents for concealing and cheating the inspectors supervising the implementation and compliance with the CWC.'[26]

In the autumn of 1993 Professor Georgi Drozd discovered a new compound, Novichok-7, which had a volatility similar to that of soman but was nearly ten times as potent. Another two binary agents, Novichok-8 and Novichok-9, were also under development. All these projects deviated from the pledge given by President Mikhail Gorbachev on 10 April 1987 that henceforth the Soviet Union would cease production of chemical weapons. Accordingly, these revelations aroused controversy, especially as Uglev maintained that Novichok agents had been used to kill a Russian banker, Ivan Kiveldi, and his secretary in 1995. External usage, though, was much more audacious: as Jean Pascal Zanders observed, 'it's almost as though the Russians are sending a message to the West that they can reach anywhere, whenever they like.'[27]

Whatever the aim, it was probably not intended that the effects of Novichok nerve agents should be revealed in an abortive assassination. The mode of attack, spraying the nerve agent on the door handle of Skripal's house,[28] was less direct than the methods employed against Markov, Litvinenko or Kim Jong-nam, and the effects, after environmental exposure, slower and less toxic. The principal victims spent nearly three hours driving into the centre of Salisbury, having a drink in the Mill pub and dining in a Zizzi restaurant before collapsing on a public bench. Like Detective Sergeant Bailey, they received intensive care at Salisbury District Hospital, aided by advice from nearby Porton Down, to restore their natural production of acetylcholinesterase. While they recovered sufficiently to be discharged, the direct spraying of nerve agent upon the wrists of Dawn Sturgess led to her demise (and revealed that a fake Nina Ricci perfume bottle with an adapted nozzle had been used to deliver the nerve agent).[29]

The attack certainly imposed huge costs upon the target area, quite apart from the levels of anxiety felt by first responders, medical staff and the local citizenry. By mid-March 2018, 500 police officers, supported by 200 military personnel, 80 ambulance staff and 50 firefighters, had been deployed in Salisbury. Once the recovery and decontamination programme, known as Operation Morlop, got underway, it focused upon twelve sites in Salisbury and Amesbury. The operation involved 800 military personnel, including the Joint Chemical, Biological, Radiological and Nuclear Task Force, assisted by specialist contractors. Military teams spent 13,000 hours in full protective gear, undertook 250 decontamination missions and gathered over 5,000 forensic samples for examination by Porton Down. Only on 1 March 2019 was the final site, Skripal's house, declared free of Novichok. As the commanding officer Lieutenant-General Tyrone Urch observed, the 355-day undertaking was '"the longest running" operation of its kind on British soil'.[30] As the policy was to destroy contaminated items, Detective Sergeant Bailey lost his house, cars and all his family possessions. By October 2018 the financial bill had soared above £7.5 million for Salisbury's recovery, with over £10 million in policing costs.[31]

More significant from a Russian perspective was the reaction of the UK government and its mustering of international support. Having given Putin's regime 24 hours on 12 March 2018 to explain the attempted assassinations, Theresa May complained two days later that 'Russia has an undeclared chemical weapons programme in contravention of international law . . . [and] has treated the use of a military-grade nerve agent in Europe with sarcasm, contempt and defiance.'[32] In seizing the initiative in what would become an Anglo-Russian information war, she unveiled an array of 'immediate actions'. These included the expulsion of 23 Russian diplomats (compared with four after the Litvinenko case), a strengthening of UK laws in connection with border detentions and money laundering, the monitoring and tracking of those travelling to the UK suspected of hostile activity, a freeze of Russian state assets where they might be used to threaten the life or property of UK nationals or residents, a revocation of an invitation to Foreign Minister Sergei Lavrov to visit the UK, and no attendance by British ministers or members of the royal family at the 2018 World Cup in Russia. By the diplomatic expulsions, May averred, 'we will fundamentally degrade Russian intelligence capability in the UK for years to come.'[33]

Britain received support from European Union (EU) states, non-EU states, NATO and above all the United States. Britain, France and the United States denounced Russia at the UN Security Council; both the EU and NATO proffered official support for the British response; and a wave of diplomatic expulsions followed. Many countries readily purged themselves of Russian spies and punished Russia for its aggressive foreign policy. By the end of March 2018, 28 states and NATO had expelled over 150 Russian diplomats, including 60 from the United States and the closure of the Russian consulate in Seattle. Russia expelled an equal number of diplomats from each of these countries, shut the British and American consulates in St Petersburg and closed the office of the British Council in Moscow. While the intelligence agencies of Britain and her allies suffered from the retaliation in kind, the collective damage done to Russian intelligence was probably as unexpected as it was unprecedented. British Foreign Secretary Boris Johnson graciously praised the 'extraordinary international response'.[34]

The information war was well underway, with Russia and the United Kingdom characterized as 'operating to tight scripts' and 'fighting to retain their global reputations'.[35] The Russian narrative had lacked credibility from the outset, moving from a raft of denials (of its involvement, of possessing any chemical weapons or of developing Novichok) to absurd claims (that another state could have produced Novichok or that allegations against Russia were a diversion from the Brexit negotiations) to more perceptive statements (that the British case lacked transparency in the absence of pictures of the patients in hospital or interviews with medical staff). The lack of iconic imagery, as in the Litvinenko case, dented the credibility of the British version, as did the maladroit commentary of the British Defence Secretary Gavin Williamson when he declared that Russia should 'go away' and 'shut up', enabling Sergei Lavrov to reply: 'Maybe he lacks education.'[36] Putin even deftly asked why, if the poison had been 'a military-grade nerve agent', the victims did not die 'on the spot',[37] a charge that could not be answered until the Amesbury revelations. In mid-March, though, Britain had taken the precaution of seeking assistance from the OPCW inspectors to provide independent verification of the British analysis.

However resilient and successful British diplomacy had been by the end of March 2018, it faced greater challenges in the following month. On 3 April 2018 the British case suffered a self-inflicted wound when Gary Aitkenhead, chief executive of the Defence Science and Technology Laboratory, Porton Down, stated that Porton could not identify the 'precise source' of the nerve agent used against the Skripals. Although he asserted that only a nation state could have produced such a complex nerve agent, 10 Downing Street moved immediately to limit the damage. Making allegations against Russia, it insisted, had drawn upon a comprehensive intelligence assessment and not just scientific analysis.[38] Only a day later Britain again found itself on the defensive because of another unpredictable element: Yulia's cousin, Viktoria. In interviews with Western and Russian media, she claimed that the Skripals had suffered only from fish poisoning, and that she wished to visit her cousin in hospital. Russian state television even broadcast a recorded telephone conversation between Yulia and her cousin, where Yulia said that 'everything is OK' and her father was 'sleeping'.[39] Britain denied Viktoria a UK visa, just as it had rejected repeated requests from the Russian embassy to provide consular access to two of its citizens.

Russian disinformation even threatened to compromise the assistance sought from the Technical Secretariat of the OPCW. The Secretariat had sent a team to Salisbury to collect blood samples from the victims, environmental samples from contaminated sites and split samples analysed at Porton Down (as they would do again after the Amesbury poisonings). It tested them in OPCW-designated laboratories and, on 12 April 2018, confirmed the findings of Porton about the identity of the 'toxic chemical' and its 'high purity' but only supplied the name and structure of the identified agent in a classified report available to states parties.[40] Two days later Sergei Lavrov revealed that BZ, an agent never made in Russia or the Soviet Union, had been found in the samples examined by the Spiez Laboratory, Switzerland. The claim produced 144,000 mentions on social media, compelling the OPCW to explain that BZ had been in the control sample, not the samples collected in Salisbury.[41]

Amesbury and the Aftermath

May and June brought a merciful release from the information war as the World Cup approached and was then held in Russia (14 June–15 July), with very few official boycotts. Even the collapse of Dawn Sturgess and Charlie Rowley in Amesbury, a mere 8 miles from Salisbury, on 30 June 2018 did not immediately disturb this hiatus. The police, fearing an accident caused by a contaminated batch of drugs, were unsure whether a crime had been committed and only on 4 July, four days before Dawn's death, did they confirm that the couple had suffered from Novichok poisoning. Faced with a murder inquiry, the police were even less communicative as they searched for further traces of Novichok in Wiltshire and waited upon Porton to determine whether this Novichok was the same agent that had poisoned the Skripals. It required Charlie Rowley, in an interview after his discharge from hospital on 20 July, to reveal that he had found the source of the nerve-agent poisonings: a discarded perfume bottle within a sealed box in central Salisbury on 27 June. He explained, too, that Dawn, having sprayed the substance on both her wrists, fell ill within fifteen minutes, while he had washed the 'oily substance' off his hands.[42]

Finding the murder weapon was a major breakthrough but the UK authorities wanted confirmation from the OPCW that the agent involved in the two incidents was the same. After this came through on 4 September,[43] a carefully choreographed release of information followed. In the House of Commons May revealed that 250 detectives had completed their case by trawling through 11,000 hours of CCTV footage and taking over 1,400 statements. As a consequence, the Director of Public Prosecutions would bring charges against two Russian nationals, who had travelled under the aliases of Alexander Petrov and Ruslan Boshirov, without making a 'futile' request for extradition. Theresa May described the movements of these men from their arrival at Gatwick Airport on 2 March: they stayed for two nights in the City Stay Hotel, Bow Road, East London, followed by trips to Salisbury over the next two days. They appeared in the vicinity of Skripal's house at 11.58, just moments before the attack on 4 March, and then returned to Waterloo station and travelled via the underground to Heathrow Airport, arriving at 18.30 before boarding flight SU2585 for Moscow. The prime minister explained how the Amesbury victims had suffered from 'the reckless disposal of the agent' but that the modified perfume bottle left 'no doubt' about the delivery method. Dismissing Russia's 'deluge of disinformation' about these incidents, she claimed that Russia had produced and stockpiled 'small quantities of these agents' in contravention of its signing the CWC, and tested various delivery methods, including 'application to door handles'. Having obtained a European arrest warrant against the two suspects, she revealed that both were officers from the GRU, and that the operation 'was almost certainly approved outside the GRU at a senior level of the Russian state'. May promised to step up Britain's 'collective efforts, specifically against the GRU', to shine 'a light on its activities' and to expose 'its methods'. 'Together' with our allies, she declared, 'we will continue to show that those who attempt to undermine the international rules-based system cannot act with impunity'.[44]

However impressive the statement, the release of CCTV images for publication in the British press maximized its impact. On the following morning newspapers carried numerous images of the two men, the perfume container, detailed accounts and maps of their movements, coupled with confirmation that traces of contamination had been found in their hotel room on 4 May.[45] Britain had seized the initiative in this round of the information war and the Russian response was woefully inadequate. Putin described the two men as 'civilians, not criminals' and looked forward to what they had to say,[46] but the ensuing interview proved risible. The suspects conceded that they had been caught on camera but insisted that they were merely tourists, visiting Salisbury Cathedral and other historic sights in the area. They denied intending to murder Skripal, knowing the where-abouts of his house or even carrying a perfume bottle, and also claimed quite implausibly that they had curtailed their first day's visit (described by the police as a reconnaissance mission) because of the 'muddy slush everywhere'.[47]

Britain, though, found little support internationally for another round of punitive sanctions. As early as 30 May 2018 Jean-Claude Juncker, head of the EU Commission, had denounced any further 'Russia-bashing', and so the EU merely doubled the number of Euro-pean arrest warrants to four, including the director and deputy director of the GRU. Meanwhile the Trump administration, despite pressure from the State Department to impose further sanctions under the Chemical and Biological Weapons Control and Warfare Elimination Act (1991), procrastinated over matters of timing.[48]

Unabashed, the British government persevered. In early October it published the real names of both suspects, namely Alexander Mishkin (alias Alexander Petrov) and Colonel Anatoliy Chepiga (alias Ruslan Boshirov), a decorated GRU officer. On 4 October 2018 Anglo-Dutch security services revealed details of a bungled cyber-attack by four GRU agents upon the headquarters of the OPCW in The Hague on 13 April. In what the British described as a 'clean up' operation after Salisbury, the two cyber specialists within the group were part of a cell in Unit 26165, called 'Sandworm', that would later mount cyber-attacks upon the Foreign Office and Porton Down. All four agents, who had travelled on diplomatic passports with mobile phones, com-puters and large amounts of cash, were caught on CCTV and detained. They were found carrying numerous incriminating items that revealed their travel movements to and within The Hague, including a taxi receipt from GRU headquarters to Moscow airport, and a treasure trove of information about their past activities.[49] Compounding this embarrassment was the disclosure the following day by Bellingcat, an investigative website, that this evidence had compromised many of their comrades. As the spies had travelled under their own names and addresses, with one of them, Alexsey Minin, registering at a GRU address, Bellingcat used this information in a trawl through Russia's vehicle-ownership database. This revealed not only Minin's name at this address but the names of 305 suspected agents, often with passport and mobile phone numbers attached.[50] Bellingcat followed up on these revelations by identifying a third suspect (and possible commander of the Skripal poisoning operation), Major-General Denis V. Sergeev, who had arrived in London on the same day as Chepiga and Mishkin, and later a possible 'fourth man', Egor Aleksandrovich Gordienko, who had worked with the unit during 2017 and 2018.[51]

If this was the *coup de grâce* in the information war, it reflected a sustained effort to punish the GRU, and by extension the aggressive foreign policy of Putin's Russia. Waging the information war deflected attention from earlier security lapses: the failure to protect Skripal properly or even install CCTV at his house, and the failure to check baggage from Moscow.[52] It sidestepped the slow response of Public Health England when it let four days elapse from the revelation of a nerve-agent poisoning on 7 March 2018 before warning up to 500 people who had visited the Mill Pub or Zizzi restaurant at the same time as the Skripals to wash their clothes and possessions.[53] It also overcame the odd infelicitous comment, the difficulties caused by Skripal's family and the lack of imagery from the Salisbury hospital. Conversely it exploited a series of blunders by the GRU and, prompted by Bellingcat, probably revealed more than it might have preferred about UK intelligence, surveillance and investigative methods. Nevertheless, it served the political imperative of punishing Russia with the adroit use of the OPCW and the marshalling of international support.

From a Russian perspective the whole enterprise was a catastrophic failure: it failed to kill the target; left extensive collateral damage, including the poison bottle; exposed the properties and effects of one of the Novichok agents without any benefit; and left trails in Britain and The Hague that exposed hundreds of GRU officers. In a remarkably candid interview, Putin insisted that 'Treason is the gravest crime possible, and traitors must be punished,' but 'I am not saying that the Salisbury incident is the way to do it.'[54] In the information war, Russia had fought largely on the defensive, either denying British allegations, spreading disinformation or concocting fabrications that were barely plausible. The tactics had some effect domestically, where a poll in October 2018 revealed that only 3 per cent of Russians thought Moscow was behind the Salisbury attack,[55] and within social media and sceptical opinion,[56] but they could not arrest the searing damage done to Russia's global reputation. International isolation, if far from complete and enduring, was a heavy price to pay for using Novichok to spread fear among Russia's dissidents abroad.

After the Salisbury debacle the poisoning of Alexei Navalny, a prominent Russian critic of the Putin regime, in Tomsk, Siberia, on 20 August 2020 might seem bizarre. Once again the poisoning with a Novichok-type agent (confirmed by a German military laboratory and independently by another two European laboratories) failed, and the victim, who had been rushed to Berlin's Charité hospital after two days' treatment in Siberia, survived. Even more remarkably, Navalny's colleagues recovered evidence of contaminated water bottles from his hotel room in Tomsk. Although Germany forced Russia onto the defensive in the ensuing information war by demanding a Russian inquiry, and confronted the regime with an image of Navalny recovering in his hospital bed, surrounded by his family,[57] international pressure may be more difficult to mobilize. While arraigning Russia in the OPCW remains an option, Germany's external relations are under the threat of sanctions from the U.S. Congress over the almost completed Nord Stream 2, the undersea pipeline that would double deliveries of gas to Germany from Russia.[58] As Putin realized, international relations ebb and flow whereas the threat from his critics remains a constant. To spread fear among the latter, and invoke retribution, Novichok remains an instrument of choice.

Conclusion:
The Evolving Nature of Chemical and Biological Warfare

Evolution in the nature and character of the challenge posed by chemical and biological weapons has been a sustained theme throughout this book. Despite the long pre-history of employing poisons in a military context, and the sinister image associated with this form of warfare often giving rise to allegations or suspicions of usage, and sometimes black propaganda, the weaponry and its potential have developed steadily since the first mass usage in April 1915. If the First World War remains the last conflict in which several belligerents employed chemical weapons in massive quantities, and refined their agents, tactics and anti-gas defences in a sustained manner, several states have exploited the casualty-causing and psychological effects of these weapons in subsequent one-sided wars and counter-insurgency operations. By combining these weapons with long-range and increasingly accurate delivery systems, they transformed the potential of chemical warfare as a force multiplier with strategic (in some instances) as well as tactical applications. States have shown, too, a continuing interest in the utility of biological weapons experimenting, developing, testing and demonstrating their potential effectiveness in some cases by all means short of actual war. As non-state actors have followed suit, employing both forms of weaponry as instruments of terror and assassination, chemical and biological weapons remain military options in the contemporary world. Technological develop-ments, particularly in the area of biotechnology, threaten to enhance this potential and pose further challenges internationally. If these developments warrant closer analysis, so too does the oft-mooted panacea of international disarmament, involving on-site inspections as a means of verifying compliance. Retaliation-in-kind or with nuclear weapons may no longer be viable deterrents but there may still be other preventive or retaliatory measures that states can adopt, if they have 'actionable' intelligence with which to counter or mitigate the effects of these weapons.

Context for Evolution

The evolution of chemical and biological warfare is a by-product of scientific, industrial and technological developments, compounded by the transformation of communication and transportation networks and of the methods of warfare. Discerning the pace and direction of change has always been difficult because the sinister reputation of this form of warfare has maximized the tendency to undertake R&D, testing, production and usage in as discreet a manner as possible. Even in the interwar years, when states conducted perfectly legitimate R&D, testing and production of chemical and biological weapons within the terms of their reservations attached to the Geneva Protocol (1925), they did so without publicizing their activities. Similarly, the tendency of states to display new weapon systems – warships, tanks, aircraft and ballistic missiles – with developing states often hailing such developments as symbols of modernity and economic modernization, has never been extended to the discovery of new war gases or the weaponization of biological agents.

This has fed all manner of suspicions about the use of poisons in the history of warfare and terrorism prior to the First World War, about unusual incidences of disease in conflicts thereafter (such as the reported outbreak of tularemia among German troops at Stalingrad), the potential for developing 'ethnic' weapons that target particular ethnic groups, and recurrent allegations of chemical warfare in counter-insurgency operations where allegations are notoriously difficult to corroborate (such as the desultory reports of chemical warfare practised by the Tamil Tigers in Sri Lanka from the early 1990s to 2006).[1] Investigative reporting has thrived in these circumstances, sometimes bringing historical issues to light from recently declassified documents, as in Harris and Paxman, *A Higher Form of Killing* (1982), or from film released long after the event, notably in the BBC series *Science at War* (1998) and BBC2's *Scotland's Secret War* (2005). Occasionally journalists highlight issues of contemporary controversy, like the BW allegations in Korea, the 'yellow rain' allegations from South East Asia or the CW attacks upon Halabja. Sometimes they provide an historical overview, as Tom Mangold did in *Plague Wars* (London, 1999), proffering 'a true story of biological warfare'. Many of these works are spiced with speculation, some of it alarmist, but the authors have nonetheless perceived that this is an evolving form of warfare, and that its potential has by no means run its course.

Advances in the fields of molecular biology and the proliferation of industrial biotechnologies have enhanced the ability to manufacture new substances or to modify old ones, and to produce these products more easily and much faster. The new technologies include the chemistries of the immune system, neurotransmitters, mammalian cell culture, protein sequencing and the more publicized technology of genetic engineering. The great breakthroughs of the 1970s, enabling scientists to identify and isolate specific genes and to manipulate their basic DNA (deoxyribonucleic acid) structures, ensured that Western governments, scientists and numerous commentators focused upon the potential application of these techniques to biological and toxin warfare. As American, British, Swedish and Canadian governments reflected upon the latest technological developments in open documents submitted to the five-yearly review conferences of the BTWC,[2] commentators used their information to consider the implications of engineering new organisms of greater virulence, antibiotic resistance and environmental stability. They described how the transfer of certain genetic traits into naturally infectious microorganisms could render otherwise harmless organisms highly virulent or alter their immunogenicity and thereby render them difficult to diagnose and more resistant to medical treatment. Bioengineering, they noted, could maximize the infectivity and pathogenicity of microbial pathogens, produce more lethal and more stable toxins, or produce some of the rarer toxins in kilogram quantities to suit military requirements. Protein engineering could modify peptides, which are the precursors of proteins and are made up of amino acids. Active in very low concentrations, these bioregulators are difficult to detect and altering them could affect many aspects of the living system from mental processes to regulatory factors such as mood, consciousness, temperature control, sleep or emotions.[3]

Advances in production technology, including computer-controlled continuous flow fermentors and hollow fibre technology, increased productivity dramatically and permitted the use of much smaller fermentors. Further advances in mammalian cell culture simplified the production of viruses and facilitated the production of large-scale yields in small facilities. Developments in particle encapsulation portended an ability to protect biological warfare agents during transport, enable them to resist damage by exposure to ultraviolet rays, and provide them with greater stability and greater protection against antibiotics. All these developments have eroded the distinction between small laboratories and production facilities, removed the need for long-term storage, and enhanced the ease of concealment. Although biotechnology has defensive potential too, in the design of new biosensors, and in qualitative improvements for protective masks, clothing, immunization and therapeutic treatments, developing novel agents seems an easier proposition than countering them with adequate defences.[4]

How quickly these developments would occur, and how quickly such agents could be weaponized, especially in aerosol form, remained a matter of debate. In the 1980s, Douglass and Lukens warned of the costs and delays that had hampered the commercialization of biotechnology, and argued that 'the road from the laboratory to arsenal is not always short or smooth'.[5] A decade later Malcolm Dando reckoned that technologies now in the hands of Western companies would become much more widespread within twenty years, and that the ability to construct 'many different kinds of new biological weaponry' would be widespread within 50 years.[6] Suspicions that the Soviets had stolen a march in this area would soon be confirmed by Soviet defectors, particularly Ken Alibek in 1992. In his autobiographical account of his career in Biopreparat, *Biohazard* (1999), Alibek recalls a remarkable briefing he attended on 'Project Bonfire' at Obolensk (1989) when a scientist revealed that 'a suitable bacterial host had been found for myelin toxin . . . Lab results had been excellent, and a series of animal experiments had been conducted in secret.' The test had shown that the infected rabbits had developed both the disease caused by the bacteria and the paralysis induced by the toxin. 'The room was absolutely silent. We all recognized the implications of what the scientist had achieved. A new class of weapon had been found.' Having introduced the gene of a toxin into a microorganism, the latter had not only manufactured the toxin but had also acted as a carrier (vector), transferring the poison to the victim. As the microorganism was *Yersinia pseudotuberculosis*, which is closely related to *Yersinia pestis* (plague), this was only a short step from inserting it into plague to produce 'a new version of one of mankind's oldest biological weapons'.[7]

Ironically, when Alibek first explained the scope and extent of the Soviet genetic engineering programmes during his debriefing in the United States, he encountered scepticism from several American scientists, who doubted that there was any need to refine these extremely lethal biological agents. Alibek retorted:

To argue that these weapons won't be developed simply because existing armaments will do a satisfactory job contradicts the history and the logic of weapons development, from the invention of the machine gun to the hydrogen bomb.

By the mid-1990s he found grim confirmation as former Soviet colleagues published articles in scientific journals, reporting on their successful insertion of the gene of Venezuelan equine encephalitis (VEE) into the vaccinia genome without affecting the vaccinia's virulence, and then the insertion of the Ebola virus into the genome of vaccinia (the vaccinia had always been seen as a surrogate for smallpox weapons research in the Soviet BW programmes). In 1997 the Obolensk scientists reported that they had developed a genetically altered strain of *Bacillus anthracis* capable of resisting anthrax vaccines, and, in earlier articles, that they had developed a multi-drug resistant strain of glanders. In all these cases, Alibek noted, the research was justified as 'entirely peaceful', intended to create a vaccine (in the Ebola case) or to improve existing vaccines.[8]

Successive US administrations now issued unambiguously frank assessments about the 'enormous potential' for making more sophisticated weapons. In *Proliferation: Threat and Response* (1997), the US Department of Defense observed that American and foreign biotechnology companies were now selling 'all-in-one kits to enable even high school-level students to perform recombinant DNA experiments', that online gene sequence databases and analytic software were available over the Internet, and that it was already 'possible to transform relatively benign organisms to cause harmful effects'. The incentive to do so lay in the extreme lethality of biological warfare agents: the 'most lethal biological toxins are hundreds to thousands of times more lethal per unit than the most lethal chemical warfare agents'. If technological hurdles still had to be overcome before novel agents could be disseminated effectively, advances in biotechnology provided 'increasing potential to control' the variable factors. These novel agents, as described by the Pentagon, could take five possible forms: benign microorganisms genetically altered to produce a toxin, venom or bioregulator; microorganisms rendered resistant to antibiotics, standard vaccines and therapeutics; microorganisms developed with enhanced aerosol and environmental stability; 'immunologically-altered' microorganisms able to defeat standard identification, detection and diagnostic methods; and combinations of these agents with improved delivery systems. The prospect of such weapons being developed, it added, raised 'the technological hurdle that must be overcome to provide for effective detection, identification, and early warning of biological warfare attacks'.[9]

Underscoring this potential, the Bush administration declared on 28 April 2004 that '[a]dvances in biotechnology and life sciences – including the spread of expertise to create modified or novel organisms – present the prospect of new toxins, live agents, and bioregulators that would require new detection methods, preventive measures and treatments.' It added prudently that

> These trends increase the risk for surprise. Anticipating such threats through intelligence efforts is made more difficult by the dual-use nature of biotechnologies and infrastructure, and the likelihood that adversaries will use denial and deception to conceal their illicit activities.[10]

Scientific scepticism ebbed gradually as the expansion of modern biotechnology led to a widespread diffusion of knowledge and technology. As numerous countries acquired the facilities for vaccine or single-cell protein production, they possessed facilities that could be subverted to produce large amounts of pathogenic micro-organisms. Scientific breakthroughs (as mentioned in the Introduction) continued apace with the full sequencing of the bacterium *Yersinia pestis* that causes bubonic plague announced in 2001, a development that could help in the development of new drugs and vaccines or be misused in the design of bioweapons. Similarly, the chemical synthesis of complete viral genomes, notably an artificial polio virus at the State University of New York in 2002, raised the possibility that other viruses with short DNA sequences would be synthesized. As van Aken and Hammond observed, this raised the possibility that several viruses could be produced artificially for biological warfare, including the Ebola virus, Marburg virus and VEE. Only 'a few highly trained experts' could attempt this, 'at least for the time being'. Much larger genome sequences such as the 200,000 base pairs of the variola genome, the smallpox virus, might conceivably be recreated *in vitro* (that is, in an experiment or other action carried out in a cell-free system), although 'it could not easily be transformed into a live infectious virus particle'. Even more alarming, they warned, was the possibility of designing new types of biological weapons that 'were entirely fictitious until a few years ago'. These included various 'non-lethal weapons', namely micro-organisms that could degrade various materials such as rubber and plastics, or kill drug-producing crops, and biochemical weapons that could serve as incapacitants. Such weapons could be employed in low-intensity or covert operations, in economic warfare or in sabotage activities. Scientific scepticism about biological warfare, if by no means eliminated, appeared to be waning: in 2009 a survey of 1,570 biologists, conducted by the American Association for the Advancement of Science, reckoned that there was a 51 per cent chance of a bioterrorist attack somewhere in the world within five years, and a 28 per cent chance that it would be a product of dual-use research.[11]

Often mentioned in this context is the theoretical option of an ethnic or race-specific agent. As early as 1970 Carl A. Larson, a Swedish geneticist, confirmed publicly that relative enzyme differences between different peoples (as reflected for example in the degree of lactose intolerance among South East Asians) might be exploited by specially designed chemical incapacitants. Some ethnic groups were also known to be particularly sensitive to certain diseases, notably the sensitivity of blacks to *Mycobacterium tuberculosis* and *Coccidioides immetis*, which cause tuberculosis and valley fever respectively.[12] As scientists become increasingly aware of the sequencing and function of the human genome in the hope of correcting genetic defects in diseases like cystic fibrosis, they acquired knowledge of cellular machinery and devised radical new treatments for a broad range of human diseases. These same capabilities might be misused in the future, possibly as Dando argued in 'twenty to fifty years' time' (from 2001), 'to make the targeting of a particular population group – with a specific vector to achieve some specific malign alteration of specific cells – a possibility'.[13]

By blurring the boundaries between chemistry and biology, the revolution in the life sciences, coupled with the development of dual-use biotechnologies, had immense potential for chemical and biological warfare. It reinforced the notion of a threat spectrum, as described by Graham Pearson, which moved from classical chemical weapons through industrial pharmaceutical chemicals, toxins and bioregulators and on to genetically modified and classical biological weapons.[14] Underpinning this linkage were the references to toxins in both the BTWC and in the references to saxitoxin and ricin among the scheduled chemicals, in Schedule 1 (the most toxic chemicals) of the CWC. Neither convention made any distinction between lethal and 'non lethal' agents; indeed, the scope of the BTWC as confirmed in the reports of various review conferences encompassed the prohibition of the production, stockpiling, acquisition and retention of microbial or other biological agents or toxins, 'whatever their origin or method of production, of types and in quantities that have no justification for prophylactic, protective, or other peaceful purposes'. If this general-purpose criterion contained a potential ambiguity in the interpretation of the term 'other peaceful purposes', so too did the general-purpose definition of chemical weapons in Article II.1(a) of the CWC, which included all 'toxic chemicals and their precursors, except where intended for purposes not prohibited'. The CWC then referred in Article II.9(d) to one of the 'purposes not prohibited' as 'law enforcement including domestic riot control purposes' but without defining the scope or context of law enforcement. These ambiguities could be exploited by the development of biochemical weapons for 'non lethal' purposes but usable in support of lethal weapons in a whole range of covert activities, including sabotage and assassination, military 'operations other than war' involving riot control, counterterrorism and economic warfare, and in the displacement of civilian populations.[15]

In this respect terrorist production and usage may be less of a fear than state-funded research laboratories developing genetically modified agents for a wide range of military purposes. The Russian special forces exemplified this possibility when they employed a gas, based upon a derivative of the potent narcotic fentanyl, to extricate hostages from the clutches of Chechen terrorists in a Moscow theatre (26 October 2002). The fact that so many died and many more were injured (see chapter Four) underlines the potential dangers of employing riot-control agents in a confined space, even if this tactic liberated the vast majority of the 800 hostages, terminated the crisis, and possibly deterred any recurrence of such an outrage. Perry Robinson fears that the issue of toxic 'non lethal' agents in support of counterterrorism may lead to a proliferation of such weapons, citing the issue of Agent CR, a riot-control agent, to British armed forces and of Agent OC to the US Marine Corps. Even more extreme was the reported willingness of Israel's special forces, charged with eliminating the terrorists who committed the Munich Olympics massacre (1972), to assassinate Wadi Haddad in 1978 with 'a lethal biological poison . . . that attacked and debilitated his immune system'.[16] Once developed, incapacitating biochemical weapons could spread beyond the confines of the military, police and special forces and find all manner of uses by military contractors, paramilitary forces, armed factions in civil wars, terrorists and even criminals. If such usage stimulated interest in 'new and improved' biochemical weapons, any distinctions between permitted and prohibited weapons might become increasingly blurred. By exploiting their pharmacology and biotechnology for counter-terrorist purposes, states could undermine the norm against the use of chemical and biological weapons.[17]

Disarmament Conventions

For many commentators, the obvious answer to these developments was to enhance the existing disarmament conventions, so buttressing the international norms against the possession and use of chemical and biological weapons. Those norms or taboos have been tested as never before by the sustained use of chemical weapons in the Syrian civil war (chapter Seven) and the use of CB weapons as instruments of assassination (chapter Eight). In spite of its near-universal membership, and many achievements, the OPCW has clearly been deceived by the chemical declarations of several states parties. Though able to complete the unprecedented task of destroying Syria's declared CW stockpile during a civil war, it proved too ponderous and punctilious in its investigations for a rapidly expanding chemical conflict. Whether the decision of a special conference of states parties to allow the OPCW to name culprits in chemical attacks in Syria (27 June 2018)[18] will make any difference remains to be seen.

The BTWC, bereft of any provision for monitoring compliance or verification, and violated by the former Soviet Union, Iraq and possibly other states, seemed most in need of additional measures. Unlike more recently negotiated treaties, such as the CWC and the Conventional Forces in Europe treaty, it lacked any provision for intrusive inspections to monitor compliance and verify that only permitted activities were taking place. The first attempt to enhance the credibility of the BTWC involved the adoption of politically binding Confidence Building Measures (CBMS) intended to prevent or remove any ambiguities, doubts or suspicions about illicit activity. Proposed at the second review conference (1986) and extended at the third (1991), the CBMS required all states-parties to file annual declarations of data about biodefence programmes, high-containment laboratories, unusual outbreaks of disease and other matters. As less than half of the states-parties submitted such declarations, and as much of the data proved incomplete and inaccurate, the third review conference mandated an Ad Hoc Group (AHG) of Governmental Experts, then known as VEREX, to examine possible verification measures from a scientific and technical viewpoint.

Convened in Geneva, it met in four sessions over 1992 and 1993 and drafted a consensus report on some potential measures, which it submitted to a special conference of BTWC parties in September 1994. The conference duly charged the Ad Hoc Group (AHG) with the task of devising a legally binding protocol to strengthen the convention. The AHG met regularly over six and a half years from 1995 to 2001, trying to resolve the complex issues involved in verifying compliance with the BTWC but without reaching a consensus. A majority of the Western Group, led by the United Kingdom, Sweden and Germany, asserted that verification was possible through declarations, visits and inspections. In the 23rd session, on 23 April 2001, the chairman Ambassador Tibor Tóth of Hungary supported this position and issued his own version of the protocol. The 210-page document required mandatory declarations of all past offensive and defensive BTW activities as well as the most relevant facilities where illegal activities might occur. It envisaged a regime of infrequent visits and clarification procedures to ensure that the declarations were accurate and that ambiguities could be addressed. A process known as managed access would seek to protect proprietary and classified information at inspected sites, and a system of noncompliance investigations would follow whenever there was well-founded concern about the possibility of noncompliant behaviour. An international bureaucracy would oversee the implementation of the protocol. Buoyed by the apparent success of the UNSCOM inspectors in uncovering Iraq's BW programme, many European commentators affirmed that BW verification was feasible, albeit as part of a 'web of deterrence' bolstered by export controls, the development of effective CB defensive measures to reduce the utility of CB weapons, and a range of robust national and international responses to any CB acquisition and/or use.[19]

Scepticism about verification, though, remained deeply etched within the Clinton and Bush administrations. The convention, as Dr Edward J. Lacey, Principal Deputy Assistant Secretary of State for Verification and Compliance, argued, was 'inherently difficult to verify'. Any 'effective' verification would require information on the intent of specific biological programmes and activities, many of which were 'dual use in nature', particularly as the production of biological agents could occur 'in a relatively small space inside a building without specific distinguishing features'. Moreover, covert activities could be concealed within legitimate biological laboratories or continued in small-scale non-declared facilities. Transparency visits, tied to the annual declarations, would not cover all declared sites and challenge inspections, whether in the field or at a facility, could suffer from delays in securing approval for the investigations, enabling evidence to be cleaned up, concealed, or 'explained away' at dual-capable facilities. Even if these provisions helped to deter some cheating, and enhance transparency, Lacey doubted that the protocol 'would improve our ability to verify compliance or non-compliance with the Convention'.[20]

Addressing the AHG in Geneva on 25 July 2001, US Ambassador Donald Mahley amplified this critique. He declared that biological weapons posed a 'unique' threat, and that it would be useless 'to patch or modify the models . . . used elsewhere' (implicitly the declarations and inspections employed in the Chemical Weapons Convention). The protocol mechanisms, he argued, would neither enhance confidence in compliance nor 'deter those countries seeking to develop biological weapons', while proving sufficiently intrusive, despite their safeguards, to 'put national security and confidential business information at risk'. Such scepticism was not new, he added: US spokesmen had voiced it repeatedly in Geneva since the initial negotiating sessions in 1995. 'New and innovative paradigms' were needed to deal with the 'magnitude' of biological activity, the 'explosively changing technology' and the 'varied potential objectives' of a biological weapons programme.[21]

As American opposition effectively thwarted the adoption of the protocol, the Bush administration incurred withering criticism at home and abroad. Denounced for its unilateralism, the administration was depicted as ideologically hostile towards arms control. This ideology, critics charged, had bolstered a consensus against the protocol at an inter-agency level within the US government and so prevented 'an effective strengthening of the Convention'.[22] Yet critics could hardly deny that the Bush administration enjoyed expert support on this issue within the United States. Fred C. Iklé, a former assistant secretary of defense in the Reagan administration, regarded the protocol as a 'fraud' since 'the 200-page draft does not include a single meaningful enforcement provision'.[23] In a special issue of the journal *Arms Control Today* (May 2001), several scientists and longstanding champions of arms control evinced doubts about the protocol. Alan P.

Zelicoff, senior scientist in the Center for Arms Control and National Security at Sandia National Laboratories and a former US delegate to the Geneva negotiations (1991–9), described the protocol as impractical since 'current technologies' as tested in mock inspections within the United States could not identify violations with a probability of 50 per cent or greater. Mike Moodie queried whether the protocol would bolster 'confidence in compliance' and 'help deter BW proliferation'. The logic of deterrence, he feared, might not apply as

> The risks of discovery of noncompliant activity are uncertain at best; the ability to reach definitive conclusions about noncompliance is questionable (especially if the proliferator handles the situation adeptly); and the potential costs for noncompliance are not convincingly high.

Underpinning these reservations were growing doubts about the value of inspections after the failure of any state to request a challenge inspection under the CWC, and the UNSCOM experience in Iraq where, as Robert P. Kadlec observed, even the most intrusive inspection regime 'failed to ensure compliance'.[24]

Ironically, this debate occurred within a few months of Richard Butler, the former chairman of UNSCOM, signing the preface of a new edition of his memoirs, *The Greatest Threat*. In this book he reflected upon the passage of two years since the ejection of UNSCOM from Iraq, and the bombing of Iraq in Operation Desert Fox. He maintained that nothing had been done 'to restore control over Saddam's weapons'. Saddam, he insisted, 'is back in the business of developing nuclear weapons . . . He has also extended the range of his missiles and manufactured chemical and biological weapons.' These emphatic assertions derived not only from an understandable suspicion of the aims and objectives of the Iraqi dictator but also, less reasonably, from an overweening confidence in the value of the inspection techniques developed by the UNSCOM team. If UNSCOM, as Butler claims, had 'become more intrusive, even, at times, aggressively so' in response to the 'false declarations, the unilateral destruction, the concealment of weapons and weapon making', it had always enjoyed unprecedented access, surveillance, sampling and inspection rights as a specialist body created by the Security Council after an imposed ceasefire (see chapter Five). Having exposed numerous gaps and inaccuracies in the Iraqi declarations, which the Iraqis could not correct after destroying their weapons, materials and much of their documentation, Butler determined erroneously that their response demonstrated a continuing pattern of concealment and deception.

He also tried to defend UNSCOM from allegations that the CIA had sought to infiltrate its activities and to use its inspectors to glean intelligence for US bombing campaigns. As these charges had compromised the integrity of the UNSCOM inspections, they had provided Saddam with a huge propaganda gift. Unable to deny charges that US officials had since admitted, Butler criticized the principal 'whistleblower', Scott Ritter, a former US Marine intelligence officer, who had led UNSCOM's Concealment Unit until his resignation on 26 August 1998. Ritter had not only revealed the intelligence links between US agencies and UNSCOM but had also written about his experiences in Iraq. He anticipated the findings of the Iraq Survey Group by denying that Iraq was producing chemical weapons or had retained any biological weapons.[25]

So 2001 was hardly a propitious year in which to promote the advantages of an international inspection regime. Critics of the Bush administration, nonetheless, insisted that the protocol was a compromise needed to strengthen a valuable but weak convention. As some of the protocol's shortcomings, notably the restrictions on mandatory declarations, had been introduced largely at American insistence 'against the inclination of major European governments', several commentators reckoned that the administration, or its successor, would have to rethink its position and endorse a variant of the protocol.[26] Kathleen C. Bailey disagreed. In a major study of American policy, she emphasized that the objections to inspections were deeply rooted within the US government (and reinforced after the results of mock inspections in the mid-1990s); that the Bush administration was merely confirming the doubts expressed by US spokesmen in the 1990s; and that a *volte face* by a future administration, though possible, would not necessarily carry the US biotechnology sector with it. This may prove a crucial caveat. Unlike the US chemical industry, which welcomed the passage of the CWC, the American biotechnology sector has always harboured fears that its highly sensitive proprietary information could be compromised by any international inspection regime. Given its influence on Capitol Hill, the industry could thwart the future ratification of any BTWC protocol by ensuring that less than two-thirds of US senators voted in favour.

The acid test, as Bailey argued, was essentially twofold. Would a new international measure, possibly some variant on the protocol already proposed, deter or curb illicit BTWC activities, and would it allow US biotechnology and pharmaceutical research, development and production, part of an industry worth $120 billion per year, to 'flourish without undue risk or burden'? If the clandestine development of biological and toxin weapons remained a feasible proposition, an international protocol might not 'affect the dedicated terrorist, subnational group, or government that is bent on obtaining BTW'. Conversely, American biotechnology companies might remain fearful lest inspections of their facilities inadvertently revealed formulae on newly developed drugs or data on processes, methodologies and matériel that could cost a company its competitive edge. Even worse, the commercial reputation of companies could be damaged if inspectors reached ambiguous conclusions after inspecting their plant. Such ambiguities might arise because legitimate R&D uses the same equipment, materiel, procedures and processes as weapons R&D; practices in the handling, storing and disposition of micro-organisms vary from site to site; and records of organisms and toxins are rarely centrally stored in laboratories (and so incomplete declarations might be adjudged erroneously to indicate illicit activity). In any case American preoccupations, stimulated by 9/11, seemed unlikely to abate, namely the enhanced investment in biodefence, domestic preparedness for biological attack, and strengthened liaison between US Centers for Disease Control and Prevention and the World Health Organization (WHO) in monitoring global outbreaks of infectious disease.[27]

Internationally, the Bush administration also launched several initiatives to restrict the possibility of terrorists acquiring weapons of mass destruction. On 1 November 2001, in the wake of the anthrax attacks in the United States, the president outlined new proposals to deal with the 'scourge of biological weapons'. Claiming that the United States and others since 9/11 have had to face 'the evils these weapons can inflict', Bush declared that 'Rogue states and terrorists possess these weapons and are willing to use them.' He recommended that all 144 state-parties to the BTWC should enact national criminal legislation against prohibited BW activities, establish an effective UN procedure for investigating suspicious outbreaks or allegations of BW usage, and devise procedures for addressing any issues of compliance concerning the BTWC. Bush urged states to seek improvements in the international response to disease control, establish national oversight mechanisms for the security and genetic engineering of pathogenic organisms, devise a universal code of ethical conduct for bio-scientists, and promote responsible conduct in the study, use, modification and shipment of pathogenic organisms.[28]

However welcome these proposals, they hardly constituted a comprehensive solution to the shortcomings of the BTWC. As voluntary measures they followed the CBMs of the 1980s and '90s, but the abject response to the latter hardly indicated that new voluntary proposals would strengthen the convention. Underpinning these measures was a pivotal assumption that guided much of the administration's subsequent policy-making, namely that 'America and the world' had witnessed 'a new kind of war' on 9/11. The readiness of a stateless network to inflict mass civilian casualties, armed only 'with box cutters, mace and 19 airline tickets', raised 'the prospect of even worse dangers – of other weapons in the hands of other men'. As Bush informed an audience at the National Defense University in February 2004, 'The greatest threat before humanity today is the possibility of secret and sudden attack with chemical or biological or radiological or nuclear weapons.' No longer could states assume that the possession of such weapons would serve the purpose of deterrence (as in the Cold War when they remained weapons of last resort):

> What has changed in the 21st century is that, in the hands of terrorists, weapons of mass destruction would be a first resort – the preferred means to further their ideology of suicide and random murder. These terrible weapons are becoming easier to acquire, build, hide, and transport. Armed with a single vial of a biological agent or a single nuclear weapon, small groups of fanatics, or failing states, could gain the power to threaten great nations, threaten the world peace.[29]

In a timely report, *World at Risk*, presented on the eve of the inauguration of the Obama administration (December 2008) a bipartisan commission, appointed by the leaders of Congress, broadly confirmed these findings. Although it approved of the US decision to withdraw from the protocol and to invest heavily in biodefence, the commission feared that the American margin of safety was shrinking and not growing. It affirmed that terrorists could acquire or develop 'weapons of tremendous destructive capability . . . without access to an industrial base or even an economic base of any kind', and that unless the world community acted decisively and with great urgency

> it is more likely than not that a weapon of mass destruction will be used in a terrorist attack somewhere in the world by the end of 2013. The Commission further believes that terrorists are more likely to be able to obtain and use a biological weapon than a nuclear weapon.[30]

Intelligence

Operationally Interpol sought to assist member states through its Bioterrorism Prevention Programme. Designed to raise awareness of the biological threat and improve response capabilities, the programme included regional workshops, training courses and exercises for hundreds of law enforcement officials across the world. In 2010 it established the CBRNE (the 'E' standing for explosives) Terrorism Prevention Programme, which covered intelligence analysis and threat evaluation, laboratory security and international investigations. It provided operational support for dealing with new technologies and disease surveillance, and in 2014 began a series of multidisciplinary workshops in different continents to bring together scientists, biosecurity professionals, law enforcement officials and health professionals.[31]

Intelligence remains a prerequisite in addressing the challenges posed by the evolving scientific potential of chemical and biological warfare and the projections of its future use by state or non-state actors. Yet the recent intelligence blunders in Japan and Iraq are hardly encouraging and failures of this magnitude have a lengthy historical pedigree. Sometimes, they reflected huge gaps in knowledge and intelligence collection (such as the shock of discovering German nerve agents after the war or of the Soviet development of novel agents and the Russian use of a fentanyl-based incapacitant). Major errors of analysis and understanding have also occurred (like the failure to anticipate the effects of the first German chlorine attack in April 1915). Belligerents have occasionally been able to conceal the usage of chemical weapons in various Third World conflicts, and political leaders have proved reluctant to act over imprecise or incomplete evidence (as in response to the Japanese or Soviet BW programmes or the Egyptian use of CW in the Yemen). Although intelligence successes have occurred from the First World War, where they sustained anti-gas protection against phosgene and many other gases, through to the 1990s in exploiting evidence from defectors over the BW programmes of the former Soviet Union and more recently in impeding the Libyan CW programme, difficulties involved in the collection, analysis and active use of intelligence derive from systemic problems associated with chemical and biological warfare.

These problems include the clandestine nature of much of the R&D, testing, production and storage of such weapons; the ability to conceal vital elements of the scientific and industrial processes within civilian facilities; the dual-use nature of many of the materials and technology involved; and the requirement for timely access to battlefield locations where alleged usage had occurred. Compounding factors include the understandable desire to encourage the investment and exploitation of emerging possibilities in the life sciences and biotechnology, and the huge potential for the use or misuse of these scientific developments. The lack of transparency derives in turn from the perception of these weapons as abnormal, with their development, acquisition and usage condemned in international treaties and conventions. However useful these norms in altering the behaviour of some states, and in deterring recourse to this form of warfare in others, they have not deterred all states and non-state actors.

Experience also confirms that if states act precipitately and make allegations over the development and use of these weapons, they are likely to be dragged into protracted and politically damaging propaganda battles. If this was evident in the 1930s when revelations about the development and usage of these weapons were made in conditions of international uncertainty and diplomatic difficulty, it was even more apparent during the Korean and Vietnam Wars when propaganda battles raged over such issues. Whenever allegations were made without clear and convincing evidence, as in the 'yellow rain' allegations, they led to damaging and distracting debates both internally and externally. If they were used to justify recourse to war, and then WMD were not found as in Iraq, the political consequences could be catastrophic for the political reputation and the international credibility of the administration concerned. Unwilling to suffer such political damage, states parties have proved reluctant to request challenge inspections under the CWC or to raise compliance concerns in connection with the BTWC. Just as US intelligence agencies doubted that they could monitor compliance with the CWC, fearing that any state determined to preserve a small, secret cw programme could use 'the delays and managed access judgments allowed by the convention' to thwart challenge inspections, they have become much more circumspect after the Iraqi debacle in their public assessments of possible cbw programmes in other countries.[32] Both Obama's administration and Cameron's government encountered massive public and political opposition when they proposed military interventions in the wake of the gas attacks at Ghouta in August 2013 (see chapter Seven). The subsequent bombings of Syrian targets by the Trump administration (7 April 2017) and by the us, aided by France and Britain (13 April 2018), were all executive decisions, avoiding any legislative debates.

There are of course less politically hazardous actions that states can and do take, not least in the sharing of information between intelligence, police, financial institutions and customs agencies of like-minded states, the promotion of export controls whether nationally or internationally, and in the criminalization of cbw activities prohibited by international treaties. Concerted intelligence analysis of advanced biochemical agents and genetically engineered organisms remains crucial in trying to avert the possibility of technological surprise, and the monitoring of natural outbreaks of disease assists in trying to control, and where possible eradicate, pathogens and pests that could harm agriculture. International action has disrupted illicit activity, including suspected wmd trafficking (see chapter Four) and a raft of terrorist plots. In January 2009 Jonathan Evans, director-general of mi5, confirmed that intelligence-led operations had smashed several terrorist conspiracies in the uk within the preceding eighteen months, including a group that considered making a 'dirty' bomb. Although some of these actions lacked sufficient evidence to prosecute, there had been 86 successful prosecutions over a two-year period.[33]

States, nonetheless, remain potentially vulnerable to the surprise and shock of terrorist outrages even when the terrorists are equipped only with firearms and explosives as in the Mumbai massacre (26–9 November 2008). Over 170 people perished in the co-ordinated attacks by ten terrorists from Lashkar-e-Taiba, a group based in Pakistan. If this revealed the shortcomings of, and scant co-ordination between, India's intelligence agencies, the same failing to act on prior warnings occurred in Sri Lanka (21 April 2019), where 253 people died and over 500 were injured in eight suicide bombings by members of isis-assisted group National Thaweed Jama'ut.

Once caught by surprise, the psychological shock mounted under the glare of the international media, which exposed the inadequate training and equipment of local police and the tardy response of India's political authorities and special forces. In other words, surprise remains a key element in the armoury of terrorists. If effective at a tactical level, it may generate strategic effects out of all proportion to the effort expended. Surprise serves as an 'operational enabler' that may maximize the degree of psychological shock, especially if magnified by the coverage of the international media. It has the potential to undermine the target government, impose disproportionate economic and social costs (not least in trying to prevent a recurrence), damage relations between states, and leave a lasting impression upon the target audience, possibly inspiring their own constituencies and attracting further recruits.[34]

Exacerbating the potential effects of a surprise attack, and any attack that dispersed chemical or biological agents would come into this category, is the vulnerability of contemporary society. If terrorism represents a form of asymmetric warfare, that is, a mode of conflict by which a weaker party can strike a much more powerful adversary where it has most difficulty in defending itself, it also exposes the vulnerabilities of the target state. Whereas the terrorist need not protect any territorial, economic or population assets, it can select from a multitude of enemy targets and attack at a time, and by a means of its own choosing, so exploiting an 'asymmetry of vulnerability'. Accordingly, even if enemy intelligence services perceive a long-term strategic threat from a terrorist network, they might struggle to identify the specific cell that might launch an attack, the timing of such an operation, and the potential target. Richard Betts illustrated this point by observing that the United States, in the wake of 9/11, had some 600,000 bridges, 170,000 water systems, over 2,800 power plants (104 of them nuclear), 190,000 miles of interstate pipelines for natural gas, 463 skyscrapers and nearly 20,000 miles of border, airports, stadiums, train tracks. 'All these', he wrote, 'usually represented American strength; after September 11 they also represent vulnerability.'[35]

Yet the events of 9/11, compounded by the WMD debacle in Iraq, have accelerated the pace of intelligence reform within the United States. The 9/11 commission highlighted both the inability and unwillingness of the intelligence community at local, state and federal level to share information, and the interagency tensions between area specialists, who concentrate upon specific geographical regions, and functional specialists, who specialize in the collection of different types of intelligence (technical, signals, human, etc). The subsequent creation of a Department of Homeland Security, and the post of National Director of Intelligence as a single source of advice for the president, represents the most extensive reorganization of US national security and intelligence since the creation of the CIA in 1947. Improvements have also been sought in intelligence collection and analysis. After the early disagreements between the intelligence agencies of the UK, US and France in Syria (see chapter Seven), the three agencies created similar networks of Syrian rebels trained and equipped to collect human tissue samples after suspected CW attacks. These spies were also expected to corroborate the time and extent of attacks by compiling non-public video evidence, and pass all samples through secure chains of custody to their handlers, and thence back to national laboratories for testing.[36]

Ashton B. Carter, a former assistant secretary of defense in the Clinton administration, described how the counterterrorism intelligence effort has evolved 'from producing papers characterizing terrorist groups to supporting operations to interdict terrorists'. The 'targeted killing' of specific terrorists across the Middle East and Pakistan testifies to his claim that 'the intelligence community has risen to the challenge of producing "actionable" intelligence on terrorists', but Carter also recognized that

> the intelligence community needs to increase the size and technical training of its workforce. Because intelligence agencies have difficulty recruiting and retaining top talent with more lucrative prospects in private industry, they need to forge better links with the outside scientific community so that advice and insight are 'on call'.[37]

Whether these developments assist in anticipating and countering any threat from terrorists armed with chemical or biological weapons may depend upon not only the efficacy of domestic surveillance, warning and security measures, but also on a continuing degree of international co-operation.

International Co-operation

The challenges posed by chemical and biological weapons, whether in the arsenals of state or non-state actors, and the possibility of transporting these weapons for dispersal in or across the borders of distant countries, underscore the primacy of international co-operation. Given the proliferation of chemical and biotechnological industries across the developing world and the global networks of many terrorist organizations, the transnational dimension of these challenges is all too apparent. The revolution in information technology keeps improving the ability of small groups to recruit, organize and deploy their tactical assets. It enables them to exploit events, disseminating images rapidly via the Internet and maximizing the impact of terrorist strikes or counter-terror blunders like the images of prisoner mistreatment from Abu Ghraib prison. Operations involving chemical and biological weapons may not have the potential for spectacle that some of the attacks with rocket-propelled grenades or improvised explosive devices (IEDs) had in Iraq, still less the second aircraft crashing into the South Tower on 9/11, when all the television companies in New York City had deployed their camera crews after the first strike some fifteen minutes earlier. Nevertheless, the panic erupting after a chemical or biological strike, as after the nerve-gas attacks in Tokyo and the anthrax posted in the United States, would become a media event and a real test for police and emergency services that most states would wish to avoid.

If such a test places a premium upon early warning of impending operations, it reflects the value of relations between the agencies of states that devote relatively modest resources to intelligence collection and analysis, and their better-funded and technologically superior American counterparts. However valuable these transatlantic links in providing advance warning of certain plots, US agencies have proven fallible in monitoring similar activities in the past: they completely missed the threat from Aum Shinrikyo and erred massively over Iraqi WMD. Accordingly, most international co-operation would seek to stifle the development of illicit chemical and biological weapons at source.

Initially like-minded states sought to do so through the creation of multilateral export controls but the history of their endeavours (see chapter Four) reflects the difficulties of relying upon consensual, voluntary agreements as an instrument of international co-operation.

The Australia Group formed in response to the use of chemical weapons in the Iran–Iraq War, and the diffusion of scientific and technological expertise, including dual-use industrial technology, within the developing world, has struggled to establish its legitimacy and effectiveness. As a cartel of suppliers, it sought to broaden its membership to dilute the impression that it was simply serving the interests of Western industrialists. As a body wedded to countering the proliferation of chemical and biological weapons, it responded to evidence of its irrelevance in Iraq by expanding the scope of its restrictions to include biological materials and equipment. Yet the existence of alternative suppliers outside the group ensures that the impact of its restrictions will perforce remain limited. Its main utility lies as a forum for informal discussion as well as the exchange of information and bargaining in support of national policies. Politically, the Australia Group demonstrates that its members support the universal norms of the BTWC and the CWC, and, by its restrictions, adds to the risks and costs of those involved in trying to bypass these norms.

The success of Aum Shinrikyo, though, in acquiring the materials and technology to produce chemical and biological weapons demonstrated the limited effects of export controls unless states monitored potential CBW activities within their own borders. 'Non-state actors', as Hans Blix observed, 'do not live on clouds . . .'

> It is reasonable from a practical point of view and fully justified legally to attach to all host states the responsibility for preventing non-state actors on their territories from acquiring and using weapons of mass destruction, the more so if the host state has legally committed itself to not having such weapons.

If the host state cannot discharge this responsibility, adds Blix, it may request assistance from other states or from the UN Security Council. If faced with non-state actors that possess international networks of communication, organization and finance, it may seek to disrupt these links through co-operative international action. The latter might involve the anti-terrorist units of metropolitan and national police forces, transnational bodies such as Europol (the European police agency), customs agencies, prosecutors and judicial authorities, intelligence and security forces.[38]

UN Security Council Resolution 1540 (April 2004) underpinned these sentiments (see chapter Six), requiring states to adopt measures that would prevent terrorists from acquiring weapons of mass destruction and their related technology. Bolstering international legal norms seems necessary in view of the rapid expansion in the number of biotechnology facilities, and the growing risks of either an accidental release of pathogens and toxins (such as the release of foot-and-mouth disease virus from the UK's facility at Pirbright in 2007) or the risks of loss, theft, misuse, diversion or intentional release. The expansion of biotechnology is particularly rapid in the United States, where scientists in some 400 institutions are studying agents of bioterrorism concern (see chapter Six). Specific risks may be evident from the significant variations in the perimeter security controls around five of America's operational BSL-4 facilities and within laboratories in sixteen Asian countries.[39]

An appropriate response would involve a combination of a national regulatory framework for the licensing of facilities that develop, possess, transfer or use human, animal or plant pathogens, and codes of conduct for biologists and biotechnologists to enhance awareness of how work in the life sciences might be misused in contravention of the BTWC and supporting national legislation. Biosecurity, nonetheless, depends fundamentally upon management teams accepting responsibility for managing risk at specific facilities, and their willingness to draft and implement security plans, preferably with the assistance of biological safety officers/advisors, and to instil a strong safety culture. In the absence of any agreed definition of biosecurity, regulation and oversight differs between states, and laboratory provisions may vary even within the same country. Excessive regulation (or the perception of excessive regulation) in one country may prompt multinational corporations to relocate their R&D facilities to other countries, and differences in biosecurity regulation may stifle international research collaboration. Accordingly, the commissioners of the *World at Risk* report have advocated that the United States should convene an international conference of all states with major biotechnology industries to promote an awareness of biosecurity. This body could authorize a global assessment of biosecurity risks with enhanced global disease surveillance networks, and propose a new set of recommendations by which states could implement their national legislation in accordance with the BTWC and their obligations under UN Security Council Resolution 1540.[40]

Another widely recognized dimension of biosecurity is the legacy from the biological weapons programme of the former Soviet Union. Under the Cooperative Threat Reduction programme, the United States has assisted in the dismantling of former biological weapons facilities in Russia and in securing stockpiles of dangerous pathogens. Moreover, the US Departments of Energy, State, and Health and Human Services have sponsored programmes to engage the services of former weapon scientists in Russia and to redirect their activities into peaceful areas of research. Designed to prevent underpaid or unemployed scientists from selling their services to terrorists or rogue regimes, the programme addresses evidence that a significant minority of Russian scientists, about twenty per cent in one survey, would be willing to do so.[41]

In recent years, this programme has had less success as the Russian government has blocked repeatedly US requests for greater transparency at the BW facilities controlled by its Ministry of Defence. Forced to curtail these efforts in Russia, the Bush administration launched a Biosecurity Engagement programme in 2006, by which it sought to promote pathogen security and collaborative bioscience research with specific countries in South Asia, South East Asia and the Middle East, where indigenous terrorist groups have exhibited an interest in acquiring biological weapons. These bilateral links to promote standards of laboratory biosafety, pathogen security, and the monitoring of outbreaks of infectious disease carried direct inducements through a grants assistance programme to promote collaborative research programmes between the US and local institutions. Initially piloted in Indonesia and the Philippines, the programme seems a potentially profitable route to pursue.[42]

All these international initiatives reflect the scope and diversity of the challenges posed by biological or biochemical weapons. The rapidity of scientific developments and their technological application underscores the continuing vulnerability of civil society to the effects of these weapons. In the struggle between offensive and defensive measures that originated in the laboratories and on the battlefields of the First World War, and continued through the 1930s, civil defence was always a massively complex undertaking. Periodically, under imminent aerial threat, states have sought to protect their civilians with elaborate civil defence measures but few modern states, other than very small ones under acute threats like Israel in the First Gulf War, have sought to follow the British example of the late 1930s and distribute respirators on a nationwide basis. Understandably the United States, in the wake of its anthrax attacks, sought to improve its surveillance, detection, emergency response, decontamination provision and medical countermeasures (both stockpiles of vaccines and therapeutic treatments). Hugely costly, this undertaking has not been emulated to the same degree elsewhere. Even authorities in the United Kingdom had to seek advice about decontamination from the US and Germany after an accidental death from anthrax in the Scottish borders in 2006. Wheelis and Sugishima aptly observe that 'Every country will need to learn to live with some measure of vulnerability and will have to balance the costs – financial, loss of openness, erosion of civil rights – of biodefense measures against their modest contributions to security.'[43]

At issue is not only the impossibility of devising perfect defences but also the risk of moving too far in the direction of counter-terrorism by devising intrusive legislation and utilizing methods of detention and interrogation that are profoundly counter-productive. Dame Stella Rimington, the former director of MI5, argued that the British government should accept the element of risk instead of 'frightening people' in order to pass laws that 'restrict civil liberties, precisely one of the objects of terrorism: that we live in fear and under a police state'.[44] Yet the counter-terror legislation secured (and sought) by the British government paled by comparison with the measures enacted under the Patriot Act and the security imposed within the United States. In the latter case General Tommy Franks, the former commander of US Central Command, who directed the wars in Afghanistan and Iraq before his retirement in 2003, warned that the reaction to an attack with WMD could be even more dramatic. It could lead, in his view, to a forfeiture of 'freedom and liberty' as the government began 'to militarize our country in order to avoid a repeat of another mass-casualty event'.[45]

Overview

Nevertheless, after recent terrorist outrages, the contemporary preoccupation with biosecurity is understandable. It reflects an awareness that the most obvious short cut by which rogue states or non-state actors could acquire biological or biochemical weapons is through an accidental or intentional diversion of materials and/or skills from dual-use research facilities. It also recognizes that an efficient delivery of weapons-grade biological material is the worst-case scenario, with a theoretical potential to inflict massive casualties over an extensive area. Surprise, though, remains a recurrent feature of chemical and biological warfare. These weapons could be employed in a multitude of ways, ranging from tools of assassination through the release of toxic agents from industrial sites and moving containers, attacks on crops and animals, the misuse of non-lethal or riot-control agents in support of other weapons, and the dissemination of agents not only through sprayers, including those from manned or unmanned aerial vehicles, but also via natural vectors in certain contexts – food, alcohol, water (see chapter Five), and insects.[46] Worst-case scenarios, however, are rare events. The next major recourse to this form of warfare might still involve chemical weapons. Six years after the nerve-gas attacks in Tokyo James M. Tour, an American scientist, demonstrated that he could order legally all the ingredients to make 280 grams of sarin from reputable chemical suppliers in the United States. To avoid handling the poisons directly, a terrorist could build a binary weapon that performed the well-known chemical reaction in the target area, with the nerve agent dispersed by an 'off-the-shelf pesticide sprayer' into the ventilation system of a building. The effects would depend upon the efficacy of the sprayer and the numbers exposed, but the casualties could range from hundreds to thousands.[47]

Far from terrorists having to choose, as is often depicted, between a conventional and CB weapon, they might choose to use both, possibly employing the latter as a 'force multiplier' causing panic or disrupting the emergency services as they responded to the effects of an explosion or an incendiary weapon. In such contexts, terrorists could release CB agents from IEDs as currently used in Iraq and Afghanistan. When the European Defence Agency reviewed the latter as a means of attacking a joint expeditionary force, operating within the urban settings of a failed state, it found all manner of difficulties. In an exercise dubbed 'Firm Foundation 2008', the agency found the lack of both an operational doctrine and appropriate equipment for specialist teams drawn from national units trained in CBRN response and in explosive ordnance disposal (EOD) – bodies long accustomed to working in isolation from one another. Not the least of the requirements was the need to develop a CBRN permeable suit that could be worn under EOD protection against blast and flame.[48]

Equipment issues are problematic, too. Most of the CBRN protection and clearance equipment remains with the armed forces, and derives from concepts developed to meet the military challenges of the Cold War. Operable only by highly trained specialists, very little of it is designed for manoeuvre against the threat from asymmetric terrorism in an urban environment. The NATO Response Force includes a CBRN battalion that provides an integrated detection and consequence management capacity and , in the wake of its Novichok poisonings (see chapter Eight), Britain reformed 28 Engineer Regiment in a counter-CBRN role.[49] At the theatre level, NATO's International Security Assistance Force (ISAF) deployed a 'flying' CBRN platoon of Czech specialists in Afghanistan, where it provided CBRN reconnaissance, sampling and decontamination tasks anywhere across the country at the request of the ISAF commander. This was particularly important in Afghan operations, where air-conditioning systems often replaced CBRN protection systems in armoured vehicles. Preparedness to meet the threat from chemical and biological remains highly variable not only in developing states but in Europe, where the number and lethality of terrorist incidents, often ISIS-inspired, surged in the period 2012–17. A survey by the European Parliament reported in 2018 that none of the European states were as prepared as the United States to counter CB terrorism. Britain was the best prepared of the EU states. It had several high-level containment facilities, stockpiles of emergency medical supplies strategically located in England, Scotland, Wales and Northern Ireland, and a Defence Chemical, Biological, Radiological and Nuclear Centre (DCBRNC) that runs eighteen training courses per year for all three branches of the military, the medical services and the fire and police services. It also had Memorandums of Understanding in place to promote cooperation in the event of an incident. Many of the other states lacked stockpiles of medical countermeasures and even adequate protection for first responders when entering a CBRN incident arena.

In some geo-strategic contexts, though, the sheer destructiveness of biological weapons, as possessed by a minor power, might serve or be thought to serve as a strategic deterrent, a view reportedly shared by the Israeli defence establishment.[50] Secondly, a response to such threats that involves a sharing of intelligence and emphasizes interoperability seems prudent, whether in the context of civil defence or in the planning of expeditionary operations. Thirdly, detecting an attack, particularly if directed at crops or livestock, might prove extremely difficult as biological attacks on agriculture would not require elaborate weaponization and might leave few indicators to distinguish them from natural outbreaks. If such attacks were directed against Western agriculture, where animals are concentrated to reduce overhead costs, the communicability of livestock diseases could have devastating economic consequences.[51] Finally, the management of any reaction to a reported CB incident, including the handling of the media and recourse to a retaliatory option, if appropriate, needs careful attention to avoid a politically maladroit over-reaction. For every confirmed use of these weapons, there are many more allegations of usage, lurid exaggerations of possible effects, and all too many instances of black propaganda.

Ever since the First World War, the use of chemical and biological weapons has been comparatively rare. Despite the claims of the disarmament lobby, this rarity has not derived from the recurrent attempts to establish international norms against chemical and biological warfare. Shortages of supply, intelligence misperceptions and later threats of retaliation-in-kind were much more important during the Second World War, and nuclear weapons marginalized all forms of weaponry between the major protagonists during the Cold War. Political, diplomatic, economic and military pressure, often upholding international norms, have curbed the CB ambitions of various states thereafter but with the increasing diffusion of the requisite scientific expertise and technological capability, some states and non-state actors remain willing to utilize these weapons, whether lethal or non-lethal, for all manner of operational purposes. Turning those aspirations into reality, as Aum Shinrikyo discovered, may still prove problematic, and a major use of these weapons against human targets may remain a 'low probability but high consequence' event. Nevertheless, aspirations to acquire these weapons are likely to endure as long as the technology keeps opening up new possibilities for their development and usage.

References

Introduction

1 'Transcript of President's Address to a Joint Session of the House and Senate', *New York Times*, 10 February 1989, pp. A17–18 at 18.
2 'President Bush Delivers Graduation Speech at West Point', 1 June 2002, www.whitehouse.gov/news/releases/2002/06/print/20020601–3.html (accessed 30 April 2006).
3 United Nations (UN) General Assembly, *Report of the Secretary-General on Chemical and Bacteriological (Biological) Weapons and the Effects of their Possible Use*, A/7575 (New York, 1 July 1969), p. 6.
4 Graham S. Pearson, 'Prospects for Chemical and Biological Arms Control: The Web of Deterrence', *Washington Quarterly*, XVI/2 (1993), pp. 145–62.
5 The National Defence Research Institute of Sweden, *Chemical Warfare Agents* (Stockholm, 1983), p. 13.
6 *Military Chemistry and Chemical Agents*, Department of the Army technical manual TM 3–215 and Department of the Air Force manual AFM 255–7 (Washington, DC, 1956), pp. 6–7.
7 *Military Biology and Biological Warfare Agents*, Department of the Army technical manual TM 3–216 and Department of the Air Force manual AFM 355–6 (Washington, DC, 1956), pp. 40–42.
8 *Report of the enquiry into the Medical and Toxicological aspects of (Orthochlorobenzylidene Malononitrile)*, part II, Cmnd 4775 (1971), pp. 16–17.
9 Stockholm International Peace Research Institute (SIPRI), *The Problem of Chemical and Biological Warfare*, 6 vols (Stockholm, 1971–5), I, pp. 41–52, 71–5; II, pp. 42–3, 58–9; *Military Chemistry and Chemical Agents*, pp. 18–19, 26–7, 31–3.
10 Jonathan B. Tucker, 'Gene Wars', *Foreign Policy*, 57 (1984), pp. 58–79 at 63; SIPRI, *The Problem of Chemical and Biological Warfare*, II, pp. 59–62.
11 SIPRI, *The Problem of Chemical and Biological Warfare*, II, pp. 35 and 37; Rodney W. Bovey and Alvin L. Young, *The Science of 2, 4, 5–T and Associated Phenoxy Herbicides* (New York, 1980), pp. 43, 217–23, 377, 393.
12 Brigadier-General J. H. Rothschild, *Tomorrow's Weapons* (New York, 1964), pp. 75–6.

13 William H. Webster, Hearings on *Global Spread of Chemical and Biological Weapons* before the Committee on Governmental Affairs and its Permanent Subcommittee on Investigations, United States Senate, 101st Congress, first session (9 February 1989), p. 10.

14 Pearson, 'Prospects for Chemical and Biological Arms Control', p. 147.

15 Office of Technology Assessment (OTA), *Proliferation of Weapons of Mass Destruction: Assessing the Risks* (Washington, DC, 1993), p. 54.

16 Rothschild, *Tomorrow's Weapons*, p. 74, and Augustin M. Prentiss, *Chemicals in War* (New York, 1937), pp. 380–82.

17 Brigadier Charles H. Foulkes, *'Gas!' The Story of the Special Brigade* (Edinburgh, 1934), p. 252.

18 Edward M. Spiers, *Chemical Weaponry: A Continuing Challenge* (Basingstoke, 1989), pp. 32–3.

19 Gaps in the evidence mean that the numbers of gas casualties are only estimates: compare Prentiss, *Chemicals in War*, pp. 657, 660, 683–4, with Paul F. Walker, 'A Century of Chemical Warfare: Building a World Free of Chemical Weapons', in *One Hundred Years of Chemical Warfare: Research, Deployment, Consequences*, ed. Bretislav Friedrich, Dieter Hoffmann, Jürgen Renn, Florian Schmaltz and Martin Wolf (Berlin, 2017), pp. 379–99, at p. 380 n.1

20 Charles J. Dick, 'Soviet Chemical Warfare Capabilities', *International Defense Review*, XIV/1 (1981), pp. 31–8.

21 Giulio Douhet, *The Command of the Air*, trans. D. Ferrari, 2nd edn (New York, 1942), pp. 180–86.

22 Ken Alibek, *Biohazard* (London, 1999), pp. 37–8.

23 SIPRI, *The Problem of Chemical and Biological Warfare*, II, p. 140.

24 US Department of Defense (DoD), *Continuing Development of Chemical Weapons Capabilities in the USSR* (Washington, DC, 1983), pp. 3–4.

25 Alibek, *Biohazard*, pp. 8, 43, 140–41. The ICBM capability is contested by Milton Leitenberg and Raymond A. Zilinskas, *The Soviet Biological Weapons Program: A History* (Cambridge, MA, 2012), pp. 309–22 but these writers admit ignorance of Soviet decision-making at the 'very highest levels', pp. 5–6.

26 UN General Assembly, *Report of the Secretary-General*, pp. 71–5, 80–81, 83–4.

27 Ibid., pp. 78 and 86; for a comparison of such effects, see Edward M. Spiers, *Chemical Warfare* (Basingstoke, 1986), appendix 3, p. 213.

28 *World at Risk: The Report of the Commission on the Prevention of Weapons of Mass Destruction Proliferation and Terrorism* (New York, 2008), p. 8.

29 Alibek, *Biohazard*, pp. 20–21; UN General Assembly, *Report of the Secretary-General*, pp. 4, 8, 86–9; Charles J. Dick, 'The Soviet Chemical and Biological Warfare Threat', RUSI: *Journal of the Royal*

United Services Institute for Defence Studies, CXXVI/1 (1981), pp. 45–51, at 47–8; Leitenberg and Zilinskas, *The Soviet Biological Weapons Program*, p. 705.

30 OTA, *Technologies Underlying Weapons of Mass Destruction* (Washington, DC, 1993), pp. 114–17; see also Joshua Lederberg, 'Biological Warfare: A Global Threat', *American Scientist*, LIX (1971), pp. 195–7, and for a synthesis of the debates in the 1980s, Malcolm Dando, *Biological Warfare in the 21st Century: Biotechnology and the Proliferation of Biological Weapons* (London, 1994), ch. 7.

31 Erhard Geissler, ed., *Biological and Toxin Weapons Today* (Oxford, 1986), ch. 2; Steven M. Block, 'The Growing Threat of Biological Weapons', *American Scientist online*, LXXXIX/1 (2001), p. 8, www.americanscientist.org/template/AssetDetail/assetid/14284?ful ltext=true&print=yes (accessed 29 August 2006).

32 Joby Warrick, 'Custom-Built Pathogens Raise Bioterror Fears', *Washington Post*, 31 July 2006, p. A1, and Scott Canon, 'Biotech Advances hold Terrifying Possibilities', *Kansas City Star*, 12 December 2005, www.kansascity.com/mid/kansascity/news/13386071.htm? template=contentModules/printstory.jsp (accessed 13 December 2005).

33 Office of the Secretary of Defense, *Proliferation: Threat and Response* (Washington, DC, November 1997), p. 81.

1 The Legacy of Gas Warfare in the First World War

1 Rupert Smith, *The Utility of Force: The Art of War in the Modern World* (London, 2005), pp. 106–7.

2 Augustin M. Prentiss, *Chemicals in War* (New York, 1937), pp. 661–2.

3 Victor Lefebure, *The Riddle of the Rhine: Chemical Strategy in Peace and War* (London, 1921), pp. 109–10.

4 Adrienne Mayor, *Greek Fire, Poison Arrows and Scorpion Bombs: Biological and Chemical Warfare in the Ancient World* (New York, 2003); Stockholm International Peace Research Institute (SIPRI), *The Problem of Chemical and Biological Warfare*, 6 vols (Stockholm, 1971–5), II, pp. 125–6, 214–15.

5 Vincent J. Derbes, 'De Mussis and the Great Plague of 1348', *Journal of the American Medical Association* (JAMA), CXCVI/1 (1996), pp. 179–82; Mark Wheelis, 'Biological Warfare before 1914', in *Biological and Toxin Weapons: Research, Development and Use from the Middle Ages to 1945*, ed. Erhard Geissler and John Ellis van Courtland Moon (Oxford, 1999), pp. 8–34.

6 Elizabeth A. Fenn, 'Biological Warfare in Eighteenth-Century North America: Beyond Jeffery Amherst', *Journal of American History*, LXXXVI/4 (2000), pp. 1552–80; for Amherst's quote, see Stephen Brumwell, *Redcoats: The British Soldier in the Americas, 1755–1763* (Cambridge, 2002), p. 188.

7 Edward M. Spiers, *Chemical Warfare* (Basingstoke, 1986), p. 14; Robert K. D. Peterson, 'Insects, Disease, and Military History', *American Entomologist*, XLI/3 (1995), pp. 147–60; Richard Holmes, ed., *The Oxford Companion to Military History* (Oxford, 2001), pp. 563–7; Philip D. Curtin, *Disease and Empire: The Health of European Troops in the Conquest of Africa* (Cambridge, 1998), ch. 8.

8 Ulrich Trumpener, 'The Road to Ypres: The Beginnings of Gas Warfare in World War I', *Journal of Modern History*, XLVII/3 (1975), pp. 460–80; see also Spiers, *Chemical Warfare*, pp. 13–14.

9 James L. McWilliams and R. James Steel, *Gas! The Battle for Ypres, 1915* (Shrewsbury, 1985), chs. 5 and 6; Brigadier James E. Edmonds and Captain G. C. Wynne, *History of the Great War: Military Operations France and Belgium, 1915* (London, 1927), I, pp. 176–92.

10 General Erich von Falkenhayen, *General Headquarters 1914–1916 and Its Critical Decisions* (London, 1919), p. 84.

11 Brigadier-General Harold Hartley, 'A General Comparison of British and German Methods of Gas Warfare', *Royal Artillery Journal*, XLVI (1919–20), pp. 492–509, at 493.

12 Compare Kim Coleman, *A History of Chemical Warfare* (Basingstoke, 2005), pp. 19–20, with Robert Harris and Jeremy Paxman, *A Higher Form of Killing: The Secret Story of Gas and Germ Warfare* (London, 1982), p. 3.

13 Rudolph Binding, *A Fatalist at War*, trans. Ian F. D. Morrow (London, 1929), p. 64.

14 Dietrich Stoltzenberg, *Fritz Haber: Chemist, Nobel Laureate, German, Jew* (Philadelphia, PA, 2004), pp. 133–42; Curt Wachtel, *Chemical Warfare* (New York, 1941), pp. 31–2; Coleman, *History of Chemical Warfare*, pp. 24–5.

15 Ludwig F. Haber, *The Poisonous Cloud: Chemical Warfare in the First World War* (Oxford, 1986), pp. 121–3; Guy Hartcup, *The War of Invention: Scientific Developments, 1914–18* (London, 1988), pp. 105–6.

16 Donald Richter, *Chemical Soldiers: British Gas Warfare in World War I* (London, 1992), pp. 24–5.

17 Gradon B. Carter, *Porton Down: 75 Years of Chemical and Biological Research* (London, 1992), pp. 7–25.

18 Prentiss, *Chemicals in War*, p. 661; Haber, *Poisonous Cloud*, p. 157.

19 Haber, *Poisonous Cloud*, pp. 156–68; Stoltzenberg, *Fritz Haber*, pp. 140–42; Andy Thomas, *Effects of Chemical Warfare: A Selective Review and Bibliography of British State Papers*, SIPRI Chemical & Biological Warfare Studies 1 (London and Philadelphia, 1985), pp. 23–9.

20 Carter, *Porton Down*, pp. 18–20; Edward M. Spiers, *Chemical Weaponry: A Continuing Challenge* (Basingstoke, 1989), p. 44.

21 Lefebure, *Riddle of the Rhine*, p. 124; see also Major S.J.M. Auld, *Gas and Flame* (New York, 1918), pp. 29, 59–60.

22 Brigadier Charles H. Foulkes, *'Gas!' The Story of the Special Brigade* (Edinburgh, 1934), pp. 93–4; Albert Palazzo, *Seeking Victory on the*

Western Front: The British Army and Chemical Warfare in World War I
(Lincoln, NE, and London, 2000), pp. 53–77.

23 Foulkes, *'Gas!'*, pp. 174–7.

24 Hartley, 'A General Comparison of British and German Methods
of Gas Warfare', p. 503; see also Spiers, *Chemical Weaponry*, pp. 73–
7; and on French artillery tactics, see Olivier Lepick, *La Grande
Guerre Chimique 1914–1918* (Paris, 1998).

25 Major Charles E. Heller, 'Chemical Warfare in World War I: The
American Experience, 1917–18', *Leavenworth Papers*, X (September
1984), pp. 88–91; Foulkes, *'Gas!'*, pp. 298–300; Prentiss, *Chemicals in
War*, p. 653.

26 Imperial War Museum, French Mss., Sir John French to Winifred
Bennett, 27 April 1915; Foulkes, *'Gas!'*, p. 19.

27 *The Times*, 29 April 1915, p. 9; H. C. Peterson, *Propaganda for War*
(New York, 1968), p. 63; J. M. Read, *Atrocity Propaganda 1914–1919*
(New Haven, CT, 1941), pp. 195–9; Spiers, *Chemical Warfare*, pp. 17–18.

28 Prentiss, *Chemicals in War*, pp. 655–8.

29 Edward M. Spiers, 'Chemical Warfare in the First World War',
in *'Look to Your Front': Studies in The First World War by the British
Commission for Military History*, ed. Brian Bond (Staplehurst, 1999),
pp. 163–78.

30 Ibid., pp. 166–7; Robert Graves, *Goodbye to All That* (London, 1929),
pp. 92–3, 129, 133–5, 137, 140, 175, 237; Siegfried Sassoon, *Memoirs
of an Infantry Officer* (London, 1930), p. 147.

31 Edgar Jones, Ian Palmer and Simon Wessely, 'Enduring Beliefs
about Effects of Gassing in War: Qualitative Study', *British Medical
Journal*, CCCXXXV (2007), pp. 1313–15; Haber, *Poisonous Cloud*,
pp. 230–38; Edmund Blunden, *Undertones of War* (London, 1928),
p. 225.

32 Edmonds and Maxwell-Hyslop, *History of the Great War*, V, p. 606;
C.R.M.F. Cruttwell, *A History of the Great War* (Oxford, 1934), p. 154.

33 Haber, *Poisonous Cloud*, pp. 227, 262, 270–71, 274, 278.

34 Amos A. Fries and Clarence J. West, *Chemical Warfare* (New York,
1921), p. 436; on the bombing of the Bolsheviks, see Spiers, *Chemical
Weaponry*, pp. 83–4.

35 Albert Palazzo, 'Plan 1919: The Other One', *Journal of the Society for
Army Historical Research*, LXXVII (1999), pp. 39–50, at p. 39; Foulkes,
'Gas!', pp. 330–31, 334; Prentiss, *Chemicals in War*, pp. 656, 683.

36 Tim Cook, *No Place to Run: The Canadian Corps and Gas Warfare
in the First World War* (Vancouver, 1999), pp. 201–2 and 210.

37 Ibid., pp. 106–10, 127–32, 137–42, 150–53, 203–5, 210, 231.

38 John Terraine, *To Win a War* (London, 1978), p. 116; Spiers,
Chemical Weaponry, p. 81.

39 However, after the German use of gas in Salonika (March 1917),
the British employed gas at the second and third battles of Gaza
(19 April and 31 October 1917) and in Palestine (14 September
1918). Yigel Sheffy, 'The Chemical Dimension of the Gallipoli

Campaign: Introducing Chemical Warfare to the Middle East',
War in History, XII/3 (2005), pp. 278–317.

40 Colonel Harry L. Gilchrist, *A Comparative Study of World War Casualties from Gas and Other Weapons* (Washington, DC, 1931), p. 7; Haber, *Poisonous Cloud*, pp. 186–7. The estimated number of Russian casualties has been disputed but without any supporting evidence; see Steven J. Main, 'Gas on the Eastern Front During the First World War (1915–1917)', *Journal of Slavic Military Studies*, 28 (2015), pp. 99–132, at 131–2.

41 Coleman, *History of Chemical Warfare*, pp. 26, 38.

42 Mark Wheelis, 'Biological Sabotage in World War I', in *Biological and Toxin Weapons: Research, Development and Use from the Middle Ages to 1945*, ed. Geissler and van Courtland Moon, pp. 35–69.

43 Ibid., p. 55.

2 Deterrence and Disarmament: Responses to Chemical and Biological Warfare, 1919–93

1 Tim Cook, '"Against God-inspired Conscience": The Perception of Gas Warfare as a Weapon of Mass Destruction, 1915–1939', *War & Society*, XVIII/1 (2000), pp. 47–69; Uri Bialer, *The Shadow of the Bomber: The Fear of Air Attack and British Politics, 1932–39* (London, 1980); and Geoffrey Best, *Humanity in War* (New York, 1980).

2 The National Archives (TNA), Public Record Office (PRO), WO 32/5190, Sir A. Lynden Bell to Sir C. H. Harington, 25 March 1919, including 'Note by the General Staff on the Use of Gas'; see also Air staff memo (22 May 1919) quoted extensively in Robin Young, 'When Churchill Championed the Use of Poison Gas', *The Times*, 3 January 1997, p. 6.

3 TNA, PRO, WO 188/143, Col. N. P. McCleland, 'Notes on the Use of Gas in Open Warfare', September 1925; Basil H. Liddell Hart, *Paris or the Future of War* (London, 1925), pp. 50–55; Col. J.F.C. Fuller, *The Reformation of War* (London, 1923), pp. 108–11, 121–35, 154–5; Edward M. Spiers, *Chemical Warfare* (Basingstoke, 1986), pp. 40–41.

4 PP [Parliamentary Papers], 'Treaty of Peace between the Allied and Associated Powers and Germany, Signed at Versailles, 28 June 1919', Cmd. 153 (1919), LIII, 221, 225; see also Lorna S. Jaffe, *The Decision to Disarm Germany: British Policy towards Postwar German Disarmament, 1914–1919* (London, 1985).

5 Edward M. Spiers, 'Gas Disarmament in the 1920s: Hopes Confounded', *Journal of Strategic Studies*, XXIX/2 (2006), pp. 281–300, at pp. 283–7, 291.

6 Ibid., pp. 287–9; FRUS [Papers Relating to the Foreign Relations of the United States] (Washington, DC, 1922), I, p. 269.

7 FRUS (1925), I, pp. 89–90; Valerie Adams, *Chemical Warfare, Chemical Disarmament: Beyond Gethsemane* (Basingstoke, 1989), pp. 49, 168–9.

8 Frederic J. Brown, *Chemical Warfare: A Study in Restraints* (Princeton, NJ, 1968), pp. 103–9.

9 Andrew Webster, 'An Argument without End: Britain, France and the Disarmament Process, 1925–34', in *Anglo-French Defence Relations between the Wars*, ed. Martin S. Alexander and William J. Philpott (Basingstoke, 2002), pp. 49–71; Hans W. Gatzke, 'Russo-German Military Collaboration during the Weimar Republic', *American Historical Review*, LXIII/3 (1958), pp. 565–97.

10 John B. S. Haldane, *Callinicus: A Defence of Chemical Warfare* (London, 1925).

11 *The Times*, 20 April 1936, p. 8; on the difficulties of gas preparations in Britain, *A Brief History of the Chemical Defence Experimental Establishment Porton* (Porton, 1961), p. 17, and in the USA, Brown, *Chemical Warfare*, ch. 3.

12 T. H. O'Brien, *Civil Defence* (London, 1955), pp. 58–9, 67–71, 76–82, 100–101, 230–33; Spiers, *Chemical Warfare*, pp. 56–7.

13 Spiers, *Chemical Warfare*, pp. 57–9, 63–5.

14 Joachim Krause and Charles K. Mallory, *Chemical Weapons in Soviet Military Doctrine: Military and Historical Experience, 1915–1991* (Boulder, CO, 1992), ch. 2.

15 TNA, PRO, WO 33/1484, 17th report of the Chemical Research and Development Department, 31 March 1937; Herman Ochsner, *History of German Chemical Warfare in World War II: Part I, The Military Aspect* (Washington, DC, 1949), p. 15.

16 Martin Hugh-Jones, 'Wickham Steed and German Biological Warfare Research', *Intelligence and National Security*, VII/4 (1992), pp. 379–402; John Bryden, *Deadly Allies: Canada's Secret War 1937–1947* (Toronto, 1989); see also Olivier Lepick, 'French Activities Related to Biological Warfare, 1919–45', Valentin Bojtzov and Erhard Geissler, 'Military Biology in the USSR, 1920–45', and Gradon B. Carter and Graham S. Pearson, 'British Biological Warfare and Biological Defence, 1925–45', in *Biological and Toxin Weapons: Research, Development and Use from the Middle Ages to 1945*, ed. Erhard Geissler and John Ellis van Courtland Moon (Oxford, 1999), chs. 5, 8 and 9.

17 Erhard Geissler, 'Biological Warfare Activities in Germany, 1923–45', in *Biological and Toxin Weapons*, ed. Geissler and van Courtland Moon, ch. 6.

18 Ibid., pp. 96–7.

19 Bojtzov and Geissler, 'Military Biology in the USSR, 1920–45', in *Biological and Toxin Weapons*, ed. Geissler and van Courtland Moon, ch. 8. See also Milton Leitenberg and Raymond A. Zilinskas, *The Soviet Biological Weapons Program: A History* (Cambridge, MA, 2012), pp. 20–23.

20 Gradon S. Carter and Graham S. Pearson, 'North Atlantic Chemical and Biological Research Collaboration', *Journal of Strategic Studies*, XIX/1 (1996), pp. 74–103.

21 John Ellis van Courtland Moon, 'US Biological Warfare Planning and Preparedness: The Dilemmas of Policy', in *Biological and Toxin Weapons*, ed. Geissler and van Courtland Moon, ch. 11; see also Barton J. Bernstein, 'America's Biological Warfare Program in the Second World War', *Journal of Strategic Studies*, XI/3 (1988), pp. 292–317.

22 Spiers, *Chemical Warfare*, pp. 62–70.

23 Compare Alibek, *Biohazard*, pp. 29–31, with Leitenberg and Zilinskas, *Soviet Biological Weapons Program*, pp. 29–32.

24 Rolf-Dieter Müller, 'World Power Status through the Use of Poison Gas? German Preparations for Chemical Warfare, 1919–1945', in *The German Military in the Age of Total War*, ed. Wilhelm Deist (Leamington Spa, 1985), pp. 171–209.

25 Spiers, *Chemical Warfare*, p. 86.

26 Brown, *Chemical Warfare*, pp. 244, 262–77; John Ellis van Courtland Moon, 'Project SPHINX: The Question of the Use of Gas in the Planned Invasion of Japan', *Journal of Strategic Studies*, XII/3 (1989), pp. 303–23.

27 Krause and Mallory, *Chemical Weapons*, p. 159; Carter, *Porton*, pp. 55–60; Victor A. Utgoff, *The Challenge of Chemical Weapons: An American Perspective* (Basingstoke, 1990), p. 129: US Department of Defense, *Continuing Development of Chemical Weapon Capabilities in the USSR* (Washington, DC, 1983), p. 1.

28 John R. Walker, *Britain and Disarmament: The UK and Nuclear, Biological and Chemical Weapons Arms Control and Programmes, 1956–1975* (London, 2016).

29 *Report of the Chemical Warfare Review Commission* (Washington, DC, June 1985), pp. xiv, 19–23, 45.

30 Judith Miller, Stephen Engelberg and William Broad, *Germs: The Ultimate Weapon* (New York, 2001), ch. 2; Simon Whitby and Paul Rogers, 'Anti-crop Biological Warfare: Implications of the Iraqi and US Programs', *Defense Analysis*, XIII/3 (1997), pp. 303–18.

31 'Nixon Bars Use of Germ Weapons', *New York Times*, 26 November 1969, p. 16; Miller et al., *Germs*, p. 62.

32 Raymond A. Zilinskas, 'The Soviet Biological Weapons Program and Its Legacy in Today's Russia', *Center for the Study of Weapons of Mass Destruction Occasional Paper* 11 (Washington, DC, 2016), pp. 18, 25–30, 40–41.

33 *Report of the Chemical Warfare Review Commission*, p. 71; on the Soviet BW programme, see Ken Alibek, *Biohazard* (London, 1999), and 'The Soviet Union's Anti-Agricultural Biological Weapons', *Annals of the New York Academy of Sciences*, DCCCXCIV (1999), pp. 18–19; Miller et al., *Germs*, pp. 75–97, 134–7; Defense Intelligence Agency (DIA), *Soviet Biological Warfare Threat*, DST-1610F-057–86 (Washington, DC, 1986).

34 Ken Alibek, 'Russia's Deadly Expertise', *New York Times*, 27 March 1998, p. A19.

35 DIA, *Soviet Chemical Weapons Threat*, DST-1620F-051–85 (Washington, DC, 1985), pp. 1–17; John Erickson, 'The Soviet Union's Growing Arsenal of Chemical Warfare', *Strategic Review*, VII/4 (1979), pp. 63–71; Krause and Mallory, *Chemical Weapons*, pp. 133–4, 139–42, 161.

36 Krause and Mallory, *Chemical Weapons*, pp. 154–8.

37 On Bush's chemical weapons policy, see Edward M. Spiers, *Chemical and Biological Weapons: A Study of Proliferation* (Basingstoke, 1994), ch. 5.

38 Hearings of the Senate Foreign Relations Committee, *Status of 1990 Bilateral Chemical Weapons Agreement and Multilateral Negotiation on Chemical Weapons Ban*, 102nd Congress, first session (22 May 1991), p. 18.

39 Ron G. Manley, 'Verification under the Chemical Weapons Convention', in *Terrorism and Weapons of Mass Destruction: Responding to the Challenge*, ed. Ian Bellany (London, 2008), pp. 180–98.

3 Chemical Warfare in Third World Conflicts

1 Martin Gilbert, *Winston S. Churchill*, IV, *1916–1922* (London, 1975), p. 274.

2 TNA, PRO, WO 106/1148, General Lord Rawlinson to Secretary, War Office, 16 September 1919; see also Edward M. Spiers, *Chemical Weaponry: A Continuing Challenge* (Basingstoke, 1989), pp. 27, 31–2.

3 TNA, PRO, WO 32/5184, Churchill minute, 12 May 1919; for this debate, see Edward M. Spiers, 'Gas and the North-West Frontier', *Journal of Strategic Studies*, VI/4 (1983), pp. 94–112.

4 Spiers, 'Gas and the North-West Frontier', pp. 97–105.

5 Gilbert, *Churchill*, IV, pp. 494, 810; IV Companion part 2 (London, 1977), pp. 1066–7, 1190, and IV Companion part 3 (London, 1977), p. 1695; and Charles Townshend, 'Civilization and "Frightfulness"; Air Control in the Middle East between the Wars', in *Warfare Diplomacy and Politics: Essays in Honour of A.J.P. Taylor*, ed. Chris Wrigley (London, 1986), pp. 142–62, at pp. 147–8.

6 Compare Kim Coleman, *A History of Chemical Warfare* (Basingstoke, 2005), p. 44, with Philip A. Towle, *Pilots and Rebels: The Use of Aircraft in Unconventional Warfare, 1918–1988* (London, 1989), p. 14, and David E. Omissi, *Air Power and Colonial Control: The Royal Air Force 1919–1939* (Manchester, 1990), pp. 21, 160, 182.

7 Sebastian Balfour, *Deadly Embrace: Morocco and the Road to the Spanish Civil War* (Oxford, 2002), chs. 2 and 5.

8 Ibid., pp. 87, 128–56.

9 John Wright, *Libya* (London, 1969), p. 158.

10 John Gooch, 'Re-conquest and Suppression: Fascist Italy's Pacification of Libya and Ethiopia, 1922–39', *Journal of Strategic Studies*, XXVIII/6 (2005), pp. 1005–32, at p. 1011.

11 The data is far from complete; see Alberto Sbacchi, *Legacy of Bitterness: Ethiopia and Fascist Italy, 1935–1941* (Lawrenceville, NJ, 1997), pp. 57–60.

12 Ibid., pp. 60–63, 71–7; Spiers, *Chemical Weaponry*, pp. 84–8; Anthony Mockler, *Haile Selassie's War* (Oxford, 1984), pp. 85–6, 409: Omissi, *Air Power*, p. 206.

13 Yuki Tanaka, 'Poison Gas: The Story Japan Would Like to Forget', *Bulletin of the Atomic Scientists*, XLIV (1988), pp. 10–19; Robert Harris and Jeremy Paxman, *A Higher Form of Killing: The Secret Story of Gas and Germ Warfare* (London, 1982), pp. 47–8.

14 Edward M. Spiers, *Chemical Warfare* (Basingstoke, 1986), pp. 65–6.

15 Compare the US estimates of 36,968 casualties (2,086 fatal) and China's claim of 10,000 deaths from over 2,000 gas attacks, Tanaka, 'Poison Gas', p. 16, with George Wehrfritz and Hideko Takayama, 'In Search of Buried Poison', *Newsweek*, 20 July 1998, pp. 27–8.

16 Tanisuga Shizuo, 'Gas Soldier', in *Japan At War: An Oral History*, ed. Haruko T. Cook and Theodore F. Cook (London, 1992), pp. 44–6.

17 Peter Williams and David Wallace, *Unit 731: The Japanese Army's Secret of Secrets* (London, 1990), pp. 41–2, 117–18.

18 Sheldon H. Harris, *Factories of Death: Japanese Biological Warfare, 1932–45, and the American Cover-Up* (London, 1994), pp. 34–6, 39, 47–8, 59, 66–7; Harris and Paxman, *Higher Form of Killing*, pp. 76–7.

19 Harris, *Factories*, pp. 60–61, 76–80, 99–100, 173–223; Williams and Wallace, *Unit 731*, chs. 10–14.

20 Williams and Wallace, *Unit 731*, ch. 16.

21 Ibid., ch. 17; Jon Halliday and Bruce Cummings, *Korea: The Unknown War* (London, 1988), pp. 182–6; John Ellis van Courtland Moon, 'Biological Warfare Allegations: The Korean War Case', *Annals of the New York Academy of Sciences*, DCLXVI (31 December 1992), pp. 53–83.

22 Stephen Badsey, 'Propaganda, The Media, and Psychological Operations: The Korean War', in *The Korean War, 1950–53: A Fifty Year Retrospective: The Chief of Army's Military History Conference, 2000*, ed. Peter Dennis and Jeffrey Grey (Canberra, 2000), pp. 150–62, at p. 160; Jeffrey A. Lockwood, *Six-Legged Soldiers: Using Insects as Weapons of War* (Oxford, 2009), pp. 187–91.

23 Van Courtland Moon, 'Biological Warfare Allegations', pp. 60–61, 69–71.

24 Lieutenant General John H. Hay, Jr, *Tactical and Materiel Innovations*, Vietnam Studies (Washington, DC, 1974), pp. 34–7.

25 Ibid., pp. 37–8; *Congressional Record*, House of Representatives, 12 June 1969, p. 15765; Spiers, *Chemical Weaponry*, pp. 101–2.

26 General William C. Westmoreland, *A General Reports* (New York, 1976), p. 366.

27 Rear Admiral William E. Lemos, Hearings on *Chemical-Biological Warfare: US Policies and International Effects* before the Subcommittee

on National Security Policy and Scientific Developments of the
Committee on Foreign Affairs, House of Representatives, 91st
Congress, first session (19 December 1969), pp. 228 and 237.

28 Towle, *Pilots and Rebels*, pp. 89–90; Steve Connor and Andy Thomas,
'How Britain Sprayed Malaya with Dioxin', *New Scientist*, 19 January
1984, pp. 6–7.

29 William A. Buckingham, *Operation Ranch Hand: The Air Force
and Herbicides in Southeast Asia 1961–1971* (Washington, DC, 1982),
pp. 200–201; Lemos, Hearings on *Chemical-Biological Warfare*, p. 242;
Paul F. Cecil, *Herbicidal Warfare: The RANCH HAND Project in Vietnam*
(New York, 1986), pp. 63–5; Gunter Lewy, *America in Vietnam* (New
York, 1978), pp. 258–9.

30 Hay, *Tactical and Materiel Innovations*, pp. 91–2; Buckingham,
Operation Ranch Hand, pp. 146–8, 199–200.

31 Buckingham, *Operation Ranch Hand*, pp. 134–6, 147–8; Cecil,
Herbicidal Warfare, p. 178.

32 'FAS Statement on Biological and Chemical Warfare', *Bulletin of the
Atomic Scientists*, xx (1964), pp. 46–7.

33 Spiers, *Chemical Weaponry*, pp. 109–12; J. B. Neilands, Gordon H.
Orians, E. W. Pfeiffer, Alje Vennema and Arthur H. Westing, *Harvest
of Death: Chemical Warfare in Vietnam and Cambodia* (New York,
1972); James B. Jacobs and Dennis McNamara, 'Vietnam Veterans
and the Agent Orange Controversy', *Armed Forces and Society*, xiii / 1
(1986), pp. 57–80.

34 Dana A. Schmidt, *Yemen: The Unknown War* (London, 1968), ch. 19.

35 Bernard G. Wertzman, 'US Says Data Show Toxin Use in Asia
Conflict', and Barbara Crossette, 'US Presents an Analysis to Back
Its Charge of Toxin Weapons' Use', *New York Times*, 14 and 15
September 1981, pp. A1 and A8 and pp. A1 and A6; see also Sterling
Seagrave, *Yellow Rain: A Journey through the Terror of Chemical
Warfare* (London, 1981).

36 US Department of State, *Chemical Warfare in Southeast Asia and
Afghanistan: Report to the Congress from Secretary of State Alexander
M. Haig, Jr., March 22, 1982*, Special Report no. 98; *Chemical Warfare
in Southeast Asia and Afghanistan: An Update: Report from Secretary
of State George P. Shultz, November 1982*, Special Report no. 104; and
*Chemical Weapons Use in Southeast Asia and Afghanistan, February 21,
1984*, Current Policy No. 553.

37 Thomas D. Seeley, Joan W. Nowicke, Matthew Meselson, Jeanne
Guillemin and Pongthep Akratanakul, 'Yellow Rain', *Scientific
American*, ccliii / 3 (1985), pp. 122–31; Julian Robinson, Jeanne
Guillemin and Matthew Meselson, 'Yellow Rain: The Story
Collapses', *Foreign Policy*, 67 (1987), pp. 100–117; Spiers, *Chemical
Weaponry*, pp. 117–21.

38 US Department of State, 'Yellow Rain Caused By Bees', Press
Guidance (Washington, DC, 1 June 1983), pp. 1–3; Gary B. Crocker,
'The Evidence of Chemical and Toxin Weapon Use in Southeast

Asia and Afghanistan', in *Biological and Chemical Warfare*, ed.
A. Heyndrickx (Ghent, 21–23 May 1984), pp. 384–412.

4 The Proliferation of Chemical and Biological Weapons

1 J. Michael McConnell, 'Annual Threat Assessment of the Director
   of National Intelligence for the Senate Select Committee on
   Intelligence', 5 February 2008, http//intelligence.senate.gov/
   080205/mcconnell.pdf (accessed 13 June 2008).
2 William H. Webster, Hearings on *Global Spread of Chemical and
   Biological Weapons* before the Committee on Governmental Affairs
   and its Permanent Subcommittee on Investigations, United States
   Senate, 101st Congress, first session (9 February 1989), p. 10; Don
   Oberdorfer, 'Chemical Arms Curbs Are Sought', *Washington Post*,
   9 September 1985, pp. A1, A6 and A7.
3 Jack Anderson, 'The Growing Chemical Club', *Washington Post*,
   26 August 1984, p. C7; Robert C. Toth, 'Germ, Chemical Arms
   Reported Proliferating', *Los Angeles Times*, 27 May 1986, pp. 1 and
   12; David B. Ottaway, 'In Mideast, Warfare With A New Nature',
   Washington Post, 5 April 1988, pp. A1 and A14.
4 Webster and Barry J. Erlick, Hearings on *Global Spread*, pp. 10–11,
   21 and 33.
5 S. J. Lundin, J. P. Perry Robinson and R. Trapp, 'Chemical and
   Biological Warfare: Developments in 1988', in SIPRI, SIPRI *Yearbook
   1988 World Armaments and Disarmament* (Oxford, 1989), pp. 100–103.
6 Gordon M. Burck and Charles C. Floweree, *International Handbook
   on Chemical Weapons Proliferation* (New York, 1991), pp. 152–60; UN
   Security Council, *Report of the Mission Dispatched by the Secretary-
   General to Investigate an Alleged Use of Chemical Weapons in
   Mozambique*, S/24065 (12 June 1992), p. 11.
7 Hearings on *National Defense Authorization Act for Fiscal year 1989
   – H.R. 4264 and Oversight of Previously Authorized Programs* before
   the Seapower and Strategic and Critical Materials Subcommittee of
   the Committee on Armed Services, House of Representatives, 100th
   Congress, second session, 1 March 1988, p. 40 and Hearings on the
   same act before the Committee on Armed Services, House of
   Representatives, 9 March 1988, p. 120.
8 Elisa D. Harris, 'Chemical Weapons Proliferation: Current
   Capabilities and Prospects for Control', in Aspen Study Group,
   *New Threats: Responding to the Proliferation of Nuclear, Chemical, and
   Delivery Capabilities in the Third World* (Lanham, MD, 1990), pp. 67–87;
   William Burns, Hearings on the *Chemical and Biological Weapons
   Threat: The Urgent Need for Remedies* before the Committee on
   Foreign Relations, United States Senate, 101st Congress, first session,
   24 January 1989, pp. 5–6.
9 Julian Perry Robinson, 'Chemical Weapons Proliferation: The
   Problem in Perspective', in *Chemical Weapons & Missile Proliferation:*

With Implications for the Asia/Pacific Region, ed. Trevor Findlay (London, 1991), pp. 19–35.

10 Julian Perry Robinson, 'Chemical-Weapons Proliferation in the Middle East', in *Non-Conventional Weapons Proliferation in the Middle East: Tackling the Spread of Nuclear, Chemical, and Biological Capabilities*, ed. Efraim Karsh, Martin S. Navias and Philip Sabin (Oxford, 1993), pp. 69–98.

11 Webster, Hearings on *Global Spread*, pp. 15–16.

12 Doug Feith, Joint Hearing on *Chemical Warfare: Arms Control and Nonproliferation* before the Committee on Foreign Relations and the Subcommittee on Energy, Nuclear Proliferation and Government Processes of the Committee on Governmental Affairs, United States Senate, 98th Congress, second session, 28 June 1984, pp. 12–13. For a summary of these reports, see Edward M. Spiers, *Chemical and Biological Weapons: A Study of Proliferation* (Houndmills, Basingstoke, 1994), pp. 22–5.

13 CRS Report for Congress RL30699, *Nuclear, Biological, and Chemical Weapons and Missiles: Status and Trends* by Paul K. Kerr (Washington, DC, 20 February 2008), p. CRS-16; Yevgeny A. Kolesnikov, 'Lessons Learned from the *Nord-OST* Terrorist Attack in Moscow from the Standpoint of Russian Security and Law Enforcement Agencies', in US-Russian Workshop Proceedings, *Terrorism: Reducing Vulnerabilities and Improving Responses* (Washington, DC, 2004), pp. 26–34.

14 CRS Report for Congress RL 30699, pp. CRS-14–15.

15 Gordon K. Vachon, 'Chemical Weapons and the Third World', *Survival*, XXIV/2 (1984), pp. 79–86; Edward M. Spiers, 'The Role of Chemical Weapons in the Military Doctrines of Third World Armies', in *Security Implications of a Global Chemical Weapons Ban*, ed. Joachim Krause (Boulder, CO, 1991), ch. 4.

16 Erlick, Hearings on *Global Spread*, pp. 32–3.

17 W. Seth Carus, 'The Proliferation of Biological Weapons', in *Biological Weapons: Weapons of the Future?*, ed. Brad Roberts (Washington, DC, 1993), pp. 19–27.

18 Ibid., p. 22; James M. Markham, 'Arabs Link Curbs on Gas and A-Arms', *New York Times*, 9 January 1989, p. A8; Keith B. Bickel, 'Poor Man's Bomb Goes Global', *Los Angeles Times*, 1 May 1998, part V, p. 5.

19 Anderson, 'The Growing Chemical Club', p. C7.

20 Office of the Secretary of Defense, *Proliferation: Threat and Response* (Washington, DC, November 1997), pp. 7, 11, 28, 39; Glenn Kessler and Robin Wright, 'Israel, US Shared Data on Suspected Nuclear Site', *Washington Post*, 21 September 2007, p. A01.

21 Chandré Gould and Peter Folb, 'The South African Chemical and Biological Warfare Program: An Overview', *Nonproliferation Review*, VII/3 (Fall/Winter 2000), pp. 10–23; Tom Mangold and Jeff Goldberg, *Plague Wars: A True Story of Biological Warfare* (London,

1999), chs. 26–7.

22 Glenn Cross, *Dirty War: Rhodesia and Chemical Biological Warfare,
1975–1980* (Solihull, 2017), pp. 79–85, 116–21, 205, 215.

23 Brad Roberts, 'Chemical Weapons and Policy', *Washington
Quarterly*, VIII/1 (1985), pp. 155–65, at p. 158; Spiers, 'The Role of
Chemical Weapons', p. 46.

24 Steve Fetter, 'Ballistic Missiles and Weapons of Mass Destruction',
International Security, XVI/1 (1991), pp. 5–42.

25 W. Thomas Smith Jr, 'Iran's missile-rattling ups the ante', *Canada
Free Press*, 13 July 2008, http://canadafreepress.com/index.php/
article/3945 (accessed 15 July 2008).

26 Spiers, *Chemical and Biological Weapons*, pp. 61–3, 147.

27 Ibid., ch. 4.

28 Michael Moodie and Brad Roberts, Hearings before the
Permanent Subcommittee on Investigations of the Committee
on Governmental Affairs on *Global Proliferation of Weapons of
Mass Destruction*, Parts 1, 2 and 3, 104th Congress, first session
(31 October and 1 November 1995 and 20 and 27 March 1996),
part 1, pp. 194, 196–200.

29 T. Skinner, 'UK Breaks up Suspected WMD Trafficking Operation',
Jane's Defence Weekly, XLIII (31 May 2006), p. 8.

30 Edward M. Spiers, *Weapons of Mass Destruction: Prospects for
Proliferation* (Houndmills, Basingstoke, 2000), p. 130; B. W. Jentleson
and C. A. Whytock, 'Who "Won" Libya', *International Security*,
XVI/3 (2005/6), pp. 47–86.

31 Jonathan B. Tucker, 'The Rollback of Libya's Chemical Weapons
Program', *Nonproliferation Review*, XVI/3 (2009), pp. 363–84.

32 Stephen G. Rademaker, 'Countering WMD and Terrorism through
Security Cooperation', 6 April 2006, http://state.gov/t/isn/rls/rm/
64173.htm (accessed 31 July 2008); see also A. C. Winner, 'The
Proliferation Security Initiative: The New Face of Interdiction',
Washington Quarterly, XXVIII/2 (2005), pp. 120–43.

33 Kathleen Bailey, Hearings on *Military Implications of The Chemical
Weapons Convention (CWC)* before the Committee on Armed
Services, United States Senate, 103rd Congress, second session
(18 August 1994), p. 124.

34 Despite joining the CWC, Libya under the Qaddafi regime concealed
a small stock of mustard-gas shells, 'Libya: Muammar Gaddafi's
Secret Stock of Chemical Weapons Found', *Daily Telegraph*, 20
January 2012.

5 Iraq's Chemical and Biological Warfare Programmes

1 Efraim Karsh and Inari Rautsi, *Saddam Hussein: A Political Biography*
(London, 1991), pp. 61, 79–83, 126.

2 Jack Anderson, 'Iraqis Trained for Chemical Warfare', *Washington
Post*, 3 November 1980, p. B13, and 'The Growing Chemical Club',

p. c7; see also Iraq Survey Group (ISG) Final Report, 'Evolution of Iraq's Chemical Warfare Program', in *Iraq's Chemical Warfare Program*, 2004, pp. 1–2, ww.globalsecurity.org/wmd/library/report/2004/isg-final-report/isg-final-report_vol3_cw.htm (accessed 27 June 2006).

3   Kenneth R. Timmerman, *The Death Lobby: How the West Armed Iraq* (London, 1992), pp. 65–7, 79–80, 154–6.

4   Ibid., p. 302; ISG, 'Evolution of CW', p. 2; William H. Webster, Hearings on *Global Spread of Chemical and Biological Weapons* before the Committee on Governmental Affairs and its Permanent Subcommittee on Investigations, United States Senate, 101st Congress, first session (9 February 1989), p. 12; Gary Thatcher and Timothy Aeppel, 'The Trail to Samarra: How Iraq Got the Materials to Make Chemical Weapons', in 'Poison on the Wind', *Christian Science Monitor* (2–8 January 1989), pp. B3, B6–B10, B14–B16.

5   Gordon M. Burck and Charles C. Floweree, *International Handbook on Chemical Weapons Proliferation* (New York, 1991), pp. 97–8; W. Andrew Terrill, Jr., 'Chemical Weapons in the Gulf War', *Strategic Review*, XIV/2 (1986), pp. 51–8.

6   UN Security Council, *Report of the Specialists Appointed by the Secretary-General to Investigate Allegations by the Islamic Republic of Iran Concerning the Use of Chemical Weapons*, S/16433 (26 March 1984), pp. 11–12; Peter Dunn, 'The Chemical War: Journey to Iran', *Nuclear, Biological, and Chemical Defense and Technology International*, I (April 1986), pp. 28–35.

7   Burck and Floweree, *International Handbook*, pp. 103–5, 116; Edward M. Spiers, *Chemical and Biological Weapons: A Study of Proliferation* (Basingstoke, 1994), p. 46; Dilip Hiro, *The Longest War: The Iran–Iraq Military Conflict* (London, 1990), p. 137.

8   UN Security Council, *Report of the Mission Dispatched by the Secretary-General to Investigate Allegations of the Use of Chemical Weapons in the Conflict between the Islamic Republic of Iran and Iraq*, S/20060 (20 July 1988), p. 10; Bernard E. Trainor, 'Chemical War: Threat in Third World?', *New York Times*, 5 August 1988, p. 8.

9   Joost R. Hiltermann, *A Poisonous Affair: America, Iraq and the Gassing of Halabja* (Cambridge, 2007), ch. 7 and pp. 185–6, 193–200; Patrick E. Tyler, 'Both Iraq and Iran Gassed Kurds in War, US Analysis Finds', *Washington Post*, 3 May 1990, p. A37; UN Security Council, *Report of the Mission Dispatched by the Secretary-General to Investigate Allegations of the Use of Chemical Weapons in the Conflict between the Islamic Republic of Iran and Iraq*, S/20063 (25 July 1988), p. 11.

10 Hiro, *Longest War*, pp. 200–201, 206–7; Thomas L. McNaugher, 'Ballistic Missiles and Chemical Weapons', *International Security*, XV/2 (1990), pp. 5–34; Al Mauroni, *Chemical and Biological Warfare: A Reference Handbook* (Santa Barbara, CA, 2003), p. 152.

11 Timmerman, *Death Lobby*, p. 197; Efraim Karsh, 'The Iran–Iraq War: A Military Analysis', *Adelphi Papers*, CCXX (1987), p. 56; Burck and

Floweree, *International Handbook*, p. 117.

12 *Chemical Weapons Use in Kurdistan: Iraq's Final Offensive*, a staff report to the Committee on Foreign Relations, United States Senate, 100th Congress, second session (Washington, DC, October 1988), pp. vii and 16.

13 Ibid., pp. 31–3; *Winds of Death: Iraq's Use of Poison Gas Against Its Kurdish Population*, report of a Medical Mission by Physicians for Human Rights (Somerville, MA, February 1989), pp. 10–12; Robert Mullen Cook-Deegan and Brad Roberts, Hearings on *Global Spread*, pp. 43–5, 313; Thatcher and Aeppel, 'The Trail to Samarra', pp. B15–B16; McNaugher, 'Ballistic Missiles and Chemical Weapons', pp. 15–21.

14 Mauroni, *Chemical and Biological Warfare*, pp. 152–3; ISG; 'Evolution of CW', pp. 3–5; George P. Shultz, *Turmoil and Triumph: My Years as Secretary of State* (New York, 1993), pp. 238–43; UN Security Council, *Resolution 620 (1988)*, S/ RES/ 620 (26 August 1988).

15 ISG, 'Evolution of the Biological Warfare Program', in *Biological Warfare*, pp. 2–3; Graham S. Pearson, 'The Iraqi Biological Weapons Program', in *Deadly Cultures: Biological Weapons since 1945*, ed. Mark Wheelis, Lajos Rózsa and Malcolm Dando (Cambridge, MA, 2006), pp. 169–90.

16 ISG, 'Evolution of BW Program', pp. 2–3.

17 Ibid., pp. 3–4; Alan Cowell, 'Iraq Chief, Boasting of Poison Gas, Warns of Disaster if Israelis Strike', *New York Times*, 3 April 1990, pp. A1, A8.

18 UN Security Council, *Eighth Report of the Secretary-General on the Status of the Implementation of the Special Commission's Plan for the Ongoing Monitoring and Verification of Iraq's Compliance with Relevant Parts of Section C of Security Council Resolution 687 (1991)*, S/ 1995/ 864 (11 October 1995), pp. 19–28.

19 Ibid., pp. 27–8; for a more critical review, see Raymond A. Zilinskas, 'Iraq's Biological Warfare Program: The Past as Future?', in *Biological Weapons: Limiting the Threat*, ed. Joshua Lederberg (Cambridge, MA, 2000), pp. 137–64.

20 James Baker with T. M. Defrank, *The Politics of Diplomacy* (New York, 1995), p. 359; Rolf Ekéus, Hearings on *Global Proliferation of Weapons of Mass Destruction* before the Permanent Subcommittee on Investigations of the Senate Committee on Governmental Affairs, 104th Congress, first session (20 March 1996), part II, p. 92; DoD, *Conduct of the Persian Gulf War* (Washington, DC, April 1992), p. Q-2.

21 General H. Norman Schwarzkopf with P. Petre, *It Doesn't Take a Hero* (New York, 1992), p. 439; DoD, *Conduct of the Persian Gulf War*, pp. 18, G-26, Q-2, Q-5, Q-7, Q-8; Mauroni, *Chemical and Biological Warfare*, pp. 155–60.

22 DoD, *Conduct of the Persian Gulf War*, pp. 244, C-2; ISG, 'Evolution of BW Program', p. 4.

23 ISG, 'Concealment and Destruction of Biological Weapons' in *Biological Warfare*, p. 2; SIPRI Fact Sheet, *Iraq: The UNSCOM Experience*

(Stockholm, October 1998).

24 Theodore A. Postol, 'Lessons of the Gulf War Experience with Patriot', *International Security*, XVI/3 (1991/2), pp. 119–71; *Gulf War Air Power Survey*, 5 vols (Washington, DC, 1993), II, p. 340.

25 General H. Norman Schwarzkopf, Hearings on *Operation Desert Shield/ Desert Storm* before the Committee on Armed Forces, United States Senate, 102nd Congress, first session (12 June 1991), p. 347; on Israel's civil defence, see Spiers, *Chemical and Biological Weapons*, pp. 121–3.

26 Schwarzkopf, Hearings on *Operation Desert Shield*, p. 334.

27 Storer H. Rowley, 'Biggest Fear was Chemical Attack', *Chicago Tribune*, 28 February 1991, p. 8.

28 ISG, 'Regime Strategic Intent', pp. 4, 8, and 'Realizing Saddam's Veiled Strategic Intent', pp. 18–19, in *Comprehensive Report*; W. Andrew Terrill, 'Chemical Warfare and "Desert Storm": The Disaster that Never Came', *Small Wars and Insurgencies*, IV/2 (1993), pp. 263–79.

29 Edward M. Spiers, *Weapons of Mass Destruction: Prospects for Proliferation* (Houndmills, Basingstoke, 2000), p. 26.

30 DoD, *Conduct of the Persian Gulf War*, p. viii.

31 Kathleen C. Bailey, *The UN Inspections in Iraq: Lessons for On-Site Verification* (Boulder, CO, 1995), p. 15; David Kay, 'Arms Inspections in Iraq: Lessons for Arms Control', *Bulletin for Arms Control* (August 1992), pp. 2–7.

32 Tim Trevan, *Saddam's Secrets: The Hunt for Iraq's Hidden Weapons* (London, 1999), pp. 383–7; Graham S. Pearson, *The UNSCOM Saga: Chemical and Biological Weapons Non-Proliferation* (Houndmills, Basingstoke, 1999), p. 217.

33 T. Weiner, 'US Spied on Iraq under UN Cover, Officials Now Say' and 'US Used UN Team to Place Spy Device in Iraq, Aides Say', *New York Times*, 7 and 8 January 1999, pp. A1 and A6, A1 and A8; Scott Ritter, *Endgame: Solving the Iraq Crisis* (New York, 2002), ch. 14.

34 Ritter, *Endgame*, p. 197; Hans Blix, *Disarming Iraq* (London, 2005), p. 29.

35 ISG, 'Realizing Saddam's ... Intent', pp. 2–3, 5.

36 Ibid.; Trevan, *Saddam's Secrets*, ch. 4.

37 UN Security Council, *Eighth Report* ... (11 October 1995).

38 ISG, 'Realizing Saddam's ... Intent', pp. 7–8.

39 Blix, *Disarming Iraq*, p. 128; Robert Jervis, 'Reports, Politics, and Intelligence Failures: The Case of Iraq', *Journal of Strategic Studies*, XXIX/1 (2006), pp. 3–52.

40 Bob Drogin, *Curveball: Spies, Lies, and the Con Man who Caused a War* (New York, 2007), pp. 126–8, 151–9, 280.

41 *The Commission on the Intelligence Capabilities of the United States Regarding Weapons of Mass Destruction* (hereafter the WMD *Intelligence Report*), 31 March 2005, p. 173, www.wmd.gov/report/wmd_report.pdf (26 August 2008).

42 *Report of the Select Committee on Intelligence on the US Intelligence Community's Prewar Intelligence Assessments on Iraq*, 108th Congress,

second session, 9 July 2004, pp. 15, 286–9.

43 *Iraq's Weapons of Mass Destruction: The Assessment of the British Government* (London, 2002), p. 5; *Review of Intelligence on Weapons of Mass Destruction; Report of a Committee of Privy Councillors*, HC 898 (14 July 2004), pp. 76–7, 80, 99, 127, 151–2, 163–76.

44 Robin Cook, *Point of Departure: Diaries from the Front Bench* (London, 2004), pp. 310–11, 379–80.

45 Bob Woodward, *Bush at War* (New York, 2003), p. 83.

46 ISG, 'Evolution of BW Program', p. 5 and annex D in *Biological Warfare*; David Kay, Hearings on *Iraqi Weapons of Mass Destruction Programs* before the Committee on Armed Services, United States Senate (28 January 2004), www.ceip.org/files/projects/npp/pdf/Iraq/kattestimony.pdf (accessed 27 June 2006).

47 UN Secretary-General, 'Secretary-General Strongly Condemns Terrorist Gas Attacks in Iraq', 19 March 2007, www.un.org/News/Press/docs/2007/sgsm10914.doc.htm (accessed 2 October 2007).

48 'Chlorine as a Terrorist Weapon in Iraq', *WMD Insights* (May 2007), http://wmdinsights.org/115/115_MEI_Chlorine.htm (accessed 22 May 2007).

6 Chemical and Biological Terrorism

1 US Department of State, *Patterns of Global Terrorism 2000* (Washington, DC, 2001), p. vi.

2 OTA, *Proliferation of Weapons of Mass Destruction*, pp. 50, 55; Harvey J. McGeorge, II, 'The Deadly Mixture: Bugs, Gas and Terrorists', *Nuclear Biological Chemical and Defense & Technology International*, I (May 1986), pp. 56–61.

3 Harvey J. McGeorge, 'Chemical and Biological Terrorism: Analyzing the Problem', *ASA Newsletter*, XLII (16 June 1994), pp. 1, 12–13.

4 Joseph Pilat, 'World Watch: Striking Back at Urban Terrorism', *Nuclear Biological Chemical Defense & Technology International*, I (June 1986), pp. 18–19.

5 Joseph F. Pilat, 'Prospects for NBC Terrorism after Tokyo', in *Terrorism with Chemical and Biological Weapons: Calibrating Risks and Responses*, ed. Brad Roberts (Alexandra, VA, 1997), pp. 1–22, at p. 8.

6 Karl Lowe, 'Analyzing Technical Constraints on Bio-Terrorism: Are They Still Important?' in *Terrorism*, ed. Roberts, pp. 53–64, at p. 62.

7 Brian M. Jenkins, 'Will Terrorists Go Nuclear?', *Orbis*, XXIX/3 (1985), pp. 507–15, at p. 511; Ron Purver, 'Understanding Past Non-Use of CBW', in *Terrorism*, ed. Roberts, pp. 65–74.

8 Purver, 'Understanding Past Non-Use of CBW', in *Terrorism*, ed. Roberts, p. 73.

9 Webster, Hearings on *Chemical and Biological Weapons Threat: The Urgent Need for Remedies* before the Committee on Foreign Relations, United States Senate, 101st Congress, first session (1 March 1999), p. 42.

10 John Deutch, Hearings before the Permanent Subcommittee on Investigations of the Committee on Governmental Affairs United States Senate on *Global Proliferation of Weapons of Mass Destuction*, 104th Congress, first session (20 March 1996), Part II, p. 75.

11 Robert H. Kupperman and R. James Woolsey, Hearings on *High-Tech Terrorism* before the Subcommittee on Technology and the Law of the Committee on the Judiciary, United States Senate, 100th Congress, second session (19 May 1988), pp. 54–5; Robert H. Kupperman and David M. Smith, 'Coping with Biological Terrorism', in *Biological Weapons: Weapons of the Future?*, ed. Brad Roberts (Washington, DC, 1993), pp. 35–46, at p. 41.

12 Harvey J. McGeorge, 'Reversing the Trend on Terror', *Defense & Terror* (April 1988), pp. 16–22, at p. 22; Dean A. Wilkening, 'BCW Attack Scenarios', in *The New Terror: Facing the Threat of Biological and Chemical Weapons*, ed. Sidney D. Drell, Abraham D. Sofaer and George D. Wilson (Stanford, CA, 1999), pp. 76–114.

13 START (National Consortium for the Study of Terrorism and Response to Terrorism), *Patterns of Terrorism in the United States, 1970–2013 Final Report to Resilient Systems Division, DHS Science and Technology Directorate* (University of Maryland, October 2014), p. 20.

14 Jonathan B. Tucker, 'Introduction' and 'Lessons from the Case Studies', in *Toxic Terror: Assessing Terrorist Use of Chemical and Biological Weapons*, ed. Jonathan B. Tucker (Cambridge, MA, 2001), pp. 13, 250–51.

15 Ehud Sprinzak and Idith Zertal, 'Avenging Israel's Blood (1946)', W. Seth Carus, 'The Rajneeshees (1984)' and John V. Parachini, 'The World Trade Center Bombers (1993)' in *Toxic Terror*, ed. Tucker, pp. 17–41, 115–37, 185–206; Judith Miller, Stephen Engelberg and William Broad, *Germs: The Ultimate Weapon* (New York, 2001), ch. 1.

16 These are more up-to-date statistics than those originally reported. Compare David E. Kaplan, 'Aum Shinrikyo (1995)' in *Toxic Terror*, ed. Tucker, pp. 207–26, at p. 221, with David E. Kaplan and Andrew Marshall, *The Cult at the End of the World: The Incredible Story of Aum* (London, 1997), pp. 182, 315.

17 Kaplan, 'Aum Shinrikyo' (1995), p. 213; Gwen Robinson, 'Sect Leader Eludes Police as Raids Uncover Lethal Haul' and 'Panic Grips Tokyo after Threat of More Gas Attacks', *The Times*, 24 and 25 March 1995, p. 11 and p. 9.

18 John F. Sopko and Staff Statement before Hearings on *Global Proliferation of Weapons of Mass Destruction*, Part I, pp. 17–18, 47–102; Kaplan, 'Aum Shinrikyo (1995)', pp. 208–9; Kaplan and Marshall, *The Cult*, pp. 17–20.

19 Sheryl WuDunn, Judith Miller and William J. Broad, 'How Japan Germ Terror Alerted World', *New York Times*, 26 May 1998, pp. A1 and A10.

20 National Academy of Sciences, *Review of the Scientific Approaches Used During the FBI's Investigation of the 2001 Anthrax Letters*

(Washington, DC, 2011), section 6.7, www.ncbi.nim.nih.gov/books/ nbk209415 (accessed 6 May 2019); Scott Shane, 'After 8 Years, FBI shuts book on Anthrax Case', *New York Times*, 20 February 2010, pp. A1 and A10. Hearings on *Global Proliferation of Weapons of Mass Destruction*, Part 1, p. 5; Kaplan,
'Aum Shinrikyo (1995)', pp. 214–21.

21 Andrew J. Grotto and Jonathan B. Tucker, *Biosecurity: A Comprehensive Action Plan* (Washington, DC, 2006), pp. 6–7; 'FBI Declares Anthrax Case Solved and Shut', *Money Times*, 22 September 2008, www.the-moneytimes.com/articles/20080921/fbi_declares_anthrax_case_solv ed_and_ shut_id-1036438.html (accessed 23 September 2008); 'Anthrax Articles from The Washington Times', 29 October 2001, 25 February and 28 August 2002 and 3 January 2003, www.anthraxinvestigation.com/washtime.html (accessed 17 October 2008);
Judith Miller, 'Bioterrorism's Deadly Math', *FrontPage Magazine* (3 November 2008), pp. 1–9, http://frontpagemagazine.com/ Articles/Read.aspx?GUID=EEBED9IF-4894-422D-B65D-48719B41E26 (accessed 4 November 2008).

22 'Staff Statement', in Hearings on *Global Proliferation of Weapons of Mass Destruction*, Part 1, p. 47; John F. Sopko, 'The Changing Proliferation Threat', *Foreign Policy*, 105 (1996–7), pp. 3–20; Kaplan, 'Aum Shinrikyo (1995)', pp. 212–14.

23 Larry C. Johnson, Hearing on *Combating Terrorism: Implementation and Status of the Department of Defense Domestic Preparedness Program* before the Subcommittee on National Security, International Affairs, and Criminal Justice of the Committee on Government Reform and Oversight, House of Representatives, 105th Congress, second session, 2 October 1998, p. 36; Mark Wheelis and Masaaki Sugishima, 'Terrorist Use of Biological Weapons', in *Deadly Cultures: Biological Weapons since 1945*, ed. Mark Wheelis, Lajos Rózsa and Malcolm Dando (Cambridge, MA, 2006), pp. 284–303.

24 Ian Reader, 'Manufacturing the Means of Apocalypse: Aum Shinrikyo and the Acquisition of Weapons of Mass Destruction', in *Terrorism and Weapons of Mass Destruction: Responding to the Challenge*, ed. Ian Bellany (London, 2007), pp. 53–80.

25 Tucker, 'Introduction', p. 8.

26 Julian P. Perry Robinson, 'Difficulties Facing the Chemical Weapons Convention', *International Affairs*, LXXXIV/2 (2008), pp. 223–39, at p. 231; see also Milton Leitenberg, Hearings on *Global Proliferation of Weapons of Mass Destruction*, part 1, p. 181.

27 Graham S. Pearson, 'Chemical/Biological Terrorism: How Serious a Risk?', *Politics and the Life Sciences*, XV/2 (1996), pp. 210–12, at p. 211.

28 Walter Laqueur, 'The New Face of Terrorism', *Washington Quarterly*, XXI/4 (1998), pp. 169–78, at p. 171; see also Mark Wheelis, 'Biotechnology and Biochemical Weapons', *Nonproliferation Review*, IX/1 (2002), pp. 48–53.

29 Ed Regis, 'Evaluating the Threat: Does Mass Biopanic Portend Mass Destruction?', *Scientific American*, CCLXXXV/6 (2001), pp. 11–13, at p. 12; Lynne Lamberg, 'Terrorism Assails Nation's Psyche', *Journal of the American Medical Association*, CCXCIV (2005), pp. 544–5; Andrew O'Neil, 'Terrorist Use of Weapons of Mass Destruction: How Serious is the Threat?', *Australian Journal of International Affairs*, LVII/1 (2003), pp. 99–112.

30 Rocco Casagrande, 'Biological Terrorism Targeted at Agriculture: The Threat to US National Security', *Nonproliferation Review*, VII/3 (2000), pp. 92–105; Paul Rogers, Simon Whitby and Malcolm Dando, 'Biological Warfare against Crops', *Scientific American*, CCLXXX/6 (1999), pp. 63–7.

31 Casagrande, 'Biological Terrorism', p. 93; BBC News Channel, 'Farm Infected with Foot and Mouth', 4 August 2007, http://news.bbc.co.uk.

32 Laurence V. Madden and Mark Wheelis, 'The Threat of Plant Pathogens as Weapons Against US Crops', *Annual Review of Phytopathology*, XLI (2003), pp. 155–76; Michael V. Dunn, 'The Threat of Bioterrorism to US Agriculture', *Annals of the New York Academy of Sciences*, DCCCXCIV (1999), pp. 184–8.

33 Dunn, 'The Threat of Bioterrorism', pp. 185–6; Thomas Frazier, 'Natural and Bioterrorist/Biocriminal Threats to Food and Agriculture', *Annals of the New York Academy of Sciences*, DCCCXCIV (1999), pp. 1–8.

34 Debora MacKenzie, 'Run, Radish, Run', *New Scientist*, CLXIV/2217 (18 December 1999), pp. 35–9, at p. 38.

35 Dunn, 'The Threat of Bioterrorism', p. 185; Madden and Wheelis, 'The Threat of Plant Pathogens', pp. 158, 165; Casagrande, 'Biological Terrorism', pp. 94–6, 99; Jeffrey A. Lockwood, *Six-Legged Soldiers: Using Insects as Weapons of War* (Oxford, 2009), pp. 241, 263.

36 'I am Not Afraid of Death', *Newsweek*, 11 January 1999, pp. 12–13, at p. 13; Alan Cullison and Andrew Higgins, 'Files Found: A Computer in Kabul Yields a Chilling Array of al Qaeda Memos', *Wall Street Journal*, 31 December 2001, pp. A1 and A3; Joby Warrick, 'Suspect and a Setback in Al-Qaeda Anthrax Case', *Washington Post*, 31 October 2006, pp. A1 and A16.

37 *WMD Intelligence Report*, pp. 269–76; George Tenet, *At the Center of the Storm: My Years at the CIA* (New York, 2007), pp. 273–4; Josh Meyer, 'Al Qaeda said to focus on WMDs', *Los Angeles Times*, 3 February 2008, pp. A1, A12–13.

38 Barton Gellman, 'Al Qaeda Near Biological, Chemical Arms Production'; Susan Schmidt and Ellen Nakashima, 'Moussaoui Said Not to Be Part of 9/11 Plot'; Paul Cruickshank and Mohamad Hage Ali, 'Jihadist of Mass Destruction'; and Warrick, 'Suspect and A Setback in Al-Qaeda Anthrax Case', *Washington Post*, 23 March 2003, pp. A1 and A10; 28 March 2003, pp. A4–5; 11 June 2006, p. B2; and 31 October 2006, pp. A1, A16; Jamal Halaby,

'Jordan militants sentenced for plotting chemical attack', 21 May 2008, http://news.yahoo.com/s/ap/20080521/ap_on_re_mi_ea/jordan_terrorism-1 (accessed 22 May 2008).

39 John V. Parachini, 'The World Trade Center Bombers (1993)', in *Toxic Terror*, ed. Tucker, pp. 185–206; Alan Cowell, 'Just One of 9 Suspects Convicted in 2003 British Poison Plot Case', *New York Times*, 14 April 2005, p. A11; John Steele, '"Chemical Bomb" Raid that Found Nothing Cost £2.2m', *Daily Telegraph*, 3 October 2006, p. 2.

40 Con Coughlin, 'Only a Matter of Time Before Terrorists Use Weapons of Mass Destruction', *Daily Telegraph*, 17 January 2006, p. 10; Sean Rayment, 'Islamists will Set Off Dirty Bomb, Spy Bosses Believe', *Sunday Telegraph*, 25 June 2006, p. 4; J. Michael McConnell, *Annual Threat Assessment of the Director of National Intelligence*, Senate Select Committee on Intelligence, 5 February 2008, http//intelligence.senate.gov/080205/mcconnell//.pdf (accessed 13 June 2008).

41 'President Delivers State of the Union Address', 29 January 2002, www.whitehouse.gov/news/releases/2002/01/print/20020129–11.html (accessed 31 April 2006).

42 'President Bush Delivers Graduation Speech at West Point', 1 June 2002, www.whitehouse.gov/news/releases/2002/06/print/20020601–3.html (accessed 31 April 2006).

43 *The National Security Strategy of the United States of America* (Washington, DC, 2002), p. 15, and (Washington, DC, 2006), pp. 18, 43; for a contrary view on deterring terrorism, see Robert F. Trager and Dessislava P. Zagorcheva, 'Deterring Terrorism: It Can Be Done', *International Security*, xxx/3 (2005/6), pp. 87–123.

44 Greg Miller, 'US Missile Strikes Take Heavy Toll on Al Qaeda, Officials Say', *Los Angeles Times*, 22 March 2009, www.latimes.com/news/nationworld/world/la-fg-pakistan-predator22–2009mar22,0,2028263.story (accessed 24 March 2009).

45 For a critique of the impact of PSI in Libya, see Tenet, *At the Center of the Storm*, ch. 15, and on Bush's counter-terrorism generally, see Edward M. Spiers, 'Chemical and Biological Terrorism and Multilateral Conventions', in *Terrorism and Weapons of Mass Destruction*, ed. Bellany, pp. 83–115.

46 UN Security Council Resolution 1540, 28 April 2004 http://disarmament2.un.org/Committee/540/index.html (accessed 28 May 2006); and UN General Assembly, 'Uniting against terrorism: recommendations for a global counter-terrorism strategy. Report of the Secretary General', 27 April 2006, A/60/825, p. 10, www.un.org/unitingagainst terrorism/contents.htm (accessed 9 May 2006).

47 David Heyman, *Lessons from the Anthrax Attacks: Implications for US Bioterrorism Preparedness* (Washington, DC, April 2002), pp. viii–xii; Grotto and Tucker, *Biosecurity*, p. ii; Art Schuler, 'Billions for Biodefense: Federal Agency Biodefense Budgeting, FY2005–FY2006',

Biosecurity and Bioterrorism: Biodefense Strategy, Practice, and Science,
III (2005), pp. 94–101.

48 Miller, 'Bioterrorism's Dangerous Math', pp. 3, 5–6; Frank Gottron
and Dana A. Shea, *Oversight of High-Containment Biological
Laboratories: Issues for Congress*, Congressional Research Service
Report (Washington, DC, 5 March 2009), pp. 6, 8; 'High-
Containment Biosafety Laboratory Safety Breaches a Growing
Concern', 4 October 2007, www.semp.us/publications/biot_
reader.php?BiotID=464 (accessed 15 April 2009).

49 United States General Accountability Office (GAO), *Biosurveillance:
Preliminary Observations on Department of Homeland Security's
Biosurveillance Initiatives*, GAO-08-960T (Washington, DC, 16 July
2008), pp. 2–3, 5; Spencer S. Hsu, 'New York Presses To Deploy
More Bioweapons Sensors', *Washington Post*, 9 January 2008, p. A3.

50 Grotto and Tucker, *Biosecurity*, p. i; Floyd Horn and Roger G.
Breeze, 'Agriculture and Food Security', *Annals of the New York
Academy of Sciences*, DCCCXCIV (1999), pp. 9–17.

51 Miller, 'Bioterrorism's Deadly Math', p. 7; Sydney J. Freedberg Jr,
Shane Harris and Corine Hegland, 'From a War On Terror
To Routine Vigilance', *National Journal* (24 January 2009),
www.nationaljournal.com/njmagazine/nj_20090124_7926.php
(accessed 8 April 2009).

7 The Recurrence of Chemical Warfare in the Middle East

1 Richard M. Price, *The Chemical Weapons Taboo* (Ithaca, NY, and
London, 1997).

2 William H. Webster, Hearings on the *Global Spread of Chemical and
Biological Weapons* before the Committee on Governmental Affairs
and its Permanent Subcommittee on Investigations, United States
Senate, 101st Congress, first session (9 February 1989), p. 12.

3 Jack Anderson and Dale van Atta, 'Iran May Turn Chemical Tables
on Iraq', *Washington Post*, 2 October 1985, p. F11; see also Gaylord
Shaw, 'Syria Reported to be Making Chemical Arms', *Los Angeles
Times*, 26 March 1986, pp. 12 and 14.

4 Robin Wright, 'Chemical Arms: Old and Deadly Scourge Returns',
Los Angeles Times, 9 October 1988, pp. 1, 18–19; 'Syria Is Producing
Chemical Weapons', *Jane's Defence Weekly*, VI/21 (29 November
1986), p. 1255.

5 Ruth Sinai, 'Syria's Chemical Weapons Equal Iraq's', *Jerusalem Post*,
20 November 1990, p. 1; James Bruce, 'Huge Weapons Race with
Israel is Driving Syria Deeper into Debt', *Jane's Defence Weekly*, VI/22
(6 December 1986), p. 1336.

6 Webster, Hearings on *Global Spread*, pp. 11 and 19.

7 Rear Admiral Thomas Brooks, Hearings on National Defense
Authorization Act for Fiscal Years 1992 and 1993 and Oversight of
Previously Authorized Programs before the Committee on Armed

Services, House of Representatives, *Seapower*, 102nd Congress,
7 March 1991, p. 107; John S. McCain, 'Proliferation in the 1990s:
Implications for US Policy and Force Planning', *Strategic Review*,
XVII/3 (1989), pp. 9–20, at p. 11; Andrew Rathmell, 'Syria's
Insecurity', *Jane's Intelligence Review*, VI/9 (1994), pp. 414–19.

8 Quoted in Dany Shoham, 'Guile, Gas and Germs: Syria's Ultimate
Weapons', *Middle East Quarterly*, IX/3 (2002), pp. 53–61, at p. 55.

9 Ibid., pp. 57–9; Anthony H. Cordesman, *Syrian Weapons of Mass
Destruction: An Overview* (Center for Strategic and International
Studies, 2 June 2008), p. 12; David E. Sanger, Andrew W. Lehren
and Rick Gladstone, 'How Syria Amassed a Nerve Gas Stockpile',
International Herald Tribune, 9 September 2013, pp. 1 and 4.

10 NTI, 'Syria' (February 2013), www.nti.org/country-
profiles/syria/delivery-systems (accessed 20 March 2013); see also
Shoham, 'Guile, Gas and Germs', pp. 57–9.

11 Cordesman, *Syrian Weapons of Mass Destruction*, p. 13; Dany
Shoham, 'Poisoned Missiles: Syria's Doomsday Deterrent', *Middle
East Quarterly*, IX/4 (2002), pp. 13–20; Alon Ben-David, 'Israeli
Attack in Syria Linked to Secret Facility', *Jane's Defence Weekly*, XLIV
(19 September 2007), p. 6.

12 Cordesman, *Syrian Weapons of Mass Destruction*, pp. 12–14; Shoham
estimated a slightly larger capability with another 60 SCUD-C missiles
armed with chemical warheads and cluster warheads for the SCUD-D,
'capable of delivering chemical or biological bomblets'. Shoham,
'Poisoned Missiles', p. 15.

13 Office of the Secretary of Defense, *Proliferation: Threat and Response*
(Washington, DC, November 1997), p. 39; see also United States
Arms Control & Disarmament Agency, *Threat Control Through Arms
Control* (Washington, DC, 1995), p. 68; Cordesman, *Syrian Weapons
of Mass Destruction*, p. 14; and Shoham, 'Poisoned Missiles',
pp. 16–17.

14 John R. Bolton, 'Remarks to the Fifth Biological Weapons
Convention Review Conference Meeting, Geneva, 19 November
2001', www.state.gov/t/us/rm/janjuly/6231.htm (accessed
9 February 2019).

15 Cordesman, *Syrian Weapons of Mass Destruction*, p. 15.

16 Jerry Gordon, 'Syria's Bio-warfare: An Interview with Dr Jill
Dekker', *New English Review* (13 January 2008), www.newenglishre-
view.org/custpage.cfm/frm/13108/sec_id/13108 (accessed
12 February 2019).

17 James R. Clapper, Director of National Intelligence, *Statement for the
Record, Worldwide Threat Assessment of the US Intelligence Community*,
House Permanent Select Committee on Intelligence, 11 April 2013.

18 Julian E. Barnes, Jay Solomon and Adam Entous, 'US Concerned as
Syria Moves Chemical Stockpile', *Wall Street Journal*, 13 July 2012,
pp. A1 and A6.

19 Neil MacFarquhar and Eric Schmitt, 'Syria threatens Chemical Attack

on Foreign Force', *New York Times*, 23 July 2012, pp. A1 and A5.

20 'Remarks by the President to the White House Press Corps', 20 August 2012, https://obamawhitehouse.archives.gov/the-press-office/2012/08/20/remarks-president-whitehouse-press-corps (accessed 15 February 2019).

21 'Obama Warns al-Assad Against Chemical Weapons, Declares 'The World Is Watching'', *CNN*, 3 December 2012, www.cnn.com/2012/12/03/world/meast/syria-civil-war/?hpt=po_c2 (accessed 4 December 2012). For comment on the 'red line' speech, see Peter Baker, Mark Landler, David E. Sanger and Anne Barnard, 'Off-the-Cuff Obama Line Put US in Bind on Syria', *New York Times*, 5 May 2013, pp. 1 and 16; and Jeffrey Goldberg, 'The Obama Doctrine', *The Atlantic* (April 2016), pp. 1–72, at pp. 3–4, 7–8.

22 Julian Perry Robinson, 'Alleged Use of Chemical Weapons in Syria', *Harvard Sussex Program Occasional Paper*, 4 (26 June 2013), p. 34.

23 Ibid., pp. 12 and 15.

24 'At Least 26 reportedly Killed in Alleged Syrian Chemical Weapons Attack', *Fox News*, 19 March 2013, www.foxnews.com/world/2013/03/19/syria-says-rebels- kill-16-in-chemical-weapons-attack (accessed 20 March 2013). For the actual numbers and confirmation of sarin used, see UN General Assembly and Security Council, *United Nations Mission to Investigate Allegations of the Use of Chemical Weapons in the Syrian Arab Republic, Final Report*, S/2013/735, A/68/663, 12 December 2013, pp. 19–20, here-after Sellström final report.

25 Toby Harnden, Uzi Mahnaimi and Marie Woolf, 'Has Syria Crossed the Red Line?', *Sunday Times*, 28 April 2013, p. 19.

26 Ibid.; see also Mary Beth D. Nikitin, Paul K. Kerr and Andrew Feickert, 'Syria's Chemical Weapons: Issues for Congress', *Congressional Research Service*, 7-5700 (20 August 2013), pp. 8–9.

27 Jon Swaine and Richard Spencer, 'US Accuses Assad Regime of Using Sarin', *Daily Telegraph*, 26 April 2013, p. 18; '"Growing Evidence" of Chemical Weapons Use in Syria – UK', *BBC News*, 26 April 2013, www.bbc.co.uk/news/world-middle-east-22305444 (accessed 13 June 2013); James Kirkup and Richard Spencer, 'MPs Demand Evidence of Sarin Use in Syria', *Daily Telegraph*, 29 April 2013, p. 13.

28 Jean-Philippe Rémy, 'Chemical Warfare in Syria', *Le Monde*, 27 May 2013, www.lemonde.fr/proche-orient/article/2013/05/27/chemical-war-in-syria_3417708_3218.html (accessed 13 June 2013); see also Perry Robinson, 'Alleged Use', pp. 21–2, 30–32.

29 Perry Robinson, 'Alleged Use', pp. 31–2; Nikitin et al., 'Syria's Chemical Weapons', p. 10.

30 Ben Farmer, 'Americans Play Down French Claims over Use of Chemical Weapons', *Daily Telegraph*, 6 June 2013, p. 20 and Nikitin, Kerr, Feickert, *Syria's Chemical Weapons*, p. 9.

31 'Dempsey Lays Out Military Options for US in Syria', *Stars and*

Stripes, 23 July 2013, www.stripes.com/middle-east/dempsey-lays-out-military-options-for-us-in-syria-1.231651 (accessed 24 July 2013).

32 Anthony Lord and David Taylor, 'An Act of Barbarism' (and other articles), *The Times*, 22 August 2013, pp. 1 and 6–7; John Hudson, 'US Spies, Experts: Chemical Weapons Likely In Syria Attack', (Foreign Policy) *The Cable*, 21 August 2013, www.the cable.foreign-policy.com/posts/2013/08/21/us_intelligence_official_finds_chemical_weapons_allegation_credible (accessed 22 August 2013); Mitch Potter, 'Syria: Shocking Images Show Aftermath of Chemical Weapons Attack that Killed Hundreds, Opposition Says', *(Toronto) Star*, 21 August 2013, ww.thestar.com/news/world/2013/08/21/more_than_200_killed_in_chemical_weapons_attack_near_damascus_say_activists.html (accessed 22 August 2013).

33 David Blair, 'Joint Intelligence Committee assessment of 27 August on Reported Chemical Weapons use in Damascus', *Daily Telegraph*, 30 August 2013, p. 6, and Ben Farmer, Philip Sherwell and Damien McElroy, 'War Chiefs Win Backing for 48-hour Barrage of Missiles', *Daily Telegraph*, 28 August 2013, p. 5.

34 Dominic Lawson, 'Forget Aarin – Assad Committed a War Crime with his First Murder', *Sunday Times*, 28 April 2013, p. 22; Stephen M. Walt, 'Room for Debate: Type of Weapons Assad Uses Shouldn't Affect U.S. policy', *New York Times*, 26 August 2013, www.nytimes.com/roomfordebate/2013/08/26/is-an-attack-on syria-justified/types-of-weapons-assad-uses-shouldn't-affect-us-policy (accessed 28 January 2015); 'Syria Crisis: Experts Split over Western Intervention', *The Guardian*, 27 August 2013, www.theguardian.com; Tim Ross, 'British Fears Grow over Legal Justification for Syria Strike', *Daily Telegraph*, 26 August 2013, www.telegraph.co.uk/news/worldnews/middleeast/syria/10267108/British-fears-grow-legal-justification-for-Syria-strike.html (accessed 28 August 2013).

35 *Parliamentary Debates (Hansard)*, DLXVI/40 (29 August 2013), cols. 1425–1556, at col. 1426 and 1430; see also Anthony Seldon, 'Ten Days that Changed the World', *Sunday Times*, 12 August 2018, pp. 13–15.

36 République Française, 'Synthèse nationale de renseignement déclassifié, Programme chimique syrien Cas d'emploi passes d'argents chimiques par le régime Attaque Chimique conduite par le regime le 21 août 2013', www.gouvernement.fr/sites/default/files/fichiers_joints/syrie_synthese_nationale_de_renseignement_declassifie_0209_2013.pdf (accessed 3 September 2013).

37 'US Government Assessment of the Syrian Government's Use of Chemical Weapons on August 21, 2013' (Washington, DC, 2013), pp. 1–4, at pp. 1 and 3.

38 Ralf Trapp, 'The Use of Chemical Weapons in Syria: Implications and Consequences', in Friedrich et al., *One Hundred Years of Chemical Warfare*, pp. 363–75, at p. 366.

39 Zeke J. Miller, 'Kerry: Obama Seeks "Accountability" for Syrian

Chemical Weapons Use', *Time*, 26 August 2013, http://
swampland.time/2013/08/26/kerry-obama-seeks-accountability
for syrian-chemical weapons-use (accessed 27 August 2013).

40 John Kerry, 'Opening Remarks Before the United States Senate
Committee on Foreign Relations', 3 September 2013,
www.state.gov/secretary/remarks/2013/09/2122603.htm
(accessed 28 May 2015).

41 Peggy Noonan, 'Why America Is Saying "No"', *Wall Street Journal*,
7 September 2013, p. A15.

42 Goldberg, 'Obama Doctrine', pp. 7, 12–13; Julian Borger and Patrick
Wintour, 'Russia calls on Syria to Hand Over Chemical Weapons',
The Guardian, 9 September 2013, www.the guardian.com/world/
2013/sep/09/Russia-syria-hand-over-chemical weapons (accessed
25 February 2019); 'Obama's Syria Speech: Full Text', *BBC News*, 11
September 2013, www.bbc.co.uk/news/world-us-canada-24044553
(accessed 23 February 2019).

43 United Nations Mission to Investigate Allegations of the Use of
Chemical Weapons in the Syrian Arab Republic, 'Report on the
Alleged Use of Chemical Weapons in the Ghouta Area of Damascus
on 21 August 2013', Note by the Secretary-General (13 September
2013), pp. 2–5.

44 Sellström Final Report, pp. 10–21.

45 OPCW, Russian Federation and the United States of America,
Framework for Elimination of Syrian Chemical Weapons, Executive
Council document EC-M-33/Nat.1. (17 September 2013) and *Progress
in the Elimination of the Syrian Chemical Weapons Programme*, Note
by the Director-General, EC-M-34/DG.1 (25 October 2013) and
EC-80/DG.4 (24 August 2015). All OPCW documents found on the
website www.opcw.org.

46 OPCW, *Progress in the Elimination of the Syrian Chemical Weapons
Programme*, Note by the Director-General, EC-M-35/DG.1 (25
October 2013) and (25 November 2013).

47 Trapp, 'The Use of Chemical Weapons in Syria', p. 368.

48 UN Security Council, *Letter dated 27 December 2013 from the Secretary-
General addressed to the President of the Security Council*, S/2013/774
(27 December 2013); Trapp, 'The Use of Chemical Weapons in
Syria', pp. 368–9; OPCW, *Progress in the Elimination of the Syrian
Chemical Weapons Programme*, Note by the Director-General, EC-M-
35/DG.1. (25 November 2013).

49 Philipp C. Bleek and Nicholas J. Kramer, 'Eliminating Syria's
Chemical Weapons: Implications for Addressing Nuclear,
Biological, and Chemical Threats', *Nonproliferation Review*, XXIII/1–2
(2016), pp. 197–230.

50 Paul F. Walker, 'Syrian Chemical Weapons Destruction: Taking
Stock and Looking Ahead', *Arms Control Today*, 14 December 2014,
www.armscontrol.org/ACT/2014.12/Features/Syrian-Chemical-
Weapons-Destruction-Taking-Stock-and-Looking-Ahead (accessed

4 March 2019); OPCW, *Progress in the Elimination of the Syrian Chemical Weapons Programme*, Note by the Director-General, EC-M-35/DG.1 (24 December 2013).

51 OPCW, *Progress in the Elimination of the Syrian Chemical Weapons Programme*, Note by the Director-General, EC-76/DG.14 (25 June 2014).

52 Elisabeth Eaves, 'Ahmet Uzumcu: Getting Rid of Chemical Weapons in Syria and Beyond', *Bulletin of the Atomic Scientists*, 9 October 2014, http://thebulletin.org/ahmet-uzumcu-getting-rid-chemical-weapons-syria-and beyond??13 (accessed 18 May 2015); OPCW, *Progress in the Elimination of the Syrian Chemical Weapons Programme*, Note by the Director-General, EC-M-44/DG.2 (25 August 2014) and EC-89/DG.1 (24 July 2018).

53 An estimate by Green Cross International's Paul F. Walker quoted in Nina Notman, 'Eliminating Syria's Chemical Weapons', *Chemistry World*, 21 May 2014, www.chemistryworld.com/features/eliminating-syrias-chemical-weapons/7390.article (accessed 5 March 2019).

54 Anthony Deutsch, 'Exclusive – Weapons Inspectors Find Undeclared Sarin and VX Traces in Syria: Diplomats', *Daily Telegraph*, 9 May 2015, https://uk.reuters.com/article/uk-mideast-crisis-syria-chemicals-exclus/exclusive-weapons-inspectors-find-und eclared-sarin-and-vx-traces-in-syria-diplomats-idUKKBNONT1Z120150508 (accessed 7 March 2019); see also OPCW, *Progress in the Elimination of the Syrian Chemical Weapons Programme*, Note by the Director-General, EC-M-44/DG.1 (25 July 2014), EC-78/DG.1 (24 November 2014) and EC-82/DG.1 (24 March 2016).

55 OPCW, *Conclusions on the Outcome of Consultations with the Syrian Arab Republic regarding its Chemical Weapons Declaration*, Report by the Director-General, EC-82/DG.18 (6 July 2016).

56 OPCW, *OPCW Fact Finding Mission: 'Compelling Confirmation' that Chlorine Gas Used as Weapon in Syria*, 10 September 2014, and OPCW, *Third Report of the OPCW Fact-finding Mission in Syria*, Note by the Technical Secretariat, S/1230/2014 (18 December 2014).

57 UN Security Council, Resolution 2235 (2015), 7 August 2015, www.securitycouncilreport.org/atf/cf/%7865BFCF98-6D27-4E9C-8CD3-CF6E4FF9%7D/s-res-2235.pdf (accessed 7 March 2019).

58 Andrew Tilghman, 'US Confirms Islamic State Use of Chemical Weapons', *Military Times*, 21 August 2015, www.militarytimes.com/news/your-military/2015/08/21/u-s-confirms-islamic-state-use-of-chemical-weapons (accessed 5 March 2019); see also Justin Huggler, Nabib Bulos and David Lawler, 'Isil Used Chemical Weapons against Kurds in Iraq, Say German Troops', *Daily Telegraph*, 14 August 2015, p. 12 and Nicola Smith, 'ISIS "Unleashes Chemical Weapons" in Battle for Kobane', *Sunday Times*, 26 October 2014, p. 31.

59 Josie Ensor, 'Isil Manufacturing its own Chemical Weapons, Warns

Watchdog Chief', *Daily Telegraph*, 4 May 2016,
www.telegraph.co.uk/news/2016/05/04/isil-manufacturing-its-own-chemical-weapons-warns-watchdog-chief (accessed 9 May
2016); see also Josie Ensor, 'Isil "Testing Chemical Weapons on
Prisoners"', *Daily Telegraph*, 23 May 2016, p. 11.

60 'INTERVIEW: The Syrian Forces and ISIL Used Toxic Chemicals as
Weapons – Report', UN News Centre, 30 August 2016,
www.un.org/apps/news/story.asp?NewsID=54795#.V9J42hxeA4o
(accessed 9 September 2016); UN Security Council, *Letter Dated
21 October 2016 from the Leadership Panel of the Organization for the
Prohibition of Chemical Weapons-United Nations Joint Investigative
Mechanism addressed to the Secretary-General*, S/2016/888
(21 October 2016).

61 Nawal al-Maghefi, 'How Chemical Weapons Have Helped Bring
Assad Close to Victory', *BBC Panorama* (15 October 2018),
www.bbc.co.uk/news/world-middle-east-45586903 (accessed 10
March 2019), hereafter BBC Panorama report, and Global Public
Policy institute (Tobias Schneider and Theresa Lütkefend), *Nowhere
to Hide: The Logic of Chemical Weapons Use in Syria* (Berlin, February
2019), hereafter GPPi report.

62 Quoted in BBC Panorama report; for the improvised chlorine
munitions, see GPPi report.

63 UN Security Council, *Letter dated 26 October 2017 from the Leadership
Panel of the Organisation for the Prohibition of Chemical Weapons-
United Nations Joint Investigative Mechanism addressed to the
Secretary-General*, S/201/904 (26 October 2017).

64 GPPi report.

65 Quoted in BBC Panorama report.

66 Ibid.

67 Travis Fedschun, 'Trump Slams Obama over Not Crossing
"Red Line" in Syria with "Animal Assad"', *Fox News*, 8 April 2017,
www.foxnews.com/politics/trump-slams-obama-over-not-crossing-red-line-in-syria-with-animal-assad (accessed 12 March 2019);
Toby Harnden and Tim Shipman, 'First Shock, then Trump's War',
Sunday Times, 9 April 2017, pp. 6–7; Bob Woodward, *FEAR: Trump
in the White House* (London and New York, 2018), pp. 146–54.

68 UN Security Council, *Letter dated 26 October 2017 from the Secretary-
General Addressed to the President of the Security Council*, S/2017/904
(26 October 2017); OPCW, *Report of the OPCW Fact-finding Mission in
Syria Regarding an Alleged Incident in Khan Shaykhun, Syrian Arab
Republic April 2017*, Note by the Technical Secretariat, S/1510/2017
(29 June 2017); Josie Ensor and Harriet Alexander, 'UK and America
Warn Assad over Chemicals', *Daily Telegraph*, 28 June 2017, p. 14;
Woodward, *FEAR*, p. 152.

69 Claire Elliott, 'Now Even Ministers Call for Vote: Pressure on
Theresa May Rises as Tories Say No to "Gesture Bombing" in
Syria', *Daily Mail*, 13 April 2018, www.dailymail.co.uk/news/

article-5614245/Pressure-Theresa-rises-Tories-say-no-gesture-bombing-syria.html (accessed 13 March 2019); on Douma attack, see GPPi report.

70 'Syria "Chemical Attack": France's President Macron Has Proof', *BBC News*, 12 April 2018, www.bbc.co.uk/news/world-middle-east-43740626 (accessed 13 March 2019); 'Media: US Has Proof that Chemical Weapons Were Used in Douma', *NBC News*, 12 April 2018, https://uawire.org/media-us-has-proof-that-chemical-weapons-used-in-douma (accessed 13 March 2019); and OPCW, *Interim Report of the OPCW Fact-finding Mission in Syria Regarding the Incident of Alleged Use of Toxic Chemicals as a Weapon in Douma, Syrian Arab Republic, on 7 April 2018*, Note by the Technical Secretariat, S/1645/2018 (6 July 2018).

71 OPCW, *First Inspections at the Barzah and Jamrayah Syrian Scientific Studies and Research Centre Facilities in the Syrian Arab Republic in Accordance with Decision EC-83/DEC.5 (Dated 11 November 2016)*, Report by the Director-General, EC-85/DG.16 (2 June 2017) and 'US-led strikes on Syria: What Was Hit?' *BBC News*, 16 April 2018, www.bbc.co.uk/news/world-middle-east-43769332 (accessed 13 March 2019), hereafter BBC News report.

72 Quoted in BBC News report.

73 Samer al-Atrush, 'Syrian Rebels Kill "Chemical Weapons Chief"', *Daily Telegraph*, 6 August 2018, p. 12 and on effects, compare GPPi Report and Ben Hubbard, 'Syrian Strike Attracts Talk, Not Changes', *New York Times*, 16 April 2018, pp. A1 and A11 and Thomas Gibbons-Neff, 'Strikes Unlikely to Halt Syria's Chemical Plans, Pentagon Report Warns', *New York Times*, 20 April 2018, p. A8.

74 Josie Ensor, 'UK and US Warn Assad over Chemical Attacks', *Daily Telegraph*, 23 May 2019, p. 15.

75 'Meet the Press Transcript', *NBC News*, 20 July 2014, www.nbc-news.com/meet-the-press/meet-the-press-transcript-july-20-2014-n160611 (accessed 13 March 2019); and David Blair, 'Assad Regime Accused of Dropping Sarin Nerve Agent Gas on Isil Insurgents', *Daily Telegraph*, 18 May 2016, p. 14.

76 OPCW, Note by the Technical Secretariat, *First Report by the OPCW Investigation and Identification Team Pursuant to Paragraph 10 of Decision C-SS-4/Dec.3 "Addressing the Threat from Chemical Weapons Use" Ltamenah (Syrian Arab Republic) 24, 25, and 30 March 2017*, S/1867/2020, p. 2.

8 Political Assassination by Poisoning

1 Nasser's killing was abandoned on account of the quantities of nerve agent required, and the likelihood of causing heavy casualties among Nasser's staff. Richard J. Aldrich, *The Hidden Hand: Britain,*

America and Cold War Secret Intelligence (London, 2001), pp. 480, 612 and 633.

2 Christopher Andrew and Vasili Mitrokhin, *The Sword and the Shield: The Mitrokhin Archive and the Secret History of the KGB* (New York, 2001), pp. 88, 361–2, and 390–91.

3 Ibid, pp. 363–70, 379–84 and 387–9.

4 Ibid, p. 389.

5 Oleg Kalugin, *Spymaster: My Thirty-two Years in Intelligence and Espionage against the West* (New York, 2012), pp. 203–12, at p. 206.

6 Nick Paton Walsh, 'Markov's Umbrella Assassin Revealed: After 26 Years, Police Hope to Bring Killer to Justice', *The Guardian*, 6 June 2005, www.theguardian.com/world/2005/jun06/ nickpatonwalsh (accessed 27 March 2019).

7 Luke Harding, *A Very Expensive Poison: The Definitive Story of the Murder of Litvinenko and Russia's War with the West* (London, 2017), pp. 184–5 and 189.

8 Ibid, pp. 188–90; see also Boris Volodarsky, *The KGB's Poison Factory: From Lenin to Litvinenko* (Barnsley, 2017).

9 *The Litvinenko Inquiry: Report into the death of Alexander Litvinenko, Chairman: Sir Robert Owen, January 2016*, hereafter Owen report, pp. 33–5, 37–8 and 40–43, www.gov.uk/government/publications/the-litvinenko-inquiry- report-into-the-death-of-alexander-litvinenko (accessed 24 March 2019).

10 Harding, *Very Expensive Poison*, pp. 117, 202 and 214; see also Owen report, pp. 110, 128–30, 132–33, 138–43, 146–7, 149, 178 and 180.

11 Owen report, pp. 48, 185, 222 and 224–5; Harding, *Very Expensive Poison*, pp. 181–2.

12 Owen report, pp. 169–70, 186, 192–201 and 209.

13 Ibid., pp. 227; see also pp. 52–5, 199 and 234 and Joel Gunter, 'Sergei Skripal and the 14 Deaths Under Scrutiny', *BBC News*, 7 March 2018, www.bbc.co.uk/news/world-europe–43299598 (accessed 27 March 2019).

14 Harding, *Very Expensive Poison*, pp. 270–71, 283 and 287.

15 'VX Marks the Spot', *The Economist*, 4 March 2017, p. 44; 'Poison Attack in Airport "Killed Kim in Minutes"', *The Guardian*, 27 February 2017, p. 17.

16 Choe Sang-hun and Rick Gladstone, '"New Victim of Palace Intrigue": Kim Jong-un's Half Brother', *New York Times*, 15 February 2017, p. A8.

17 John V. Parachini, 'Assessing North Korea's Chemical and Biological Weapons Capabilities and Prioritizing Countermeasures' before the Committee on Foreign Affairs Subcommittee on Terrorism, Nonproliferation and Trade and the Subcommittee on Asia and the Pacific, United States House of Representatives, 17 January 2018.

18 'Kim Jong-nam: Indonesian Woman Freed in Murder Case',

BBC News, 17 March 2019, www.bbc.co.uk/world-asia–47520443 (accessed 27 March 2019) and Nicola Smith, 'Suspect in Murder of Kim's Brother Walks Free', *Daily Telegraph*, 4 May 2019, p. 15.

19 'Russian Spy: What Are Novichok Agents and What Do They Do?' *BBC News*, 19 March 2018, www.bbc.co.uk/news/world-europe–43377698 (accessed 28 March 2019); Guy Faulconbridge and Michael Holden, 'What Is Known, And Not Known, About Poisoning of Ex-spy in Britain', *Reuters*, 5 April 2018, www.reuters.com/article/us-britain-russia-explainer/what-is-known-and-not-known-about-poisoning of-ex-spy-in-britain-idUKKCNIHC130 (accessed 28 March 2019).

20 Hansard, 'Salisbury Incident', DCXXXVII (12 March 2018), cols. 620–21.

21 Hansard, 'Salisbury Incident', DCXXXVII (14 March 2018), cols. 855–7.

22 Neil Buckley, David Bond and Henry Foy, 'Agents of Fear', *Financial Times*, 10 March 2018, p. 9; 'Former Russia Agent, Living in Retirement, Yet Still in Spy Game', *New York Times*, 15 May 2018, p. A5; Mark Urban, *Skripal Files: The Life and Near Death of a Russian Spy* (London, online edition, 2018).

23 Marc Bennetts, 'Russian Warning Don't Move to England', *The Guardian*, 10 March 2018, p. 12.

24 Jonathan B. Tucker, *War on Nerves: Chemical Warfare from World War I to Al Qaeda* (New York, 2006), pp. 315–22; Will Englund, 'Ex-Soviet Scientist Says Gorbachev's Regime Created New Nerve Gas in '91', *Baltimore Sun*, 16 September 1992, p. 3A and 'Russia Still Doing Secret Work on Chemical Arms Research Goes On as Government Seeks U.N. Ban', *Baltimore Sun*, 18 October 1992, p. 1A.

25 Vil S. Mirzayanov, *State Secrets: An Insider's Chronicle of the Russian Chemical Weapons Program* (Denver, CO, 2008), pp. 121–2, 138 and 142–8.

26 Ibid., pp. 148, 167 and 219; see also Tucker, *War of Nerves*, pp. 253–4.

27 '"Novichok" Poison', *Chemical and Engineering News*, XCVI (19 March 2018), p. 3; Tucker, *War of Nerves*, pp. 273, 320–21; Mirzayanov, *State Secrets*, pp. 167–8, 326–7; and Andrew Roth, 'Nerve Agent was Used in 1995 Murder, Claims Former Soviet Scientist', *The Guardian*, 23 March 2018, www.theguardian.com/uk-news/2018/mar/23/nerve-agent-was-used-in–1995-claims-former-soviet-scientist (accessed 8 April 2019).

28 Joe Riddle, 'Poison Found on Front Door Handle', *Salisbury Journal*, 5 April 2018, p. 5.

29 Robert Mendick, Martin Evans, Kate McCann, Con Coughlin and Dominic Nicholls, 'Russian Agency Behind Poison Attack "Is Acting with Impunity"', *Daily Telegraph*, 6 September 2018, pp. 1 and 3; see also Mark Urban, 'Russian Spy Poisoning: How the Skripals Were Saved', *BBC News*, 29 May 2018, www.bbc.co.uk/news/uk–44278609 (accessed 2 April 2019).

30 'Salisbury Decontamination Work "Completed" After Nerve Agent

Attack', *Forces Network* (1 March 2019), www.forces.net/news/salisbury-be-declared-decontaminated-novichok (accessed 3 April 2019); see also Steven Morris and Caroline Bannock, 'Police Contact 131 people over Salisbury Nerve Agent Fears', *The Guardian*, 15 March 2018, www.theguardian.com/uk-news/2018/mar/15/police-contact–131-people-over-salisbury-nerve-agent-fears (accessed 2 April 2019).

31 Rebecca Hudson, 'Breakdown of £7m Spend on Recovery', *Salisbury Journal*, 17 October 2018, pp. 1–2 and 'Policeman Speaks Out About Nerve Agent Poisoning Ordeal', *Salisbury Journal*, 29 November 2018, p. 5.

32 Hansard, DCXXXVII (12 March 2018), col. 621 and (14 March 2018), col. 856.

33 Ibid., (14 March 2018), col. 856.

34 Steve Rosenberg, 'Spy Poisoning: Nato Expels Russian Diplomats', *BBC News*, 27 March 2018, www.bbc.co.uk/news/world-asia–43550938 (accessed 3 April 2019); Julian Borger, 'Spy Poisoning: Allies Back UK and Blast Russia at UN Security Council', *The Guardian*, 15 March 2018, www.theguardian.com/world/2018/mar/14/uk-spy-poisoning-russia-tells-un-it-did-not-make-nerve-agent-used-in-attack (accessed 12 April 2019).

35 Patrick Wintour, 'The Russians Seem to Be Using Viktoria as a Battering Ram to Try to Gain Access to Yulia', *The Guardian*, 6 April 2018, p. 7.

36 'Spy Poisoning: Putin Most Likely Behind Attack – Johnson', *BBC News*, 16 March 2018, www.bbc.co.uk/news/uk–43429152 (accessed 30 July 2018); see also Urban, *Skripal Files*, ch. 21.

37 'Vladimir Putin: "Nonsense" to Think Russia Would Poison Spy in Britain', *The Guardian*, 18 March 2018, www.theguardian.com/uk-news/2018/mar/18/vladimir-putin-nonsense-to-think-russia-would-poison-spy-in-uk (accessed 4 April 2019).

38 Sam Coates, Catherine Philp, 'May Battles to Preserve Alliance against Russia', *The Times*, 4 April 2018, pp. 1 and 6.

39 Patrick Wintour, 'Yulia Skripal's Cousin' and 'Yulia Skripal's Cousin Viktoria Denied UK Visa to Visit Poisoned Relatives in Hospital', *The Independent*, 6 April 2018, www.independent.co.uk/news/uk/politics/viktoria-skripal-uk-visa-denied-home-office-sergei-salisbury-visit-hospital-yulia-a8292481.html (accessed 4 April 2019).

40 OPCW, Note by the Technical Secretariat, *Summary of the Report on Activities carried out in support of a request for Technical Assistance by the United Kingdom of Great Britain and Northern Ireland (Technical Assistance Visit TAV/02/18)*, S/1612/2018, 12 April 2018.

41 'OPCW Rejects Russian Claims of Second Salisbury Nerve Agent', *The Guardian*, 18 April 2018, www.theguardian.com/uk-news/2018/apr/18/opcw-rejects-russian-claims-of-second-salisbury-nerve-agent (accessed 12 April 2019) and Urban, *Skripal Files*, Ch. 21.

42 Steven Morris and Kevin Rawlinson, 'Novichok Victim Found

Substance Disguised as Perfume in Sealed Box', *The Guardian*, 24 July 2018, www.theguardian.com/uk-news/2018/jul/24/ novichok-victim-ill-within-15-minutes-says-partner-charlie-rowley (accessed 6 April 2019) and 'Salisbury Poisoning: Police "Identify Novichok Suspects"', *BBC News*, 19 July 2018, ww.bbc.co.uk/news/ uk-44883803 (accessed 6 April 2019).

43 OPCW, Note by the Technical Secretariat, *Summary of the Report on Activities carried out in support of a request for technical assistance by the United Kingdom of Great Britain and Northern Ireland (Technical Assistance Visit TAV/03/18 and TAV/03B/18 'Amesbury Incident')*, S/1671/2018, 4 September 2018.

44 Hansard, 'Salisbury Update', DCXLVI (5 September 2018), cols. 167–70.

45 Francis Elliott, Fiona Hamilton, Tom Parfitt, 'May Vows Revenge on Russia', *The Times*, 6 September 2018, pp. 1, 6–9; Mendick et al., 'Russian Agency Behind Poison Attack', pp. 1–3; and Rebecca Hudson, 'Novichok Attack Suspects Named', *Salisbury Journal*, 6 September 2018, pp. 1 and 6.

46 'Skripal Poisoning, Putin Says Suspects "Civilians, Not Criminals"', *BBC News*, 12 September 2018, www.bbc.co.uk/news/world-europe-45494627 (accessed 6 April 2019).

47 'Skripal Suspects: 'We Were Just Tourists in Salisbury', *BBC News*, 13 September 2018, www.bbc.co.uk/news/world-europe–45509097 (accessed 6 April 2019).

48 David Boffey, 'Russia-bashing Must Stop, Says Jean-Claude Junker', *The Guardian*, 31 May 2018, ww.theguardian.com/ world/2018/may/31/russia-bashing-must-stop-says-jean-claude-juncker (accessed 8 April 2019) and 'Skripal Poisoning: Trump Admin Yet to Impose New Russia Sanctions Required by Law', *NBC News*, 24 January 2019, www.nbcnews.com/politics/ national-security/trump-admin-has-not-imposed-new-sanctions-required-by-law-n962216 (accessed 8 April 2019).

49 Steven Swinford and Robert Mendick, 'Russia's Cyber Raiders Foiled in Humiliation for Putin', *Daily Telegraph*, 5 October 2018, pp. 1 and 4–5 and Robert Mendick and Alec Luhn, 'Second Salisbury Assassin', *Daily Telegraph*, 8 October 2018, p. 2.

50 Dominic Nicholls, Anna Mikhailova and Alec Luhn, 'Embarrassment for Putin as 305 "Spies" Are Named', *Daily Telegraph*, 6 October 2018, p. 16.

51 Asher McShane, Ella Wills, 'Third Suspect in Skripal Poisoning Case Identified as Russian Military Intelligence Officer', *Evening Standard*, 14 February 2019, www.standard.co.uk/news/uk/ third-suspect-in-skripal-poisoning-case-identified-as-russian-military-intelligence-officer-a4067396.htnl (accessed 27 March 2019); Mark Urban, 'Skripal poisoning: Third Man Commanded Attack', 28 June 2019, www.bbc.co.uk (accessed 3 March 2020); and Robert Mendick, '"Fourth man" in Salisbury Attack on Skripals',

Daily Telegraph, 26 February 2020, p. 18.

52 Rebecca Hudson, 'Former MI6 Boss Says Threat Against Sergei Skripal Was Much Higher than We Expected', *Salisbury Journal*, 22 November 2018, www.salisburyjournal.co.uk/news/ 17242323.former-m16-boss-says-threat-against-sergei-skripal-much-higher-than-we-expected (8 April 2019) and 'Ben Wallace Quoted in 'Skripal Poisoning: Putin Says Suspects "Civilians Not Criminals"'.

53 Rebecca Hudson, 'Warning for Hundreds: Questions over Health Advice Delay', *Salisbury Journal*, 15 March 2018, p. 8.

54 Lionel Barber and Henry Foy, '"The Liberal Idea Has Become Obsolete": Vladimir Putin Exclusive Interview', *Financial Times*, 28 June 2019, p. 1.

55 'Only 3% of Russians believe Moscow Was behind Skripal Attack, Poll says', *Reuters*, 25 October 2018, www.themoscowtimes.com/ 2018/10/25/only–3-percent-russians-believe-moscow-was-behind-skripal-attack-poll-says-a632 (accessed 8 April 2019).

56 Mary Dejevsky, 'One Year On, the Skripal Poisoning Case Is Still Riddled with Questions That No One Wants to Answer', *The Independent*, 4 March 2019, www.independent.co.uk/voices/ skripal-poisoning-salisbury-attack-yulia-russia-novichok-putin-a8807191.html (accessed 8 April 2019).

57 Justin Huggler and Theo Merz, 'Germany Confirms Navalny Was Poisoned with Novichok', *Daily Telegraph*, 3 September 2020, pp. 1 and 3; Nataliya Vasilyeva, 'Novichok Poison Found on Navalny's Hotel Water Bottle', *Daily Telegraph*, 18 September 2020, p. 13.

58 'The Lady May Toughen Up', The Economist, 12 September 2020, p. 27.

Conclusion: The Evolving Nature of Chemical and Biological Warfare

1 Peter Katona, 'The Historical Impact of Terrorism, Epidemics and Weapons of Mass Destruction', in *Countering Terrorism and WMD: Creating a Global Counter-Terrorism Network*, ed. Peter Katona, Michael D. Intriligator and John P. Sullivan (London, 2006), pp. 13–32; Ken Alibek, *Biohazard* (London, 1999), pp. 30–31; Alexander Kouzminov, *Biological Espionage: Special Operations of the Soviet and Russian Foreign Intelligence Services in the West* (London, 2005), pp. 150–58; Markus Binder, 'Sri Lankan Government Alleges Tamil Tigers Preparing for Chemical Warfare', WMD *Insights* (October 2007), pp. 1–4, http://wmdinsights.org/119/119_SAI_ SRI_SriLankan.htm (accessed on 6 November 2007).

2 For a comprehensive synthesis of this material, see Malcolm Dando, *The New Biological Weapons: Threat, Proliferation and Control* (Boulder, CO, 2001).

3 Macha Levinson, 'Custom-made Biological Weapons', *International Defense Review*, XIX (1986), pp. 1611–15.

4 Ibid., pp. 1612, 1615; Office of the Secretary of Defense, *Proliferation: Threat and Response* (Washington, DC, November 1997), pp. 83–4.

5 Joseph D. Douglass, Jr. and H. Richard Lukens, 'The Expanding Arena of Chemical-Biological Warfare', *Strategic Review*, XII/4 (1984), pp. 71–80, at p. 75.

6 Malcolm Dando, *Biological Warfare in the 21st Century: Biotechnology and the Proliferation of Biological Weapons* (London, 1994), p. 156.

7 Alibek, *Biohazard*, pp. 163–4; see also 'Soviets Violate Ban on Biological Warfare – Stunning Advances in Biotechnology', *Army Chemical Journal*, III/1 (Spring 1987), pp. 42–3.

8 Alibek, *Biohazard*, pp. 260–62.

9 Office of the Secretary of Defense, *Proliferation*, pp. 81–3.

10 Executive Office of the President, *Biodefense for the 21st Century*, Homeland Security Presidential Directive 33 (Washington, DC, 28 April 2004), www.fas.org/irp/offdocs/nspd/hspd-10.html (accessed 19 January 2009).

11 Gary Stix, 'Plague Redux', *Scientific American*, CCLXXXV/6 (2001), p. 15; Jan van Aken and Edward Hammond, 'Genetic Engineering and Biological Weapons', *EMBO reports*, IV (June 2003), www.pubmedcentral.nih.gov/articlerender.fcgi?artid=1326447 (accessed on 15 January 2009); Peter Aldhous, 'Are Fears over Bioterrorism Stifling Scientific Research?', *New Scientist*, 5 February 2009, www.newscientist.com/article/dn16539–are fears-over-bioterrorism-stifling-scientificresearch.htr (accessed 20 March 2009).

12 Carl A. Larson, 'Ethnic Weapons', *Military Review*, L/11 (1970), pp. 3–11; A. Condera, 'Biological Weapons and Third World Targets', *Science for the People*, XIII/4 (1981), pp. 16–20.

13 Dando, *The New Biological Weapons*, pp. 125–9, at p. 129.

14 Graham S. Pearson, 'Prospects for Chemical and Biological Arms Control: The Web of Deterrence', *Washington Quarterly*, XVI/2 (1993), p. 149.

15 Alan Pearson, 'Incapacitating Biochemical Weapons: Science, Technology, and Policy for the 21st Century', *Nonproliferation Review*, XIII/2 (2006), pp. 151–88; Aken and Hammond, 'Genetic Engineering and Biological Weapons', pp. 5–6.

16 Julian P. Perry Robinson, 'Difficulties Facing the Chemical Weapons Convention', *International Affairs*, LXXXII/2 (2008), pp. 228–9; Aaron J. Klein, *Striking Back: The 1972 Munich Olympics Massacre and Israel's Deadly Response* (New York, 2005), pp. 104–11, 205–8.

17 Pearson, 'Incapacitating Biochemical Weapons', pp. 169–71.

18 OPCW, 'CWC Conference of States Parties Adopts Decision Addressing the Threat from Chemical Weapons Use', 27 June 2018.

19 Dando, *The New Biological Weapons*, pp. 144–9; Pearson, 'Prospects for Chemical and Biological Arms Control', pp. 155–61; Marie Isabelle Chevrier, 'A Necessary Compromise', *Arms Control Today* (May 2001), www.armscontrol.org/act2001_05/chevrier.asp (accessed on 5 April 2006).

20 Edward J. Lacey, Testimony before the Subcommittee on National Security, Veterans Affairs, and International Relations, Committee on Government Reform, US House of Representatives, 10 July 2001, www.state.gov/t/vci/rls/rm/2001/5168.html (accessed on 17 February 2006).

21 Ambassador D. Mahley, 'Statement by the United States to the Ad Hoc Group of the Biological Weapons Convention States Parties, Geneva, Switzerland', 25 July 2001, www.state.gov/t/ac/rls/rm/2001/5497.htm (accessed on 19 February 2006).

22 Elizabeth Olsen, 'US Rejects New Accord Covering Germ Warfare', *New York Times*, 26 July 2001, p. A7; Malcolm R. Dando, *Preventing Biological Warfare: The Failure of American Leadership* (Houndmills, Basingstoke, 2002), pp. 174–9, at p. 177.

23 Fred C. Iklé, 'The New Germ Warfare Treaty Is a Fraud', *Wall Street Journal*, 27 July 2001, p. A8.

24 Alan P. Zelicoff, 'An Impractical Protocol'; Mike Moodie, 'Building on Faulty Assumptions'; and Robert P. Kadlec, 'First Do No Harm', *Arms Control Today* (May 2001), www.armscontrol.org/act2001_05/zelicoff.asp; 05/moodie.asp; and 05/kadlec.asp (accessed on 5 April 2006).

25 Richard Butler, *The Greatest Threat: Iraq, Weapons of Mass Destruction, and the Growing Crisis of Global Security* (New York, 2001), pp. vii, 52, 80–81, 178–85, 218–19; Scott Ritter, *Endgame: Solving the Iraq Crisis* (New York, 2002), pp. 219–22.

26 Chevrier, 'A Necessary Compromise'; John Steinbruner, Nancy Gallagher and Stacy Gunther, 'A Tough Call', *Arms Control Today* (May 2001), www.armscontrol.org/act/2001_05/steinbruner.asp (accessed on 5 April 2006).

27 Kathleen C. Bailey, 'Why the United States Rejected the Protocol to the Biological and Toxin Weapons Convention', National Institute for Public Policy (October 2002), pp. 9–24, www.nipp.org/publications.php (accessed on 19 December 2003).

28 'President's Statement on Biological Weapons', 1 November 2001, http://whitehouse.gov/news/releases/2001/11/print/20011101.html (accessed on 14 May 2006).

29 'President Announces New Measures to Counter the Threat of WMD', 11 February 2004, www.whitehouse.gov/news/releases/2004/02/print/20040211–4html (accessed on 11 May 2006).

30 *World at Risk: The Report of the Commission on the Prevention of Weapons of Mass Destruction Proliferation and Terrorism* (New York, 2008), pp. xii, xv, xxviii, 25, 41–2.

31 Ronald K. Noble, 'Keeping Science in the Right Hands', *Foreign Affairs*, XCII/6 (2013), pp. 47–53.

32 *Current and Projected National Security Threats to the United States*, Hearing before the Select Committee on Intelligence of the United States Senate, 105th Congress, first session (5 February 1997), p. 88; Douglas Jehl, 'US Intelligence Review Is Softening Some Judgments About Illicit Arms Abroad', *New York Times*, 18 November 2003, p. A13.

33 Floyd P. Horn and Roger G. Breeze, 'Agriculture and Food Security', *Annals of the New York Academy of Science*, 894 (1999), pp. 14, 16; 'A Glimmer of Hope from the Dark World of MI5', *The Telegraph*, 7 January 2009, www.telegraph.co.uk/comment/telegraph-view/4143720/A-glimmer-of-hope-from-the-dark-world-of-MI5.html (accessed on 8 January 2009).

34 *The Lessons of Mumbai*, RAND Occasional Paper (Santa Monica, CA, 2009), pp. 1–2, 9–12; Deborah Haynes, 'Sri Lanka Attacks Could Signal New International Campaign of Terror' *SKY News*, 23 April 2019, www.sky.com/story/sri-lanka-attacks-could-signal-new-international-campaign-of-terror-11701179 (accessed 3 May 2019).

35 Gregory B. O'Hanyon and Daniel R. Morris, 'Warning in the Age of WMD Terrorism', in *Countering Terrorism and WMD*, ed. Katona, Intriligator and Sullivan, pp. 51–68.

36 Adam Entous, Siobhan Gorman and Cassell Bryan-Low, 'Networks of Spies Aid Syria Gas Probe', *Wall Street Journal*, 24–5 August 2013, pp. A1 and A5.

37 Ashton B. Carter, 'How to Counter WMD', *Foreign Affairs*, LXXXIII/5 (2004), pp. 72–85, at p. 85; Richard L. Russell, 'A Weak Pillar for American National Security: The CIA's Dismal Performance against WMD Threats', *Intelligence and National Security*, XX/3 (2005), pp. 466–85.

38 Hans Blix, *Disarming Iraq* (London, 2005), p. 288; John P. Sullivan, 'Fusing Terrorism Security and Response', in *Countering Terrorism and WMD*, ed. Katona, Intriligator and Sullivan, pp. 272–88, at pp. 282–4.

39 US GAO, *Biosafety Laboratories: Perimeter Security Assessment of the Nation's Five BSL-4 Laboratories* (Washington, DC, September 2008), GAO-08-1092, pp. 4–10; 'Asian Biosafety Practices Fall Short of International Standards', 10 August 2006, www.genengnews.com/news/bnitem.aspx?name=4490582 (accessed on 13 August 2006).

40 *World at Risk*, pp. 38–9; House of Commons Innovation, Universities, Science and Skills Committee, *Biosecurity in UK Research Laboratories*, sixth report of session 2007–8 (London, 16 June 2008), pp. 9, 17–19; Frank Gottron and Dana A. Shea, *Oversight of High-Containment Biological Laboratories: Issues for Congress*, Congressional Research Service Report (Washington, DC, 5 March 2009), p. 23.

41 Deborah Yarsike Ball and Theodore P. Gerber, 'Russian Scientists and Rogue States: Does Western Assistance Reduce the Proliferation Threat?', *International Security*, XXIX/4 (2005), pp. 50–77.

42 *World at Risk*, pp. 36–7.

43 Wheelis and Sugishima, 'Terrorist Use of Biological Weapons', in *Deadly Cultures: Biological Weapons since 1945*, ed. Mark Wheelis, Lajos Rózsa and Malcolm Dando (Cambridge, MA, 2006), p. 303; 'War Experts Gave Anthrax Advice', BBC News Channel, 24 November 2008, http://news.bbc.co.uk/2/hi/uk_news/scotland/south_of_scotland/7746436.stm (accessed on 13 January 2009).

44 Tom Whitehead, 'We Risk Police State, Says Former Spy Chief', *Daily Telegraph*, 17 February 2009, pp. 1–2.

45 Dominic Nicholls, 'Defence Base Closures Called Off in Wake of
    Novichok Attack', *Daily Telegraph*, 1 March 2019, p. 2.
46 L. V. Madden and M. Wheelis, 'The Threat of Plant Pathogens
    as Weapons Against us Crops', *Annual Review of Phytopathology*,
    XLI (2003), pp. 155–76; Jeffrey A. Lockwood, *Six-legged Soldiers:*
    Using Insects as Weapons of War (Oxford, 2009), ch. 26.
47 George Musser, 'Better Killing through Chemistry', *Scientific*
    American, CCLXXXV/6 (2001), pp. 10–11.
48 Brooks Tigner, 'Finding Common Ground: Europe Seeks to
    Consolidate CBRN and EOD Protection', *Jane's International Defence*
    Review, XLII/1 (2009), pp. 32–3.
49 S. N. Chatfield, 'Members States' Preparedness for CBRN Threats:
    Terrorism (Brussels: Policy Department for Citizens' Rights and
    Constitutional Affairs, European Parliament, 2018), pp. 13, 20–21,
    34.
50 Susan B. Martin, 'The Role of Biological Weapons in International
    Politics: The Real Military Revolution', *Journal of Strategic Studies*,
    XXV/1 (2002), pp. 63–98; Avner Cohen, 'Israel and Chemical/
    Biological Weapons: History, Deterrence, and Arms Control',
    Nonproliferation Review, VIII/3 (2001), pp. 27–53, at pp. 37 and 47.
51 Rocco Casagrande, 'Biological Terrorism Targeted at Agriculture:
    The Threat to us National Security', *Nonproliferation Review*, VII/3
    (2000), pp. 95–6.

Select Bibliography

Alibek, Ken, *Biohazard* (London, 1999)

Brown, Frederic J., *Chemical Warfare: A Study in Restraints*, 2nd edn (New Brunswick, NJ, 2006)

Carter, Gradon B., *Porton Down: 75 Years of Chemical and Biological Research* (London, 1992)

Coleman, Kim, *A History of Chemical Warfare* (London, 2005)

Cook, Tim, *No Place to Run: The Canadian Corps and Gas Warfare in the First World War* (Vancouver, 1999)

Cross, Glenn, *Dirty War: Rhodesia and Chemical Biological Warfare, 1975–1984* (Solihull, 2017)

Dando, Malcolm, *Biological Warfare in the 21st Century: Biotechnology and the Proliferation of Biological Weapons* (London, 1994)

—, *The New Biological Weapons: Threat, Proliferation and Control* (Boulder, CO, 2001)

Friedrich, Bretislav, Dieter Hoffmann, Jürgen Renn, Florian Schmaltz and Martin Wolf, eds, *One Hundred Years of Chemical Warfare: Research, Deployment, Consequences* (Berlin, 2017)

Geissler, Erhard, ed., *Biological and Toxin Weapons Today* (Oxford, 1986)

— and John Ellis van Courtland Moon, eds, *Biological and Toxin Weapons: Research, Development and Use from the Middle Ages to 1945*, SIPRI Chemical and Biological Warfare Studies XVIII (Oxford, 1999)

Haber, Ludwig F., *The Poisonous Cloud: Chemical Warfare in the First World War* (Oxford, 1986)

Harris, Robert, and Jeremy Paxman, *A Higher Form of Killing: The Secret Story of Gas and Germ Warfare* (London, 1982)

Harris, Sheldon H., *Factories of Death: Japanese Biological Warfare, 1932–45, and the American Cover-Up* (London, 1994)

Hiltermann, Joost R., *A Poisonous Affair: America, Iraq, and the Gassing of Halabja* (Cambridge, 2007)

Krause, Joachim, and Charles K. Mallory, *Chemical Weapons in Soviet Military Doctrine: Military and Historical Experience, 1915–1991* (Boulder, CO, 1992)

Lederberg, Joshua, ed., *Biological Weapons: Limiting the Threat* (Cambridge, MA, 2000)

Leitenberg, Milton, and Raymond A. Zilinskas with Jens H. Kuhn, *The Soviet Biological Weapons Program: A History* (Cambridge, MA, 2012)

Lockwood, Jeffrey A., *Six-legged Soldiers: Using Insects as Weapons of War* (Oxford, 2009)

Mayor, Adrienne, *Greek Fire, Poison Arrows and Scorpion Bombs: Biological and Chemical Warfare in the Ancient World* (New York, 2003)

Miller, Judith, Stephen Engelberg and William Broad, *Germs: The Ultimate Weapon* (New York, 2001)

Palazzo, Albert, *Seeking Victory on the Western Front: The British Army and Chemical Warfare in World War I* (Lincoln, NE, and London, 2000)

Prentiss, Augustin M., *Chemicals in War* (New York, 1937)

Robinson, Julian Perry, 'Alleged Use of Chemical Weapons in Syria', *Harvard Sussex Program Occasional Paper*, 4 (26 June 2013)

Schneider, Tobias, and Theresa Lütkefend, *Nowhere to Hide: The Logic of Chemical Weapons Use in Syria* (Berlin, 2019)

Spiers, Edward M., *Chemical and Biological Weapons: A Study of Proliferation* (Houndmills, Basingstoke, 1994)

—, *Chemical Warfare* (Basingstoke, 1986)

—, *Chemical Weaponry: A Continuing Challenge* (Basingstoke, 1989)

—, *Weapons of Mass Destruction: Prospects for Proliferation* (Basingstoke, 2000)

Stockholm International Peace Research Institute, *The Problem of Chemical and Biological Warfare*, 6 vols (Stockholm, 1971–5)

Tucker, Jonathan B., ed., *Toxic Terror: Assessing Terrorist Use of Chemical and Biological Weapons* (Cambridge, MA, 2000)

—, *War of Nerves: Chemical Warfare from World War 1 to Al-Qaeda* (New York, 2006)

Walker, John R., *Britain and Disarmament: The UK and Nuclear, Biological and Chemical Weapons Arms Control and Programmes, 1956–1975* (London, 2016)

Wheelis, Mark, Lajos Rózsa and Malcolm Dando, eds, *Deadly Cultures: Biological Weapons since 1945* (Cambridge, MA, 2006)

Wilkinson, Mark, *Before Intelligence Failed: British Secret Intelligence on Chemical and Biological Weapons in the Soviet Union, South Africa and Libya* (London, 2018)

Zilinskas, Raymond A., 'The Soviet Biological Weapons Program and Its Legacy in Today's Russia', Center for the Study of Weapons of Mass Destruction Occasional Paper, 11 (Washington, DC, July 2016)

Acknowledgements

Three forms of acknowledgement are appropriate for this work. The first is to Ian Bellany for inviting me to contribute to his volume on *Terrorism and Weapons of Mass Destruction* (London, 2007) and to the United States Institute for Peace for hosting the conference in Lancaster in 2006 associated with that volume. As these invitations enabled me to update my research on terrorism, I was able to respond positively when commissioned to write this book.

The second acknowledgement is to Martha Jay and her colleagues at Reaktion Books for the invitation to write this work, involving still further research and reflections about how the debate on chemical and biological weapons has evolved in the contemporary era. It has been a pleasure to work with them.

The final acknowledgement is to Fiona, my wife, and Robert and Amanda, for enduring the preparation of yet another book. I am, as ever, deeply indebted to them.

Index